THE LOST
BATTALIONS

THE LOST BATTALIONS

A BATTLE THAT COULD NOT BE WON.
AN ISLAND THAT COULD NOT BE DEFENDED.
AN ALLY THAT COULD NOT BE TRUSTED.

TOM GILLING

ALLEN&UNWIN

SYDNEY · MELBOURNE · AUCKLAND · LONDON

First published in 2018
This edition published in 2019

Allen & Unwin
83 Alexander Street
Crows Nest NSW 2065
Australia
Phone: (61 2) 8425 0100
Email: info@allenandunwin.com
Web: www.allenandunwin.com

 A catalogue record for this
book is available from the
National Library of Australia

ISBN 978 1 76087 616 6

Set in Minion by Midland Typesetters, Australia
Printed and bound in Australia by SOS Print + Media Group

10 9 8 7 6 5 4 3 2

The paper in this book is FSC® certified.
FSC® promotes environmentally responsible,
socially beneficial and economically viable
management of the world's forests.

For Aidan

CONTENTS

CONTENTS

AUTHOR'S NOTE

There is significant variation in the spelling of place names in the former Netherlands East Indies, Burma and Siam. Where countries, cities and towns have been renamed since the war (e.g., Batavia is now Jakarta), I have generally used the wartime name rather than its modern equivalent.

Keeping Fit in the Tropics

Follow these simple rules to avoid tropical diseases. Tropical malaria can be avoided by an intelligent soldier. Take atebrin tablets as ordered, after a meal, and followed by a drink of water. Always carry a supply of atebrin tablets, and if separated from your unit, take one every day. If you forget one day, take two the next day. Sleep under a mosquito net.

Always from dusk until dawn, unless sleeping under a net, wear slacks, gaiters and long sleeved shirt (sleeves rolled down) and apply repellent lotion to face and hands every 3 hours. Always carry a bottle of repellent lotion. Treat your clothes with Anti-Mite Fluid. Follow the directions for its use exactly and avoid Scrub Typhus. To avoid dysentery and typhoid do not drink water unless it has been boiled or chlorinated. Keep flies and other insects off your food and keep eating utensils clean. Wash your body as much and as often as possible, to avoid tropical skin diseases. Carry your own soap always. Carry an extra pair of socks and underwear. Wear the socks on alternate days.

Australian Military Forces *Record of Service Book*, revised August 1944

Chapter 1

BROTHERS IN ARMS

———•———

On Good Friday, 11 April 1941, nine hundred officers and men of the 2/3rd Machine Gun Battalion steamed out of Sydney Harbour aboard the military transport ship *MM*, destination unknown. The *MM*—'a monster', in the words of Alf Sheppard of B Company, 'larger than any ship any of us had ever seen before'—was painted grey, but its drab exterior could not disguise the fact that it was the luxury ocean liner *Ile de France*, which had been commandeered by Britain after the fall of France. In total it carried more than 4000 soldiers.

Accompanying the *Ile de France* out of Sydney Harbour were three more requisitioned ocean liners, *Queen Elizabeth*, *Mauretania* and the Dutch *Nieuw Amsterdam*. The *Queen Mary* was waiting for them at Jervis Bay, 170 kilometres down the New South Wales coast, with the soldiers of the 2/2nd Pioneer Battalion, a newly formed unit like the machine gunners. (A few of the Pioneers had been squeezed aboard the *Queen Elizabeth*.)

Between them the five converted liners carried 25,000 soldiers—the largest Australian military force to be sent overseas since the First Australian Imperial Force in 1914. Private Desmond Jackson, who had joined the machine gunners at the age of 20, described the convoy as a 'fleet of giants'.

Raised in South Australia, Victoria, Tasmania and Western Australia, the machine gun battalion was led by an Adelaide lawyer, Lieutenant Colonel Arthur Seaforth Blackburn. Nearly a quarter of a century earlier, Blackburn had been awarded the Victoria Cross by King George V at Buckingham Palace for his bravery in France, where he led repeated attacks on German strongpoints outside the village of Pozières. Reports of Blackburn's extraordinary exploits on the Western Front appeared in newspapers big and small all over Australia. In a letter published in October 1916 by the *Richmond River Express and Casino Kyogle Advertiser* (and reprinted in many other papers), Blackburn recalled the 'fearful scrap' at Pozières, where he and his men

> fought solidly for three days and nights, almost without stopping, and drove our way foot by foot through the village ... Goodness only knows how I got out of it alive, as 17 times the man behind me was killed, and 22 men behind me were wounded ... While working my way up the trench, I came upon a lad of 19 chained by the hand and waist to a machine gun. Fancy having to chain your men to guns. No wonder the beggars are hard to drive out, as they are all quite convinced that we take no prisoners and will kill them all.

At the age of 49, Blackburn was determined to prove to his newly formed machine gun battalion that he was not past it. In forced marches, the 'skinny-legged' colonel always led from the front, astonishing men young enough to be his sons with his physical stamina and sheer bloody-mindedness.

As well as being an experienced and resourceful soldier, Blackburn was a skilled organiser—a talent that would prove indispensable to the troops aboard the trouble-prone *Ile de France*. Veterans described sewerage problems, a shortage of drinking water and a diet consisting almost exclusively of boiled potatoes and porridge. 'After about a week on these rations we were almost on the verge of mutiny,' Private Tom Keays recalled in the 2/3rd Machine Gun Battalion history, *From Snow to Jungle*. After Blackburn took over domestic arrangements, 'the cooks were hastily replaced by our own army cooks and the meals were much more palatable thereafter'.

To Des Jackson it was an 'uneventful' voyage, but danger was rarely far away. Fear of attack by German raiders meant that a total blackout applied to ships off the New South Wales coast. Escorted by a warship, the heavy cruiser HMAS *Australia*, the converted liners carried little in the way of armament. Eight of the battalion's Vickers machine guns were manned round the clock to protect the *Ile de France* from attack by enemy aircraft—'a popular duty', one soldier remembered, as it meant escaping from the darkness and suffocating heat below deck. Life jackets and full water bottles had to be carried at all times, and there were regular emergency drills.

After picking up the *Queen Mary* off Jervis Bay, the convoy steamed south. Although many of the *Queen Mary*'s interior fittings had been stripped out when she was converted to a troop ship, the men of the 2/2nd Pioneer Battalion were surprised to discover her luxurious accommodation largely intact. Corporal Harry Walker, the middle child of eleven from Alma, in Victoria, was impressed with the size of the ship but would suffer along with his mates as the ship neared the equator. 'It was designed for the cold Atlantic Ocean run,' Walker said in his tape-recorded memoirs. 'There wasn't sufficient air conditioning for the tropics, and boy did we swelter.'

Problems in the engine room of the *Ile de France* slowed the rest of the convoy, and heavy seas made the voyage through the Southern Ocean a misery. When troops were denied shore leave at Fremantle, Blackburn had to act quickly to prevent a riot. A note in the unit diary reads, '2030. Disturbance by certain personnel re conditions on boat. Mostly reinforcement personnel and as far as can be ascertained no members of this unit took part.'

The battalion reached full strength when the men of D Company, who had been in Perth on pre-embarkation leave, joined at Fremantle. The diary notes ruefully, 'Endeavours to reduce number of personnel on board failed.'

The *Ile de France* was too big to dock and had to be provisioned by lighter. For security reasons letters home had been strictly censored since the battalion left Sydney, but after arriving in Fremantle some of the machine gunners had the bright idea of throwing letters over the side to avoid the censors. Arch Flanagan, a Tasmanian from C Company, told Blackburn's biographer, Andrew Faulkner, 'A bloke on one of the boats said "got any letters . . . I'll post them for you." Well, I don't know whether he was a German spy but the next thing the letters were with the colonel.' Flanagan was not the only man to get a rollicking from an angry Blackburn, although he protested that the letters 'contained no more information about the convoy than every wharfie in Fremantle knew'.

Secrecy had been an overriding concern ever since the convoy left Sydney. 'Most secret' orders issued before departure from Fremantle stated that 'too much stress cannot be placed upon the importance of preventing any leakage of information in respect of movement overseas'. Messages in bottles were banned from being thrown overboard, since an enemy raider could theoretically plot the convoy's course by picking up 'two or more bottles containing dated messages'.

Life for the soldiers on the *Ile de France* began to improve after the convoy set sail for Colombo, although Blackburn professed to find it 'extremely dull'. An ill-judged ban on all forms of gambling ordered by Blackburn's superior officer, Lieutenant Colonel Stillman, was quietly dropped (no doubt on Blackburn's advice). An order requiring 'officers, NCOs, sentries, picquets and patrols' to suppress forbidden games wherever they were found was replaced by a milder ban on gambling 'during training hours'. The battalion history records that after Fremantle 'the aft lounge was set up to cater for Bingo, two-up, Vingt-et-Un, Crown and Anchor and roulette, amongst other games, to be played after working hours'. Under the new regime, the lounge resembled 'a smoke-filled Dante's Inferno'.

As the convoy entered the tropics, the heat became stifling. All ranks were warned that sunburn was a 'self-inflicted wound'. A shortage of fresh water meant that troops could only wash clothes in seawater. On 14 April orders were issued for the fresh water supply to be cut off daily between 9 a.m. and 6 p.m. Soldiers were instructed to 'fill water bottles daily before 0900 hrs for drinking purposes'. After a series of accidents, a general warning was issued of the 'danger of throwing orange or other fruit peelings in corridors and in stairways'.

On the *Queen Mary*, conditions below deck became so unbearably hot, according to the Pioneers' battalion history, that all training was cancelled during the day to allow the troops to get some relief on deck. At night, 'stripped to the waist and perspiring freely', men queued up at the wet canteen for beer at five pence a pint, but 'the conditions under which it was consumed were so unpleasant that few rejoined the queue'. In any case, getting drunk could cost a soldier his life: ship's orders stated that if anyone fell overboard the ship would not stop to pick them up. Sleeping in the heat was virtually impossible, and all over the ship furtive groups huddled over cards, with bundles of cash changing hands every night. Soldiers caught using 'empty bottles as urinals' were threatened with immediate arrest. 'The officers and nurses were more fortunate,' the battalion history reports. 'Their after-dinner leisure was spent in the large air-conditioned Tourist Lounge, or in the Cocktail Bar, where iced drinks were served by white-coated stewards.'

On 22 April the *Nieuw Amsterdam*, full of New Zealand troops, peeled away from the convoy, steaming for Singapore. During their brief stay on the island, the New Zealanders barely ventured outside the naval base. One wrote home:

The afternoon was spent on a small route march to a swimming bath about two miles from the boat, I will say the swim was good, but the march had me beat, it was too hot, enough to melt a man into a grease spot. There was no leave for us so one night we rushed the gangway and made an escape onto land where we could get a bit of fresh air. Myself I never want to see the place again.

Switching to the *Aquitania*, the New Zealanders reached Colombo harbour just five days after the Australians on the *Ile de France* and the *Mauretania*. The *Queen Mary* and *Queen Elizabeth* had to sail to Trincomalee on the far side of the island. The huge sister ships stayed a mere two days for refuelling, and the frustrated Pioneers were not allowed on shore.

The bustling, shabby city of Colombo was an eye-opener for troops who had never set foot outside Australia. Alf Sheppard remembered the snake charmers, the hawkers selling trinkets and souvenirs, and the madcap driving of the local taxi drivers. 'Woe betide anyone who got in their way,' Sheppard wrote. 'The horns, never still, made a nerve-wracking din.' Cheap meals were laid on at a seafront hotel, free buses ran to nearby tourist attractions, and the 'European ladies of the colony' served up tea and sandwiches at the troops' canteen. Soldiers were banned from visiting districts where smallpox was prevalent.

The Pioneers on board the *Queen Mary* and *Queen Elizabeth* were now several weeks ahead of the machine gunners. In the first week of May the Pioneers reached Port Tewfik, at the southern end of the Suez Canal. From there they were sent to Palestine, rattling south by train along the bank of the Suez Canal before crossing the canal at night in barges. Their destination was a newly built camp about 16 kilometres north of Gaza called Hill 95.

Lacking the speed of the British liners, the lumbering *Ile de France* was constantly at risk of attack by Axis aircraft and submarines lurking in the Gulf of Aden and the Red Sea. The machine gunners' diary records a conference between Blackburn and his company commanders on the subject of anti-aircraft protection: 'Dangers now rapidly becoming real; will be particularly so during the last 48 hrs of voyage.'

The danger of enemy attack was dramatically illustrated a few weeks later, when the requisitioned White Star liner *Georgic* was hit by German bombers while at anchor in Port Tewfik. A bomb exploded in the hold, starting an inferno that quickly spread to ammunition stored in the ship's dummy funnel. Ruptured fuel tanks fed the flames. Engineers managed to start the ship's engines, allowing the crew to drag the *Georgic* away from the main shipping lane and onto a sandbar, where the stricken ship was left to burn itself out. The blackened liner was eventually refloated and sent to India for repairs.

Many of the machine gunners were itching to be sent to the Western Desert, where Australian and Commonwealth troops were being besieged by Rommel's Afrika Korps at Tobruk. Instead they were ordered to join the Pioneers in Palestine.

Formed at Puckapunyal, Victoria, the 2/2nd Pioneer Battalion had been trained to perform engineering tasks such as road building and mine clearing, but a shortage of reserves meant the battalion would do more shooting than digging.

Hill 95 was close to the Gaza Ridge, where the Australian Light Horse under Lieutenant General Harry Chauvel had charged Turkish trenches in 1917. Nights were cold, but days were hot, dry and dusty. Several of the men were struck by the unfamiliar smell in the air, which some swore to be camel dung.

Tents were camouflaged and slit trenches dug; troops were forbidden to use the slit trenches as rubbish pits. There was some confusion over dress. An order requiring soldiers to wear shirts did not mention trousers, and some soldiers had been caught without any. The machine gunners' diary notes, '[A]s a few individuals appear to think that they are complying with the order by wearing shirts only, all troops will also be warned that shorts or trousers will be worn as well as shirts.'

Like other units sent to Palestine, the machine gunners were warned to guard their weapons and ammunition from the locals. 'They were expert thieves and it was necessary to take every possible precaution to prevent theft, including chaining rifles to tent poles at night,' wrote John Bellair. Negligence by an officer responsible for securing weapons led straight to a court martial. A guilty verdict usually saw the officer returned to Australia in disgrace, 'services no longer required'.

Thieves caught red-handed by the Pioneers were roughly dealt with. 'One unfortunate Arab who was apprehended was handed over to Maj. Lang and subjected to the indignity of a blanket toss,' the battalion history records, 'the blanket being removed after the last toss to allow the hapless victim to crash to the ground.'

Pilfering of weapons was not the only irritation the Australians faced in Palestine. Bellair recalled how 'drink of the worst kind was to be had in some of the surrounding villages—home-made firewater sold in bottles bearing respectable labels. Although there was a reasonable supply of Australian beer, men who wanted something stronger tried the local liquor, usually only once ... One member of the battalion, however, drank some of the stuff walking back to camp, lay down and went to sleep in the snow and was frozen to death. This tragedy was a grim enough warning to stop people buying it.'

At weekends, ten men per company were given leave to visit Jerusalem and Tel Aviv, the latter reminding some Pioneers of St Kilda beach in Melbourne.

NCOs worked hard to get their men into shape. The machine gunners' diary records 'PT, rifle exercises and route marches during the day'. Clothing and equipment was issued, including Vickers guns with new sights, transport vehicles and a staff car for Blackburn. The Pioneers were taught how to handle the Bren light machine gun and the Thompson submachine gun, which had been issued for the first time. Rumours circulated that the machine gunners would be sent to Crete to bolster British, Commonwealth and Greek troops defending the island against imminent German invasion. Meanwhile the Pioneers' commanding officer, Lieutenant Colonel Wellington, took his officers to Metulla, a town on the Syrian border, where they climbed a lookout tower and gazed across the parched Syrian countryside to the twin forts of Khiam and Merdjayoun—a reconnaissance trip that would prove valuable in the weeks to come.

At 7 p.m. on 4 June 1941 the machine gun battalion was told it would be taking part in Operation Exporter, the invasion of Syria. The Pioneers would join in but would not fight as a battalion, each of its four companies instead supporting a different brigade.

Since the fall of France, Syria had been under Vichy control. Around 34,000 Australian, British, Indian and Free French soldiers faced more than 50,000 Vichy troops supported by German and Italian planes. Few among the British high command expected the Vichy troops to fight. The Free French commander expected them to come over en masse to the allied side. Even Field Marshall Wavell, the Allied commander in the Middle East, appeared convinced that the campaign could be won with 'propaganda leaflets and display of force'.

Australians formed the bulk of the invaders—a fact that it was hoped would further demoralise the Vichy troops. While the Allies were supported by ships, they had no tanks and only a handful of anti-tank guns—a disadvantage that would be the cause of many Australian casualties.

Safe from the fighting, 150 kilometres away in a swanky Jerusalem hotel, the British commander, General Henry Maitland 'Jumbo' Wilson, overruled the Australian commander, Lieutenant General John Lavarack, by dividing his forces in three. In his official history of Australia's role in the war, Gavin Long notes that while a strategy of simultaneous attacks might have worked against dispirited defenders, against a determined enemy it risked sabotaging the chance of overall success. In the event, Vichy troops manoeuvring behind the divided Allied advance would briefly threaten not just to push the Allies out of Syria but to chase them across the border into Palestine.

A lack of transport prevented the machine gun battalion from taking part in the initial thrust. Private Bill Schmitt's uncle, a First World War veteran, had urged him to join the machine gunners because 'they're not right up the front like the infantry'. But Blackburn's machine gunners were not on the sidelines for long.

Private Keith 'Chook' Fowler, who had initially been rejected by the army on medical grounds, recalled, 'Blackie couldn't get us into action quick enough. He liked the honour and the glory.'

Far from streaming across to join their Free French compatriots, the Vichy French were up for the fight, eager to redeem the country's military honour after the capitulation to Hitler.

On 11 June the machine gunners suffered their first casualties during an attack by enemy aircraft. Private William McGregor was killed; Sergeant Stan Owen and Privates Harold Gobbie, Fred Mitchell and Fred Cullinger were wounded.

Private Fowler had a different battle on his hands. Born in Adelaide and brought up by an aunt after his father 'cleared off', Fowler had been assigned to B Company, which had been mainly raised in Victoria. By his own admission pretty uneducated, Fowler was given a hard time by his comrades after he was made 'No. 2'—the gunner's right-hand man—on the company's 'No. 1' gun, a position they felt should go to someone more senior, or maybe smarter.

There wasn't much to envy about being the No. 2 man on a Vickers machine gun crew. Apart from being shot at by enemy gunners, the main hazard was deafness. The Vickers could fire up to 500 rounds a minute. Sergeant Ron Graetz, another No. 2 man, recalled the noise being so loud that 'for days and days afterwards, you could see blokes' lips moving but you couldn't hear anything.' Graetz, who fought alongside Fowler in Syria, suffered permanent hearing damage.

Despite the hazards, Fowler's comrades begrudged him the No. 2 role. 'They thought I should be the "No. 5", at the arse end,' Fowler recalled in 'Machine Gun Memoirs'. One soldier in particular, classically educated, set about cutting Fowler down to size, deliberately bamboozling him with quotes from Shakespeare. During an enemy barrage, the other man, Fred Souter, broke down and started weeping uncontrollably. 'What did I do? I went up and consoled him, put my arms around him, held him and said, "It's all right, Fred, you'll be OK." Then I broke down too. The whole thing just exploded in my head.' The trauma of the barrage was so great that Fowler went temporarily blind.

On 15 June Blackburn was given orders to hold or destroy a strategically important bridge over the Jordan River. The bridge was 45 kilometres away, and Blackburn was told to have his men dug in and ready to fight by dawn. Vichy planes were active at night, and the column obeyed a strict blackout: on Blackburn's instructions, windscreens were pulled out and brake lights destroyed. With no moonlight to guide them, the only way Blackburn's drivers could stay on the road was by having a navigator hanging out of the cabin to watch the edge. In the rush to reach the bridge, two motorcycles fell over a precipice and a signals lieutenant died after being crushed between two trucks.

Thirty kilometres away, 1500 Vichy troops with 40 tanks were attacking the town of Quneitra. With the assault on the bridge expected at any minute, Blackburn was ordered to deliver desperately needed ammunition to the British Royal Fusiliers defending Quneitra. The town fell before the ammunition arrived, only to be recaptured 24 hours later with the support of Blackburn's machine gunners. Recalling his entry into the devastated town, Blackburn described

a French tank burning and nearly red hot ... overturned lorries, British and French, three smashed armoured cars, dead horses, piles of ammunition ... and several ordinary cars riddled with bullets. In spite of this most of the shops were open. Australians, those off duty, were wandering along the streets buying. Locals were calmly cleaning up, sorting their belongings, shopping and seeming indifferent to the war.

The Syrians were not always so unperturbed. Blackburn witnessed streams of civilians escaping with their belongings from towns ruined by the fighting. 'It is difficult to describe the look of hurt misery in these people,' he wrote in a letter home. 'They are thoroughly cowed and horribly anxious to make you think they are on your side. Poor devils, they would necessarily be exactly the same to the enemy if they recaptured the place.'

After the fall of Quneitra, the machine gunners were ordered to join an advance by Free French, Indian and British troops who had been held up outside Damascus. Again, it was Vichy tanks and armoured cars that were the main problem, stopping the Free French in their tracks and threatening to decimate an Indian brigade armed with nothing more than rifles. Even with the promise of Australian machine gun support, the Free French commander, Colonel Casseau, was reluctant to move. With nearly 1000 yards (914 metres) of apparently unoccupied land in front of them, the machine gunners defied conventional tactics and advanced by them-selves, pushing aggressively into no man's land and clearing out any enemy positions they encountered for the Free French to occupy. According to the unit diary, 'By this means some considerable progress was made with the advance and the Free French finally advanced some 3 or 4 miles.'

The Pioneers, meanwhile, had been involved in bloody fighting for the Vichy stronghold of Fort Merdjayoun. The fort was captured by the Allies, retaken, and recaptured, but the cost was high. While the British guns failed to breach the walls, Vichy artillery ripped into the hapless Pioneers. In a single day of fighting outside the fort's massive walls—Corporal Harry Walker remembers them being 'about six feet thick all made of rock'—the Pioneers lost 27 killed, 46 wounded and 29 captured. 'That was a stupid bloody arrangement,' machine gunner Allan Gardiner told Blackburn's biographer. 'They sent in the ... Pioneers that many bloody times. Poor buggers. Jeez they got knocked around. I don't think they recognised how strongly held the fort was. They were Foreign Legion blokes ... and they had tanks and we didn't.'

With Merdjayoun finally in Allied hands, the Pioneers were sent to capture a ridge north-east of the town, with the machine gunners again in support. Intelligence suggesting that the ridge was weakly defended proved to be false. The Pioneers found themselves up against 2000 Vichy troops. The result was the same as at Merdjayoun: the Australians were mown down. The Pioneers' battalion history records that 53-year-old Staff Sergeant Wally Peeler, like Blackburn a Victoria Cross recipient from the 1914–18 war, went into no man's land that night to recover the wounded, bringing back four soldiers who had survived all day in the baking Syrian sun.

On 21 June the mayor of Damascus emerged under a flag of truce to offer a formal surrender of the city and its police force. As the senior 'British' officer present, Blackburn joined Colonel Casseau in taking the surrender, despite the fact that (as he later admitted) he had 'no authority whatever' to be present. At the ceremony the French commander made 'a special little speech acknowledging the glories of Australia—so I gathered, which I was pleased to accept (not understanding one word of French) in a short speech in Australian—which they all equally solemnly pretended to understand and accept!'

Taking the Vichy surrender was 'quite a moment for our redoubtable CO', Private Des Jackson recalled proudly. 'It was also . . . the day that the Germans invaded Russia.' (Jackson was one day out—Hitler's invasion of the Soviet Union, Operation Barbarossa, began on 22 June.)

The Vichy capital had fallen, but the fighting did not end until 11 July. During this time the Pioneers were involved in a fierce battle for Damour, the French administrative capital, 30 kilometres south of Beirut. The fall of Damour on 9 July, after Australian troops encircled the town, left the road to Beirut open. The armistice was signed at Acre three days later. By then Operation Barbarossa was nearly three weeks old. While there was now little prospect of the Germans invading Syria, the hard-won territory had to be secured and held. Together with the Pioneers, Blackburn's machine gunners became part of the Allied occupying force.

The Syrian campaign had been a strange one. It was not just French soldiers who felt their loyalties divided. Taken prisoner during the fighting outside Merdjayoun, a group of Pioneers was evacuated to the safety of Beirut by their Vichy captors. Passing through lines of Vichy reserves, they were met by a number of British fighters serving with the French Foreign Legion. The battalion history records that the British mercenaries 'paused to exchange friendly greetings. Such was the nature of the Syrian campaign.'

Like many of his mates, Private Jackson revelled in the opportunity to play the tourist when not on duty. As well as visiting 'famous places such as Homs, Aleppo, Beirut, Jerusalem and Tel Aviv', Jackson took the opportunity to explore the Roman ruins at Palmyra and at Baalbek, in Lebanon's Bekaa Valley.

The occupation brought its own hardships. Sandflies, sandfly fever and so-called 'Syrian sores' were a constant nuisance. An outbreak of sandfly fever among Pioneer companies stationed at El Mina, the port of Tripoli, led to 'a vast increase in the number of daily sick'. Many Australian soldiers contracted malaria; some had already died of the disease. Mosquito nets were handed out and troops were issued with quinine. The battalion history notes that soldiers were 'warned not to eat a Syrian dish called *ghibee* made of minced raw meat, barley and various spices. It was palatable but could cause intestinal worm infection. Brothels in the town of Elmina were declared out of bounds for obvious reasons.'

A Commission of Control was set up with headquarters in Beirut. The Australian officers on the commission got along well with their purported enemies, the Vichy French; less well with their allies the Free French, who claimed much of the glory and most of the spoils despite having played only a bit part in the fighting. Furious at the way the Free French had grabbed the lion's share of captured equipment and weapons, a company of Australian machine gunners carried out a smash-and-grab on the British Ordnance Stores in the Lebanese town of Rayak, liberating for their own use badly needed spares and military hardware.

From early October the machine gunners were billeted in Fih and Bterram, small Lebanese villages not far from the coast south of Tripoli. They were there when momentous news arrived of the Japanese attack on the US Pacific Fleet at Pearl Harbor on 7 December 1941. In the New Year the battalion moved to a new camp, Hill 69 near Gaza. There, as Private Jackson recalled, 'we began the rather strange procedure of training for jungle warfare in a desert'.

Chapter 2
DESTINATION UNKNOWN

The fighting in Syria left 416 Australian soldiers dead and more than 1100 wounded. The Machine Gun Battalion's losses—nine dead and 34 wounded—were relatively light beside those of the infantry battalions and the Pioneers. Seventy-three officers and men of the 2/2nd Pioneers were killed, with another 102 wounded in action and others evacuated sick. Small wonder, as Blackburn's biographer put it, that 'Blackburn's men speak of the Pioneers in terms of reverence'. In the months to come, the bond between the two units would be tested under circumstances that no Australian soldier—not even Blackburn—could have foreseen.

Japan's entry into the war had deadly implications for Australia, which had grown used to sheltering behind Britain's supposedly impregnable island fortress of Singapore. The Australian government had lobbied hard—but with little success—for Britain to send more planes to defend the island in the event of an attack. Within hours of the raid on Pearl

Harbor, Japanese bombers attacked Singapore. Two days later, Japanese planes caught the British battleships *Prince of Wales* and *Repulse* in the open sea off the east coast of Malaya, sinking both ships with torpedoes. Japanese troops landed in Malaya and advanced rapidly down the peninsula towards Singapore. Besides the tin mines and rubber plantations in Malaya, the Japanese had their eyes on another prize: the rich oilfields of the Netherlands East Indies.

For more than a year, the Dutch had been resisting Japan's increasingly strident diplomatic demands for oil from the NEI. Anticipating that Japan would sooner or later resort to force, the Dutch had attempted to strengthen their forces in the NEI, but their appeals for armaments were considered a low priority by the Allies' two major arms manufacturers, Britain and the United States. The Americans, still nominally committed to a policy of non-intervention, would not give any guarantee of support in the event of Japanese aggression towards the NEI. Britain, with its shared imperial interests, was more amenable, but in return for Churchill's vague promises of military support the Dutch were locked into a broader Far Eastern strategy centred on Fortress Singapore.

Details were hammered out between military officials from Britain, Australia and the Netherlands at the Singapore Conference in February 1941, which led to the Dutch agreeing to commit four squadrons of aircraft to Singapore in the event of war with Japan, disastrously weakening its already enfeebled air force in the NEI. In return, Australia agreed to deploy matching squadrons to Ambon and Timor. In his book *Allies in a Bind: Australia and Netherlands East Indies relations during the Second World War*, Jack Ford argues that this was 'far more of a concrete commitment than either the Americans or the British were prepared to give'.

Immediately after the Japanese attack on Pearl Harbor, the Dutch honoured their promise by sending four squadrons to Singapore—a move that was to have profound ramifications for the defence of the NEI.

According to the battalion history, the entry of Japan and the United States into the war 'caused much discussion and speculation' among the machine gunners in Syria. The war had suddenly come much closer to home. As the Australians tucked into a Christmas dinner of roast turkey and plum pudding—served, as tradition required, by the officers and sergeants—decisions were being made in London, Washington and Canberra that would have terrible consequences for all of them.

British, Indian, Australian and Malay troops were in headlong retreat from the Japanese in Malaya. The speed of the Japanese advance had created an air of panic in Canberra, and the Australian government wanted its soldiers home. At midnight on 31 January 1942, the men at Hill 69 clambered into cattle trucks bound for El Kantara on the Suez Canal, where they would cross the canal before boarding an Egyptian train for Port Tewfik. The order to leave came so suddenly that the machine gunners took only their rifles and personal kit. The battalion's Vickers guns, equipment and vehicles were left behind on the understanding that they would be sent on.

Privates Neil MacPherson, Bluey Rowe and Hugh Sorley were among a group of 52 West Australians from the Training Battalion in Dimra who found themselves transferred to the 2/2nd Pioneer Battalion as replacements for the men lost in Syria. Along with the machine gunners, the Pioneers believed they were on their way home.

MacPherson was one of five brothers from Perth whose parents had emigrated from Scotland to take up a group settlement block at Margaret River. His father, a First World War veteran, had been promised 500 acres (202 hectares)—'a huge block, but nobody told him it was timbered'. Like many other migrant settlers, MacPherson's parents had lost their land during the Depression when they couldn't keep up the interest payments on their mortgage. In the years after the Depression, his father was often unemployed. Australian soldiers were generally bigger, fitter and healthier than their counterparts in the British army, but at nineteen, MacPherson knew what it was like to go hungry.

The machine gunners shivered as overnight temperatures in the Sinai plunged to zero. But worse was to come. The engine that was to take them to Port Tewfik broke down and the soldiers were ordered to remain on the train until it was fixed. 'We spent a miserable day crammed together in ancient wooden coaches, impatiently waiting for the journey to begin,' Private Jackson recalled. 'Eventually at 3 p.m. there was a bustle of activity and after many shouts and much fuss, the engine gave a whistle, the buffers thudded against each other and the train clanked out of El Kantara about six hours behind schedule.' For many of them, those six hours would be the difference between life and death.

Near Ismailia, the train rattled past the barbed-wire perimeter of an Allied camp holding German and Italian prisoners of war. Some of the Australians hurled abuse at the enemy soldiers as they passed. While the Italians 'replied vociferously', the Germans merely ignored them. It was an encounter that would stick in the mind of one of the machine gunners, Private Jack Thomas, who had been earning 15 shillings a week as an office boy in Broken Hill when he decided to enlist. 'I held those men in disrespect,' Thomas recalled of the prisoners corralled behind barbed wire. 'I looked at them with an air of conquest. I learned what humility was all about when, within a year, I became a prisoner of war myself.'

Arriving at Port Tewfik, the machine gunners discovered that the ship they were supposed to board, the *Mauretania*, had sailed without them. After a night in tents, they were instructed to leave their kitbags in piles on the stone jetty. It was a hectic scene. Barrage balloons filled the sky above a harbour crowded with small freighters manoeuvring gingerly between the hulks of sunken troop transports. Lying at anchor was a large, modern single-funnelled passenger ship that Jackson recognised as the Orient liner *Orcades*.

The machine gunners were marched aboard in time for lunch: 33 officers and around 600 other ranks. Others had been transferred as

reinforcements to another machine gun battalion and would fight at
El Alamein. Blackburn's battalion joined their comrades from the Syrian
campaign, the Pioneers, and a smattering of troops from other units.
Altogether there were 3400 soldiers on a ship meant to carry 2000. Private
Jackson lit a cigarette and had a look around. Hearing the noise of the
anchor being weighed, he thought, 'Surely we wouldn't sail without our
kitbags.'

Jackson was not the only one worried. The men's kitbags and officers'
valises were stuck on two railway trucks, in full view of the troops preparing to sail. Blackburn asked the skipper, Captain Fox, to delay sailing until
the battalion's baggage could be loaded but was rebuffed. Tied up in port,
the *Orcades* was an easy target for enemy aircraft and Fox was responsible
for the lives of more than three thousand Australian troops, as well as
several hundred others on board. He was anxious to get away.

The *Orcades* left Port Tewfik on 1 February 1942. Sailing without
their personal baggage was bad enough, but much of the machine gun
battalion's fighting equipment—including all its Vickers guns and ammunition—was also left behind, together with vehicles and drivers. Over
the following days most of the missing equipment would be crammed
aboard other ships, mostly slow freighters, but none of it ever reached the
machine gunners.

Things were not much better for the Pioneers. Ammunition above
50 rounds per man (1000 rounds per light machine gun) was supposed
to be loaded onto the *Orcades* with the baggage party, but 'owing to bad
organisation on the part of the embarkation staff, the Bn [battalion] sailed
without the baggage party, ammunition reserve and kitchen gear. All other
units on the boat in the same condition.' The lack of cooking utensils 'was
very keenly felt . . . as without them we were unable even to boil water for
tea.' In the absence of proper utensils, the men boiled water in biscuit tins.

It was not only military equipment that had to be abandoned. Private
Jim Wastell, a stretcher bearer and medical orderly, played trombone in

the battalion's much-admired band. After the Syrian armistice, Wastell had been presented with a French trombone rescued from the citadel at Homs. As the battalion history records, 'He packed it carefully in his kitbag which was left on the wharf at Port Tewfik. He did not see his kitbag or his trombone again.'

Having endured the discomforts of the *Ile de France*, few complained about conditions on the *Orcades*. The food was good, but the overcrowding meant there were limited opportunities for physical training. Private Jackson was not the only one excited at the thought of returning home, with or without equipment, to help defend Australia against the advancing Japanese. After two and a half days' sailing, the *Orcades* passed through 'Hell's Gate', the straits dividing the Red Sea from the Gulf of Aden, and swung east. The Pioneers' unit diary records that on 4 February, 'security pamphlets on jungle warfare opened'. Four days later 'notes on NEI issued and lectures to troops given'. The Australians were ordered into tropical kit.

Reports of a ship being torpedoed 50 nautical miles from Colombo put everyone on high alert. Since the *Orcades* had no naval escort, Captain Fox had to rely on speed and cunning. As the ship steamed across the Indian Ocean, changing course every few minutes to foil enemy submarines, the troops pored over jungle warfare manuals. While their destination was still unknown, it was beginning to seem unlikely that it would be Australia. A clue to where they might end up came on 8 February, when officers were issued with a pamphlet entitled 'The Customs and the Peoples of the Netherlands East Indies'.

Other military pamphlets that went the rounds contained advice about jungle warfare. Max 'Geezer' McGee, a machine gunner from Adelaide who had joined up at the age of 20, recalled listening to lectures about how short-sighted and poorly armed the Japanese soldiers were. Apparently, 'they could not see at night, they could not fire and hit anything over 200 yards'. McGee attributed this useless information to the British, who were already being taught a lesson in jungle fighting by the Japanese in Burma and Malaya.

The next day the Pioneers were re-issued with the weapons they had deposited in the ship's armoury after leaving Port Tewfik. On 9 February the *Orcades* sailed into Colombo harbour. Crowded with merchantmen and warships, the port was shrouded with oily black smoke. Colombo had been bombed. When the Australians arrived, parts of the town were still burning.

The machine gunners had stopped at Colombo en route from Australia to the Middle East, but it was all new to the Pioneers. Plans for shore leave had to be abandoned when orders came through that they would only be staying long enough to take on supplies. Within 24 hours the *Orcades*, escorted by the cruiser HMS *Dorsetshire*, was steaming through the harbour boom and out into the Bay of Bengal.

Two divisions of Australian soldiers were now on their way back from the Middle East, but their destination was still a mystery. 'As a private soldier,' Thomas recalls, 'you're not the first to be told where you're going.' As the convoy zigzagged across the Indian Ocean, Rangoon, Sumatra, Java, Darwin and even Fremantle seemed possible destinations.

One of the fastest troop ships of the war, the *Orcades* was now far ahead of the rest of the fleet. On 13 February Colonel Blackburn warned his men to prepare for attack by enemy submarines, planes and warships. The same day an Australian ship, HMAS *Hobart*, took over from the *Dorsetshire*—a switch that some interpreted, wishfully, as confirmation that they were heading home.

By now news of the unfolding catastrophe in Malaya was known to everyone on board the *Orcades*. Blackburn received urgent orders to land at Oosthaven, a harbour on the southern tip of Sumatra. The Japanese, eager to secure Sumatra's oil wells, were preparing to drop paratroopers to take the airfield at Palembang, 300 kilometres north. Blackburn's force was to get to the airfield first and hold it. Blackburn called his senior officers together. It was a 'suicide mission', one officer who was there remembered being told. According to signals officer Edward Starrett, Blackburn left it to individual officers to decide how to inform their men, but he urged them to 'spend 10 minutes or so to settle down and absorb the situation' before speaking to them.

On the morning of 15 February, the troops awoke to find the ship sliding between tiny offshore islands towards a jungle-fringed coast. 'We didn't understand what was happening,' Corporal Harry Walker recalled. 'We were always kept in the dark.' Keith Ford and his mates 'thought we were going to Australia and we were until we did a left hand turn in the middle of the Indian Ocean'.

At around 9 a.m., they anchored a few kilometres off the Sumatran coast. On the same day, news came over the ship's loudspeakers that Singapore had fallen. 'It was a stunning moment,' Private Jackson recalled.

Plans were hurriedly made to disembark the troops, although for what purpose it was hard to say. With most of their weapons and equipment left behind at Port Tewfik, the Australians had little with which to defend themselves, let alone stop the relentless advance of the Imperial Japanese Army.

The machine gun battalion, Jackson wrote, 'had no machine guns of any type, no mortars and no hand grenades. About 100 men, who had no firearms at all, were expected to fight with bayonets and knives . . . the prospect of fighting a formidable opponent in unfamiliar jungle country, virtually unarmed, was not exactly attractive.'

On a personal level, however, things were looking up for Private Jackson. After some time as acting corporal, Jackson was confirmed in his new rank with a corresponding jump in his pay.

The Pioneers were luckier than the machine gunners, having managed to bring some of their Bren guns from Syria, but the force as a whole was desperately short of weapons and ammunition. 'The ammunition worked out at 8 rounds per man and the chances of success at practically nil,'

Lieutenant Wally Summons wrote in his wartime memoir, *Twice their Prisoner*. The only advice given to troops without rifles was to pick up the one dropped by the man in front after he had been shot. Some of the rifles were from the First World War or even earlier; a few had to be issued without ammunition. Some of the machine gunners were armed with nothing but wooden clubs or pickaxe handles.

Jack Thomas was one of those armed with a Canadian-made Ross rifle—a weapon that dated back almost to the Boer War and was often fitted with a piece of rope for a sling. Thomas remembers feeling 'a certain amount of apprehension' at the thought of going up against Japanese machine guns with 'a single shot rifle, no magazine, and a pocketful of rounds'.

If Blackburn was dismayed by the thought of trying to defend Sumatra with sticks and obsolete rifles, he didn't show it. Complaints about equipment and weapons got short shrift from the commanding officer. Lieutenant Jack Goodrick, not yet out of his teens when war broke out, told Blackburn's biographer, 'There were occasions when you thought . . . he's mad. He had no sense of danger judging by some of the things he said and did. He could never be overwhelmed . . . He took everything in his stride.'

The landing force was ferried ashore on a small Dutch freighter. Japanese bombers were only minutes away but fortunately none appeared, otherwise there would have been carnage on the deck of the *Orcades*. As it was, the most troublesome foe was the swarms of mosquitoes that attacked the troops as they neared the shore.

It was dark when the freighter reached the wharf. A monsoonal downpour drenched the troops huddled together on deck. Australian morale was not improved by the sight of a row of British armoured cars parked on the pier, apparently waiting to be loaded onto ships. By the time Blackburn's troops had begun going ashore, news came through that the Japanese had already captured the airfield at Palembang and seized the nearby oilfields.

The smell of panic was in the air. Corporal Walker recalled, 'We got to Oosthaven just on dark to be met by one surprised service man. His greeting was: "What are you doing here? This place has been evacuated. The Allies have capitulated. I'm waiting here for a tug boat to take me off."'

Before Blackburn's prediction of a 'suicide mission' could come true, the order to land was reversed. 'The powers that be decided the Japs were too close,' Neil MacPherson recalls.

A signal ordering the troops to re-embark was received by the captain of the destroyer *Encounter*, which was lying at anchor in the harbour. The advancing Japanese were now reported to be less than 20 kilometres from Oosthaven. The British were getting out and Blackburn's troops, with their pickaxe handles and Boer War rifles, were ordered to join them. 'Needless to say, no one was sorry,' Jackson wrote.

Around the harbour confusion reigned. In the sheds Wally Summons saw 'a few cases stencilled with "Britain delivers the goods" and some tired troops sleeping on the ground'.

The rain was still falling, and the tropical night was so dark it was almost impossible to distinguish the outlines of the numerous ships at anchor. The *Orcades*, showing no lights in case of enemy air attack, lurked somewhere in the blackness out to sea—if she hadn't already sailed.

A coral reef gave protection to ships inside the harbour but made entering and leaving hazardous. Walker remembered the freighter's captain refusing to go back out to sea without a pilot. 'The pilot had shot through. I didn't know what had happened to him . . . the captain eventually took us back without a pilot and it was about midnight when we got back to the *Orcades*. We were relieved to find the ship waiting for us.'

According to the machine gunners' history, the Dutch captain had been extraordinarily lucky to find the liner at all: 'A single flash of lightning had illuminated the huge black outline of the troopship and given him his bearings.'

It was after midnight before the troops were re-embarked and plied with hot cocoa and sandwiches. A few hours later the *Orcades* was racing across the Sunda Strait, which separates the islands of Sumatra and Java. Its destination was Tandjong Priok, the port of Batavia (now Jakarta). Once again, there was no sign of Japanese planes, despite the number of Allied ships converging on the port from Sumatra and Singapore.

The *Orcades* reached Tandjong Priok in the early afternoon of 16 February. In the distance, just visible against the horizon, a huge Japanese invasion fleet was moving slowly along the coast towards Bali and Timor. Held for 48 hours on the *Orcades*, the Pioneers and machine gunners waited impatiently to learn their fate. Australian stragglers and deserters from the rout in Singapore were running amok on the wharves, looting stores and jeering at the new arrivals. Blackburn rounded up those who were willing to join him and had the rest sent to the lock-up. Two badly holed British cruisers lay at anchor in the harbour. Keith Ford was one of many 'hoping to Christ' that the *Orcades* would just weigh anchor and leave. Corporal Jackson felt there was still a chance of returning to Australia. Java, he believed, was as good as lost already. Two fighting battalions armed with rifles and clubs, bolstered by an assortment of drivers, engineers, cooks, members of a mobile laundry and stragglers from Singapore, would be no match for the Japanese, so why land them at all?

Chapter 3
GREATCOATS WILL BE WORN

Three weeks earlier, on 27 January 1942, the commander of the Australian I Corps, General John Lavarack, had been called to a meeting with the British commander of Allied forces in Southeast Asia, General Archibald Wavell. At the time, Blackburn's Pioneers and machine gunners were still several days away from leaving Suez. Wavell had arrived in Batavia in early January and set up headquarters at Lembang, near the major town of Bandoeng in West Java.

The commander of Allied forces had a low opinion of the fighting ability of his enemy. David Day, in his book *The Great Betrayal: Britain, Australia and the onset of the Pacific War 1939–42*, quotes Wavell advising Singapore's Commander-in-Chief, Sir Robert Brooke-Popham, that with sufficient air support 'You ought easily to be able to deal with any Japanese attack on Malaya,' and adding, 'I should be most doubtful if the Japs ever tried to make an attack . . . and I am sure they will get [it] in the neck if they do.'

Even after the NEI campaign was over, Wavell continued to disparage Japanese air power. In his 'Despatch by the Supreme Commander of the ABDA [American-British-Dutch-Australian] Area to the Combined Chiefs of Staff on Operations in the South-West Pacific', Wavell wrote, 'I have always maintained, and still do, that the Japanese air force is comparatively weak and can be overcome whenever the Allies manage to concentrate a sufficient air force under favourable conditions'. This was a remarkable assessment given the lethal airborne attacks on Pearl Harbor and on the British battleships *Prince of Wales* and *Repulse*.

Of all the territories Japan's Southern Army was planning to capture—the Philippines, British Malaya, Burma, the Dutch East Indies and Timor—Japanese military chiefs had identified Malaya and Java as the most difficult. In the official Japanese history of the invasion of the Netherlands East Indies, translated into English in 2015, the Chief of the Army General Staff, Hajime Sugiyama, is quoted as saying that the Java operation would be 'very difficult'. On 30 December 1941 Sugiyama told the Chief of the Navy General Staff, Osami Nagano:

[I]n the Malaya operation, owing to divine aid and the close cooperation between the Army and the Navy, we were able to achieve brilliant military gains by conducting a surprise attack on the enemy. However, as for the Java operation that we will conduct shortly, we must expect that it will be extremely difficult compared to the Malaya operation, owing to the facts that the enemy has rapidly been reinforcing its defence in the area these days, that it is more difficult to make a surprise attack on Java than on Malaya, and that the enemy is getting familiar with our ways of conducting landing operations.

Since the attack on Pearl Harbor, American troops in the Philippines had been forced back into the Bataan peninsula; the Japanese had occupied Kuala Lumpur and invaded Burma, and New Guinea had been bombed. By late January it was becoming clear, even to General Wavell, that he had seriously underestimated the Japanese. Lavarack did not go alone to the meeting on 27 January but took along his chief of staff, Major General Berryman, and his senior intelligence officer, Lieutenant Colonel Wills. Both Berryman and Lavarack were horrified by events in Malaya and scornful of Allied preparations for the defence of Java. Wavell's initial plan had been for the Australian 6th and 7th Divisions returning from the Middle East to defend the southern part of Sumatra (the 7th Division) and the 'middle belt' of Java (the 6th Division). Lavarack did not agree with the corps being split, but when he took his objections to the Australian government he was told to obey Wavell's orders but to press for the divisions to be united as soon as the situation permitted.

Wills, the intelligence chief, was equally unimpressed, insisting that the two Australian divisions could not arrive in time to save Sumatra and Java from the Japanese and warning that any Australian troops landing before a Japanese attack would be 'lost', putting 'the defence and safety of Australia itself' in jeopardy.

The escalating disaster in Malaya, which seemed certain to end with the loss of Singapore, ruled out any possibility of the 6th and 7th Divisions landing in Java. But that still left the question of what to do with Blackburn's band of Pioneers and machine gunners, who were at that moment on their way to Suez and, so they imagined, across the Indian Ocean to Australia.

Wills later recalled that at the meeting in Lembang, 'Wavell . . . told us that Singapore was about to fall and 6th and 7th Divisions were not to come to Java. We were to get out, but a small force of Australians under Blackburn was to stay for political reasons to bolster Dutch resistance and to prolong it as long as possible.' Wills, an old friend of Blackburn's from Adelaide, offered to stay and fight, but his offer was refused.

The news from Malaya continued to worsen. By 13 February the fall of Singapore looked imminent. In an 'appreciation' written for the chief of the Australian general staff, General Sturdee, Lavarack confirmed that even with two Australian divisions he would be unable to hold Java. Wavell gave a similar opinion to the Combined Chiefs of Staff in Washington and the War Office in London.

The fate of Blackburn's battalions still hung in the balance. Notes from Australian I Corps headquarters at Tjisaroea in Java show that as late as 16 February '[n]othing definite has been decided with regard to the role of the personnel contained in the *Orcades*'.

Meanwhile Sturdee had written a compelling paper of his own in which he scathingly described the two Dutch divisions in Java as more like 'Home Guards than an Army capable of undertaking active operations'. While the Dutch, although 'inexperienced and not highly trained', would probably put up a fight, Sturdee commented that the rank and file were 'natives whose fighting qualities are doubtful under conditions of modern warfare'. It was unlikely, he said, that the Javanese were 'as good as British Indians, who so far have not been very successful against the Japanese'. Noting that the benign topography, well-developed communications and abundant natural resources would all favour the Japanese invaders, Sturdee concluded that the prospects of successfully defending Java were 'far from encouraging'. Even if it could be held, Java did not fit any of the military criteria for a continental base from which to launch a concerted Pacific campaign with American help against the Japanese: this could only be done from Australia.

Acting on Sturdee's and Lavarack's advice, the Australian Prime Minister, John Curtin, cabled Churchill in London requesting that the Australian 6th and 7th Divisions in transit from the Middle East, along with the 9th Division in Palestine, be returned to Australia.

The next day Wavell sent his own cable to Churchill, advising against the landing of the Australian divisions on Java. 'Burma and Australia are absolutely vital for war against Japan,' Wavell wrote. 'Loss of Java, though severe blow from every point of view, would not be fatal. Efforts should not therefore be made to reinforce Java which might compromise defence of Burma or Australia.' While concluding that the risk of deploying the returning Australians in Java was both tactically and strategically 'unjustifiable', Wavell added a significant rider: 'I fully recognize political considerations involved.'

Those 'political considerations' would determine the fate of the soldiers on the *Orcades*. Convinced that landing them at Batavia would be futile, Lavarack tried to prevent the troops from being disembarked. Wavell, anxious not to 'compromise' relations with the Dutch and fearful of damaging Allied 'prestige', ignored him. In Australia, General Sturdee presciently warned the government that once Blackburn's men had been landed and distributed around Java it would be nearly impossible to get them out.

Unfortunately for Blackburn's ragtag force, its destiny was being overshadowed by the larger question of what to do with the Australian divisions returning from the Middle East. While Curtin was adamant that they should all come home, Churchill wanted at least one Australian division to bolster the desperate Allied defence of Burma. The US president, Franklin Roosevelt, pressured the Australians to agree, offering to send American troops to Australia in return. But Curtin, too shrewd to accept the airy promise of untested Americans in the place of battle-hardened Australian soldiers already on ships, refused.

Churchill resorted to moral blackmail in an attempt to change Curtin's mind, insisting it was in direct response to Curtin's demand for Singapore to be reinforced that the British 18th Division had been ordered to fight there rather than in Burma, and that Australia therefore bore a 'heavy share' of responsibility for its loss. His cable to the Australian prime minister began:

I suppose you realise that your leading division, the head of which is sailing south of Colombo to the Netherlands East Indies at this moment in our scanty British and American shipping, is the only force that can reach Rangoon in time to prevent its loss and the severance of communication with China. It can begin to disembark at Rangoon on the 26th or 27th. There is nothing else in the world that can fill the gap.

By the time the cable was sent, Churchill had already taken the extraordinary step of diverting ships carrying the Australian 7th Division to Rangoon on the off-chance that Curtin and his war cabinet would buckle. They didn't, and after further angry cables between the two governments the convoy was refueled and eventually arrived safely in Australia minus one ship: the *Orcades*.

On the wharf at Tandjong Priok, the tug of war continued. Amid the constant wail of air-raid sirens, the troops were kept aboard the ship while Blackburn and Wavell argued over their disembarkation. Private Bill Schmitt recalled, 'I had a rifle, five rounds of ammunition, and the clothes I stood up in. It was hopeless—the biggest mess-up you've ever seen.'

Sergeant Redmond 'Red' Sheedy told Blackburn's biographer that he and his mates were ordered off the ship several times, re-embarking each time. 'This went on about five times. I thought "we're not going to land here", so I left half my stuff on board.' In his memoir Max McGee recalled, 'For two days Blackie refused to order us off the ship. In the end he was promoted to brigadier and ordered off . . . he then had to obey or face a court martial. He was too good a soldier to do that. So we lost the fight.' McGee was just a machine gunner and not privy to details of the conversation between Colonel Blackburn and General Wavell, but there is no doubt Blackburn's men believed their leader had done all he could to get them home.

Australian efforts to prevent the landing caused deep and lasting resentment among the British, with Wavell's Chief of Staff, General

Pownall, excoriating the Australian government for its 'damnable attitude' and suggesting that the attempted withdrawal from Java had shown Australians—'the most egotistical conceited people imaginable'—in their 'true colours'.

Eventually, on 19 February, the troops on the *Orcades* were ordered to disembark. They were supplied with rations for three days. Along with the Pioneers and machine gunners (still without machine guns) were units from the 2/6th Field Company, the 2/2nd Casualty Clearing Station and the 105th General Transport Company, plus the stragglers from Singapore whom Blackburn had persuaded to join up. In his 'Report on Operations of the AIF in Java Feb/Mar 1942', Blackburn estimated the total strength of AIF troops under his command at 'approx. 2,500' and described them as 'very insufficiently equipped'.

On the same day that Blackburn's men landed, news came through that Japanese planes had bombed Darwin, presenting a ticket home to some anti-aircraft gunners who were to have landed with the rest. The combined force was to be called Blackforce after its commanding officer. Vague assurances were given about a plan to evacuate the force if and when the decision was made to abandon Java, but it is doubtful that Blackburn—an experienced and decorated soldier fighting his second world war—would have put much faith in it.

So many orders had been given, reversed, and given again during the long wait to disembark that after the order 'Greatcoats will be worn' was given, only to be countermanded, some men decided they'd had enough. 'It was all too much for [Private Buck] Peters,' reported the machine gunners' historian, 'who peeled off his greatcoat, hurled it overboard and shouted, "That will make up your bloody minds for you!" They landed . . . wearing gas capes.'

Jack Thomas remembers five Catalina flying boats passing overhead. 'As they flew over they saluted us. We didn't know whether they were on a mission or just saying hello.' Chances are the Catalina pilots and their passengers were on their way—or soon would be—to what they hoped would be safety in Australia. During the last weeks of February 1942, a shuttle service brought several thousand evacuees from Java to Broome in Western Australia, many in flying boats. But the north of Australia lay within range of Japanese fighters. Less than a fortnight after Blackforce landed in Java, Broome became the target of Australia's second most destructive air raid after the bombing of Darwin. In just 20 minutes Japanese Zero fighters destroyed 24 Allied planes, killing a number of civilians who were trapped in flying boats on the harbour.

Blackburn's battalions had little to fight with, and there was no prospect of their being reunited with equipment travelling on other ships. Luckily the wharves were crowded with vehicles, weapons and equipment intended for the troops in Malaya. Blackburn's scroungers quickly went to work to make sure that Blackforce had everything it needed. Colonel Ted Lyneham got a Chevrolet staff car, Blackburn a 'fine house' in Batavia for his headquarters.

General Lavarack, with no soldiers to command, was preparing to leave; Wavell would soon follow. Choosing not to say goodbye to Blackburn in person, Lavarack sent him a letter in which he professed to 'deeply regret' having to leave Blackburn 'stranded' on Java 'with a mere handful of Australians'. Lavarack assured him he had done 'everything possible to prevent your disembarkation' but said 'General Wavell was determined to have you ashore . . . for reasons of prestige and morale'. For a soldier commanding a 'suicide mission', it wasn't much of a send-off.

Not all the Dutch appeared pleased by the arrival of the Australians. Private Jack Cocking was part of a contingent from the 2/4th Machine Gun Battalion that was temporarily attached to the 2/3rd Battalion. At Tandjong Priok, Cocking remembered 'friction' with the Dutch on the wharves, who refused to give the Australians any ammunition and declared they would not fight the Japanese. After landing, Cocking's group was assigned to guard fuel dumps in the Batavia area before being instructed to 'spread over the island and give the impression to Jap [reconnaissance] planes that the island was strongly held'.

With General Wavell out of the picture, the Dutch Commander-in-Chief, General Hein ter Poorten, took command of all Allied land forces on Java. According to the machine gunners' historian, General Ter Poorten's appointment was 'a gesture to the Dutch, but an inevitable one'. Although Blackburn was in charge of the Australians, he had to take his orders from Ter Poorten as well as from the local Dutch commander, Major General Schilling, and the British commander, Major General Sitwell.

Corporal Harry Walker, newly elevated to acting sergeant, remembered hearing rumours about 'all the Americans' preparing to land in Java as reinforcements. All that materialised, however, was a battalion of Texans from a US field artillery regiment, 550 men shipped away from the safety of Brisbane and now marooned with the Australians.

(It was not only the Australians who were being fed misinformation. On 2 March a telegram was received at the Japanese Sixteenth Army headquarters advising that 'according to the statement of the captain of a British destroyer, who was taken prisoner as a consequence of the naval engagement off Surabaya, two divisions of the Australian Army had completed their landing on Java at [Tjilatjap] several days ago.' According to the official Japanese history, the generals became 'agitated' at this unexpected report. The landing of two Australian divisions, if true, represented a serious threat to the two Japanese battalions that were moving inland. 'If it had been Dutch East Indies Army divisions, it would have been no problem, but the Australian Army could not be treated lightly.' The entire staff of Sixteenth Army headquarters became 'more and more anxious' until the Chief of Staff, Major General Okazaki, declared that 'the information of the landing of the Australian Army is a lie' and that 'judging from the recent operations of our aircraft, submarines and other units, as well as from the strategic positions of the enemy and ours, it is absolutely unthinkable'.)

Blackforce was initially ordered to defend the Dutch airfields and civilian airports against enemy paratroopers. The Australians had scrounged some useful equipment but had few heavy weapons. Neil MacPherson remembers being armed with 'a tommy gun and .303 rifle'. Tommy guns were handy weapons to use against enemy soldiers but not much good for shooting down aircraft.

Blackburn knew he could rely on the machine gunners and Pioneers but expected little of the nearly 180 stragglers from Singapore, whose poor morale and 'indifferent' training made their ability to fight if 'heavy pressure was put on them' appear 'very doubtful'. Fearing the worst, he assigned them to a reinforcement draft.

Private Jack Thomas was ordered with a platoon of machine gunners to defend Kemajoian airport. Although it was Batavia's main civilian airport, Kemajoian lay well outside the built-up districts of the city. Thomas remembers the area being covered with 'coconut and banana palms, nothing residential, a bit swampy'. The machine gunners got straight to work digging slit trenches. The Dutch had not bothered with slit trenches, and it did not take long for the Australians to discover why: in such boggy land they quickly filled with water. Nevertheless, the trenches offered some protection from bombs and strafing.

Nights were an uncomfortable experience, and not because of the Japanese. Thomas's platoon slept in bamboo huts known as attap after the palms used to make their roofs and walls. 'We had a few clothes. I still had my greatcoat, which wasn't very convenient in the tropics. I found a place to lie down, a sort of woven bamboo mat. Almost straight away I began to itch all over. The place was crawling with vermin. We were all infested in no time at all. We were more concerned about the vermin than we were about the enemy.'

The next morning, 22 February, the airport was attacked by 27 carrier-borne Zeros. 'One of our blokes, Sergeant Stock, got killed, several others were wounded by shrapnel.' Thomas did not see any Dutch fighter planes but he remembers a single transport plane—probably the same one mentioned in the battalion history: '[T]he KLM pilot of a large transport plane . . . taxied over to them and announced that he was about to take off for Australia.' The pilot asked, 'Does anyone want to come?' but found no takers.

In the aftermath of the bombing, a lone Zero came over to inspect the damage. 'A few of the boys had a pot at it,' Jack Thomas recalls. 'There was a bloke with a Browning on the back of a truck who got off a few shots.' The Dutch garrison, however, simply vanished. Thomas remembers them as 'absent'.

After two days, Thomas's platoon was ordered to move to Buitenzorg (now Bogor). Since they had no transport of their own, they had to commandeer a truck. When they stopped for the night, a Dutch general came out to give the Australian machine gunners a pep talk. 'He said, "we'll seek out the enemy and hit him and when we hit him we'll hit him hard"', remembers Thomas, 'and then he disappeared.'

On the morning the Japanese attacked Kemajoian airport, more Zero fighters raided Semplak airfield, near Buitenzorg, strafing troops and destroying aircraft on the ground. At Tjilitan airfield, Corporal Frank McGrath told two Pioneers, Neil MacPherson and his red-haired mate Bluey Rowe, to dig a weapon pit in the middle of a clearing. Recounting the story for the West Australian government's ANZAC centenary project, MacPherson said that Corporal McGrath wanted a Bren gun set up on a tripod to fire at the Zeros strafing the airfield. MacPherson and Rowe had dug down a few feet into the red clay when the air-raid alarm started wailing. Three Japanese pilots screamed in low over the trees, firing straight at the gun pit, which would have stood out like a bullseye in the centre of the green clearing. As the three Zeros roared overhead, the two Pioneers flattened themselves against the dirt and stayed there until the attackers flew off. When they climbed out of the gun pit, they found the clay walls pocked with bullet holes at chest height. McGrath told them to camouflage it next time.

At Tjilitan many of the Singapore stragglers absconded from their posts, leaving a dangerous gap in the Pioneers' defences. (They were found to have fled at the sound of automatic gunfire, which turned out not to be Japanese but to have come from a British anti-aircraft unit testing their Bren guns.) Blackburn gave the entire reinforcement draft a trademark roasting, but nearly a third of the draft—52 men—refused to fight. These men, the Pioneers' battalion history records, 'were escorted from the position lest their low morale and deplorable fighting spirit contaminate their more worthy comrades-in-arms.' Most were tossed in a Dutch lock-up and returned to Australia in one of the last ships to get out of Java. The rest were officially transferred to the Pioneers' battalion and in later fighting impressed everyone with their 'courage and steadfastness'.

A bigger problem, at least in Australian eyes, was the reliability of their Dutch allies. With around 65,000 soldiers on Java, the Netherlands East Indies army represented by far the strongest force facing the Japanese. But other numbers told a different story. The Dutch army comprised roughly 40 Indonesian soldiers for every European, and 300 years of often brutal colonial occupation meant that many Indonesians were more inclined to see the Japanese as liberators than invaders. Harry Walker noticed that 'many of the Javanese and Euro-Asians changed into civilian clothes and didn't want any part of the action against the Japs'.

General Sitwell would note in his report on the Java campaign that even before the Japanese landed, the Dutch army in Java 'for various reasons' had been 'heavily depleted in white personnel'. Dutch attempts to re-arm since about 1936 had been stymied, and as a result 'they were not yet prepared for modern war'. As for the Dutch air force, 'Though pilots were individually gallant, they had little training in formation fighting and manoeuvre, and the machines with which they were equipped were known to be inferior to those used by the Japanese.'

Australians guarding the aerodromes were amazed to discover that Dutch officers left their posts each night to sleep in their comfortable homes in Batavia before returning in the morning. As the machine gunners' history records, 'This difference in attitude towards their duties as soldiers did not increase our troops' respect for their allies.'

Australian troops were similarly unimpressed with the efforts of Dutch fliers. Walker recalled, 'We had a few planes, the Tomahawks. They would disappear after the air-raid siren came on and would keep out of sight until the air raid was over . . . Without air defence or air attack we were in an absolutely hopeless position.' Walker's criticism was not entirely fair. Whether the Dutch pilots were up for the fight or not, their Tomahawks were no match for the carrier-borne Japanese Zeros. Most of the allied planes that were not evacuated were destroyed on the ground.

Not surprisingly, Blackburn saw little value in dispersing his troops to defend an air force that had scant military value. To the Japanese, however, capturing the airfields was vital. A Japanese army report—Monograph No. 66—identifies the occupation of Kalidjati airfield as a key objective for the invasion force:

> Due to the distance from the Army base in Sumatra it was recognized that aerial support from that base would be inadequate during the Central Java Operation. Consequently, it was of the utmost importance that Kalidjati airfield should be occupied as expeditiously as possible.

In his book *Allies in a Bind*, an account of the war written primarily from a Dutch perspective, Jack Ford reveals that the mistrust among Allied forces on Java was mutual. The fall of Singapore, Ford writes, 'had a disastrous affect on Dutch morale especially amongst the KNIL [the Royal Netherlands East Indies Army]. So much of the defence plans had been based around British assurances that Singapore would be held . . . A feeling of fatalistic resolution as regards their eventual defeat and anger at being betrayed by their Allies fell upon the Dutch.' The morale of the Dutch army on Java was eroded, Ford suggests, by constant Japanese air raids and by 'a growing feeling amongst the Dutch' that 'the Allies had let them down and were mainly interested in running away'.

The Australian commander might have argued against being on Java, but 'running away'—as his record in Syria and France attested—was not the way Blackburn fought his wars. The intrinsic dysfunctionality of the ABDA alliance would soon be apparent.

The day after the Semplak airfield raid, Blackburn again asked the local Dutch commander, General Schilling, to take the Australians off garrison duty in order to train for the larger fight against the Japanese that now seemed 'inevitable'. Twenty-four hours later, Blackburn got his wish: his troops were to be consolidated under one 'central command'. In his report on the Java campaign, Blackburn noted that as a result of discussions with Schilling, Sitwell and Ter Poorten, 'it was finally decided to use Blackforce as a "Striking Force" to attack Japanese invading forces in western Java wherever and whenever opportunity offered.'

Blackburn hurried to confer with his Commander-in-Chief, who was already clearing his desk before flying to India to take charge of the defence of Burma. He recalled being ordered by Wavell to give 'every assistance possible' to Dutch forces fighting the Japanese. Wavell told Blackburn that 'every hour gained by resisting the invasion would be of value to the Allied cause in the South West Pacific in general and to Australia in particular'.

Churchill conveyed the same message to the British forces left behind on Java, cabling the RAF commander, Air Vice-Marshal Maltby, his 'best wishes for success and honour in the great fight that confronts you. Every day gained is precious, and I know that you will do everything humanly possible to prolong the battle.'

Blackburn informed Lavarack, now safely back in Australia, that Blackforce had orders to 'fight to the end' and there was to be 'no withdrawal from the island or surrender'.

Japanese land forces were now preparing to invade Java from both the east and west. A bold attempt by the Dutch Admiral Doorman to intercept the Eastern Force resulted in the loss of two Dutch cruisers, a Dutch destroyer and two British destroyers in the battle of the Java Sea. The next day HMAS *Perth* and the USS *Houston* went to the bottom of the Sunda Strait, but only after sinking four Japanese transports and damaging others. Four American destroyers survived the battle and escaped to Fremantle. The British heavy cruiser HMS *Exeter* was attacked and sunk soon afterwards. Any chance of the Allies being able to mount a significant air defence of Java evaporated when the USS *Langley*, an ex-aircraft carrier converted to carry cargo, was sunk with the loss of 40 P-40 Kittyhawk fighters. Another 27 Kittyhawks, crated and ready for assembly, reached shore aboard the *Sea Witch*, but the US technicians who could have put them together had already been evacuated to Australia. The ship's crew pushed the crates into the sea to keep them out of enemy hands.

The Japanese navy now held absolute command of the seas around Java. A full-scale invasion was only hours away. Waiting for the Japanese were the roughly 2500 men of Blackforce and a Dutch force ten times bigger and—at least in some Dutch minds—well prepared to repel the invaders.

Eighteen months earlier, a Dutch rubber official, J.A. Schiotling, had arrived in Australia by boat from Sarawak. His visit was widely reported in the Australian press, along with his fighting comments that Dutch authorities in the Netherlands East Indies were 'vigilant' about the possibility of a Japanese attack and were 'ready to meet any emergency'. An invasion, Schiotling told Australian reporters, 'would be no easy matter, for all possible landing places bristle with shore batteries . . . the military strength of the Dutch East Indies is considerable.' The civilian population, he said, was prepared for the fight and 'everyone in Java had built air-raid shelters at their homes. Blackouts were systematically practised, and all inhabitants, including natives, were throughly drilled in air-raid precautions.'

Noting that oil was 'the chief attraction for Japan in the East Indies', the *Sydney Morning Herald* quoted Schiotling's assurance that 'All men of the 1904–05–06 classes are standing by. They have had months of training. All other men have received notice for general mobilisation. No Dutch citizen is allowed to leave unless he has a very good reason.'

Refusing to be cowed by the Japanese, Schiotling also insisted that there was 'no question of the Dutch East Indies wavering in the struggle against Germany'.

Schiotling's blustering assertions were carried by several newspapers in South Australia, Tasmania and Victoria—the home states of the bulk of the Pioneers and machine gunners now marooned on Java. Some of Blackburn's men might have remembered reading them. Whether they still believed them was another matter.

Chapter 4

THERE ARE NO JAPANESE WITHIN 100 MILES

By 27 February Blackforce was dug in at a tea plantation close to the village of Leuwiliang, roughly 20 kilometres west of Buitenzorg, where Blackburn had established his battalion headquarters.

The naval actions in the Java Sea and the Sunda Strait had put the Japanese landings back by 24 hours but they only delayed the inevitable. The invaders, many of them battle-hardened from fighting the Americans in the Philippines, came ashore on the night of 28 February 1942. The Eastern Force landed 160 kilometres west of the port city of Surabaya on the north coast, half of the force moving on Surabaya and the rest crossing the island to take the south coast port of Tjilatjap. The Western Force also split in two, the 230th Regiment landing at Eretanwetan, east of Batavia, and quickly seizing Kalidjati airfield; and the 2nd Division coming ashore at Bantam Bay and Merak with the aim of taking Batavia and Buitenzorg. The official Japanese history of the invasion puts the number of Japanese troops that landed on Java during the first ten days of March, including airfield duty units and shipping units, at about 55,000. (Blackburn's report envisaged a much larger Japanese force of '8–10 divisions'.)

Until now, the only Japanese that most of Blackburn's men had seen were the pilots of the Zeros that bombed and strafed the airfields. The first Japanese soldier many Australians laid eyes on would be the one who took them into captivity. But Singapore had showed what the Japanese army was capable of, and the possibility of an ambush never felt far away. 'Troops gossip,' recalls Jack Thomas. 'War can be a bit boring sometimes. You spend some of your time being very active and other times just contemplating what might happen, listening to false news, discussing ideas you pick up from here and there.'

Thomas's platoon was travelling towards Buitenzorg when they heard reports of enemy soldiers nearby. 'We were told there were Jap troops about 250 yards away in the scrub along a dirt road. There was a ditch running beside the road going towards where the Japs were supposed to be.' Thomas and his mates tossed around the idea of crawling along the ditch to see if the Japanese were really there, but 'wisdom prevailed' and they decided against it. 'It got dark,' Thomas recalls. 'Not just dark but black. Half a dozen of us were stuck there with no orders. The sergeant came back and told us there was a Bren gun carrier [a light armoured vehicle] and we had orders to get moving. So we backed out of there without finding out if there were any Japs or not.' Not a shot had been fired but Thomas remembers feeling 'very apprehensive'.

The Dutch plan was for a fighting withdrawal from the invasion beaches to the north-flowing Tjiudjung River, where the allies would hold a defensive line before falling back to strongholds along the Tjianten River, 35 kilometres further east, to defend Batavia and Buitenzorg. (In the event the Japanese landings at Bantam Bay and Merak went ahead unopposed.) In keeping with Ter Poorten's 'scorched earth' policy, bridges, ports and oil installations were to be destroyed.

While the main Dutch army slowed the Japanese advance, Blackforce was to act as a mobile reserve, hitting the Japanese advancing along the southern road towards Buitenzorg and, provided the Dutch did not lose control of key roads, intercepting the enemy force closing on Batavia and striking it from behind.

Events on the ground did not go to plan. Japanese Monograph No. 66 states that some units of the invasion force were 'greatly hindered by the enemy's destruction of bridges and roads'. But the overall pace of the advance caught the Allies by surprise. The Japanese swiftly overran the small and lightly armed British force defending the airfield at Kalidjati, who were unaware the Japanese had even landed on Java (the Dutch had neglected to inform them) until they saw enemy armoured cars barrelling across the grass towards them. The Australians, too, would quickly discover the deficiencies of Dutch intelligence.

In *Allies in a Bind*, Ford states that due to a calamitous shortage of communications equipment the KNIL was left to rely on the civilian postal, telephone and telegraph services, all of which were collapsing as a result of Japanese bombing and the widespread desertion of the Indonesian staff. Dutch commanders, he writes, were 'so desperate for motor transport' that they had to requisition buses, many of which were driven by Indonesians 'who tended to desert their vehicles when enemy aircraft appeared'. According to the Australians, the situation was even worse. The Pioneers' history records that 'on one occasion [Lieutenant] Summons in his capacity as Intelligence Officer sought information from Dutch Headquarters concerning enemy movements, and was told that the morning newspaper had not yet been delivered'.

While Blackburn planned his audacious double attack, his Dutch allies were preparing to pull the rug out from under him. After landing at Eretanwetan, the Japanese 230th Regiment had advanced so quickly that the Dutch generals feared the major city of Bandoeng was about to be lost. Just after midnight on the night of 1 March, Blackburn received a call from Schilling informing him that 'not only would no NEI forces now be available but that he had received orders that all NEI forces from Buitenzorg must withdraw to Bandoeng'. The southern road, which had been crucial to Blackburn's plans, was going to be left undefended. Without Dutch support, Blackburn had no choice but to withdraw to a new position where he would be able to defend his own flanks 'without help from other forces'. With the approval of his Dutch superiors, Blackburn prepared to move to a spot south of Buitenzorg before Schilling rang again with the news that 'fresh plans had now been made'. Blackforce cancelled his orders to withdraw, turned his columns around and 'raced forwards' to a defensive position on the east bank of the Tjianten River at Leuwiliang.

The machine gunners' history describes the area as 'a patchwork of villages, large paddy fields ankle-deep in water, and plantations of coconuts, rubber and other trees, many of which hid native houses'. There were also 'patches of thick jungle'. An 80-metre stone bridge supported the main central road running west–east across the island.

The Australians, still unaware of the Japanese landings, wanted the bridge left intact to enable mobile operations against the enemy. Allied intelligence reports after the disastrous campaign in Malaya and Singapore had stressed the speed of the Japanese advance and the way their commanders bypassed obstacles and outflanked strong defensive positions. Blackburn had studied the reports and knew that mobility was the key to preventing his small force from being outflanked and encircled.

After perusal of some notes, issued by I Aust Corps, on the normal Japanese tactics, it was obvious that my force, numerically weak and ill-equipped, would almost certainly be overwhelmed if defence tactics such as had been used in the Middle East and to which my troops were accustomed, were adopted. As the normal Japanese tactics employed in the advance had been to envelop all opposition, I disposed my force

in depth, one Coy [company] holding the prepared defensive positions astride the road with another Coy in support, also astride the
road, about ½ to ¾ mile in rear. The balance of my force was kept
mobile in armoured cars and on carriers and trucks, ready for immediate employment in a counter-encirclement role.

Keeping the bridge open was an essential part of Blackburn's plans,
but it conflicted with General Ter Poorten's 'scorched earth' policy of
destroying vital infrastructure. The Pioneers' commanding officer, Lieutenant Colonel John Williams, arrived at Leuwiliang just in time to see the
bridge blown. 'Soon after first light,' the battalion history records, 'there
occurred one of the many acts of faulty co-operation between units of
the Allied forces which was to contribute so much to the rapid collapse
of all resistance in Java. Contrary to the express instructions of the
C.O. [commanding officer], Dutch army engineers partially demolished
the bridge at Leuwiliang.' According to Blackburn, 'it appeared that the
NEI commander at Leuwiliang had not been informed that Blackforce
was taking over.'

With the destruction of the bridge, Blackburn was denied the very
tactical advantages—surprise and mobility—that he had successfully
argued for just days earlier. Not only that, but he found himself backed
into the kind of static defence that had already proved a failure against
the Japanese. Blowing the bridge, Blackburn wrote, 'prevented any mobile
offensive action by Blackforce west of Leuwiliang ... made my plan of
attack incapable of execution', and left the Japanese forces 'virtually in
undisputed command' of all key roads connecting the two west–east
roads across western Java.

Oblivious to the approaching enemy, Corporal Jackson 'waited tensely,
wondering what was happening. The questions uppermost in our minds
were: have the Japanese landed and if so, in what numbers and where?
Nobody, not even Brigadier Blackburn, had the answers.'

Determined to make the best of a defensive battle he had wanted to avoid, Blackburn deployed his strongest troops, the Pioneers, along both sides of the road, supported by two companies of machine gunners, with three more companies kept further back in reserve. Ammunition, at least, was not a problem. 'We had trucks full of it,' Private Bill Haskell recalled. 'We weren't short of ammo.'

To counter the threat of encirclement, Blackforce was spread across an area roughly 12 kilometres wide. Patrols—lightly armed in the absence of any information that the Japanese had landed—roamed as far as 10 kilometres in front of the Australian line. The vehicles scrounged from the docks at Tandjong Priok gave Blackburn at least some mobility. After reports of headlights moving east on the main road, an armoured car drove nearly 50 kilometres without seeing any sign of the enemy.

The Dutch troops supposed to have taken up positions on the Australians' left had disappeared. 'They left the flank in the air,' Len Croxton recalled. Blackforce was on its own. With no possibility of air support, Colonel Williams told his company commanders that their orders were to 'stand and fight' and not to give ground 'under any circumstances'. If overrun, survivors were to make for Bandoeng or to hide out in the mountains of south Java.

Corporal Jackson recalled that day, 2 March, passing 'peacefully'. The Dutch area commander advised Blackburn, 'As far as I know there are no Japanese on the island; I guarantee that there are no Japanese within 100 miles.'

The Japanese, however, were much closer and already making preparations for the assault.

The next day, 3 March, patrols were sent out at hourly intervals from 7.30 a.m. Local police were enlisted to probe the area forward of the demolished bridge. According to the Pioneers' history, the police reported seeing 'a Japanese clad in native attire at a ford some 1000 yards north of the bridge. The Japanese had been directing natives back over the hills.'

The report was received 'with some scepticism'. At 11.50 a.m., a signal was received from battalion headquarters at Buitenzorg: 'Dutch Intelligence report indicates no Japanese landings on Java.'

Jackson reports that when this information was given to the platoon, 'we took it at face value: it was a relief to hear that the island was still free of the enemy'. Their relief was short-lived. Just five minutes later, five Japanese light tanks rolled into view to inspect the remains of the partially demolished bridge. The Australians reacted at once, using anti-tank rifles to knock out two of the enemy tanks and scattering the soldiers on the ground. The Pioneers' unit diary records drily that at 1205 hours on 3 March, 'Report to [Brigade] HQ that Japanese were at Lewiliang'.

Before long Japanese troops could be seen arriving in the area in lorries, but they were careful to remain out of rifle range. Blackburn's plea for the demolition of a dam further west had been refused, and the Japanese invasion force was now streaming along the main road.

Concrete defences gave some protection to the Pioneers on the east bank of the river. Private MacPherson was among the group that drove off the Japanese tanks with anti-tank rifles. Afterwards, he says, 'the Japs did what they always did—they pulled back and moved along the river and crossed over.'

Within half an hour, a forward patrol of machine gunners led by Lieutenant Tim Brettingham-Moore came under fire from Japanese mortars. Jackson recalled 'ambling along a narrow jungle road, feeling very relaxed, when suddenly six mortar bombs exploded all around us.' None of the Australians was hit, but the shock of being mortared by an enemy that was not supposed to exist was 'enormous'. Jackson and his mates quickly fanned out and lay flat on the jungle floor, bracing themselves for the infantry attack they expected to follow. Meanwhile a Japanese patrol attempted to wade across the river 250 metres south of the bridge but was driven back by the Pioneers.

It was not until an hour later that Blackforce received information that a large Japanese invasion force had landed unopposed on the night of 28 February–1 March on the north-western tip of Java, 120 kilometres from where they were standing. Despite the blown bridges and damaged roads, the Japanese had covered the distance in just 36 hours. Monograph No. 66 reports that they

found the Leuwiliang Bridge already destroyed and approximately two companies of Australian soldiers manning pillboxes on the east side of the bridge. To the rear of Leuwiliang on a line several kilo-meters long running north and south from Tjibatok [a village close to the river] there were prepared positions consisting of pillboxes guarded by approximately 1500 Australian troops.

With their defence plans in ruins, the Dutch generals panicked. An order came from General Ter Poorten for the bulk of Blackforce to move 150 kilometres east to join Dutch troops in a counterattack against the Japanese forces advancing on Bandoeng, leaving only a 'skeleton force' to defend Leuwiliang. Such an attack—unprepared, against an enemy whose exact strength and position were unknown, in terrain unfam-iliar to Blackburn or any of his officers—was almost guaranteed to fail. Blackburn protested and eventually had the order rescinded.

During the afternoon the Texan artillerymen from the 131st Field Regiment arrived. Machine gunner Reg Monks remembered them wearing 'high-heeled boots and cowboy belts' and toting .45 revolvers in holsters. 'Good on yuh, Aussies,' one of them greeted the machine gunners. 'You bottle 'em up and we'll give 'em the works.'

It was the Pioneers who were in most urgent need of artillery support. A large Japanese force was massing across the river from the demolished bridge, opposite the Pioneers. The Americans aimed their powerful 75-millimetre guns over the heads of the enemy troops, destroying the vehicles at the rear. The rest of the column, caught between the blazing tanks and trucks and the river, then became sitting ducks for the Texan gunners. According to First Lieutenant David Hilner, the battery 'proceeded to level the other vehicles and men at will', sweeping the west bank back and forth 'with devastating effect'. Blackburn commented later, 'Some 160 rounds were fired . . . and the accuracy of the fire could not possibly have been improved.'

Aware that the Japanese would be searching for weakness in the Australian flanks, Blackburn sent a company of machine gunners a couple of kilometres down the north–south road to defend the perimeter. As the afternoon wore on without any sign of an attack, Captain John Kennedy, the company commander, and two lieutenants, John Redward and John Hayne, set off in an armoured car on a scouting mission along a jungle track. Like other company commanders, Kennedy had read the Dutch intelligence report stating that there had been no Japanese landings on Java. Blackburn's careful dispersal of his forces over a wide area meant that few had so far set eyes on the enemy. At dusk Kennedy and his companions had not returned. The men assumed the worst: the missing officers had been either killed or captured by the Japanese. The battalion history records, 'This was a great blow to the company.' A patrol was sent out in the rain to look for traces of the missing officers but found nothing. It would be many weeks before their fate was known.

By the end of the day, the machine gunners had lost three officers. Four Pioneers were dead. Blackburn is alleged to have told the Dutch General Schilling, 'My boys have been fighting all day and enjoyed it very much.'

For all Blackburn's bravado, the machine gunners on the left flank weren't having much fun, many of them spending the night in waterlogged rice paddies, knee deep in mud. Kennedy's second-in-command, Captain Dick a'Beckett, took charge of C Company, sending a dozen men down the track to keep watch overnight for any attack. Sporadic gunfire could be heard in the distance, but the sector remained quiet until just before dawn, when Japanese soldiers who had forded the river during the night emerged from the darkness and attacked a hut where members of the 2/6th Field Company had sheltered from the rain. Lieutenant Brettingham-Moore reported men being cut to pieces by a Japanese officer 'who went crazy with his sword'. He and a'Beckett had visited the hut just minutes earlier; otherwise, they would have 'shared in this terrifying experience'. Only two of the engineers got out of the hut alive.

Other Japanese soldiers poured out of the coconut plantation 100 metres south of the Blackforce positions, shrieking as they splashed across the paddy fields towards a large hillock defended by two platoons of machine gunners. Four men were killed as the Japanese broke through the outposts, but the attack failed to dislodge the Australians on the hillock and after a fierce fight the Japanese withdrew to the plantation. A'Beckett was one of the Australians wounded and had to be evacuated. That left Brettingham-Moore, a law student before he joined up, as C Company's sole officer. Just 21 years old, Brettingham-Moore commanded the company 'like a veteran', Corporal Jackson recalled. There were two more attacks in the murky pre-dawn light, but both times the Japanese were driven back. When daylight came, Brettingham-Moore risked his life wading through the paddy fields to check on another platoon, while two men crawled through the long grass in front of the coconut plantation to lob grenades into a Japanese machine-gun post.

Max McGee, still recuperating after a bout of dengue fever, got lucky after finding himself in the sights of an enemy sniper. The bullet narrowly missed his head before smacking into his haversack, when it 'punctured a tin of bully beef' before shattering against his pocket knife, one fragment denting his pannikin and the other putting a hole in his emergency ration tin.

In another sector, the Japanese were trying to pass themselves off as locals. The Pioneers' unit diary records 'a number of men (apparently natives) bathing in the river and idling on the opposite bank. One man walked about in the water for some hours with a fishing net, but he was more interested in scrutinising our bank of the river than in catching fish.'

While exploring a section of the river bank, machine gunners from A Company discovered Japanese boot prints in the mud. The company came under mortar attack. To Private Jack Thomas, it felt 'very much an end of the world situation'. Thomas told Blackburn's biographer, 'We fixed bayonets but there was nothing to charge at. We were on the move all the time—no fixed positions—we were never dug in.' As for all the rubbish they had been told on the *Orcades* about Japanese soldiers being short and short-sighted, Private Bob Smith recalled, 'a lot of them were six footers'.

Monograph No. 66 confirms that as soon as they arrived at Leuwiliang, the Japanese began planning an 'enveloping' attack on Blackburn's positions. But the Pioneers and machine gunners put up such strong resistance during the initial phase of the battle that 'all attempts to cross the river on the south side of Leuwiliang were frustrated'. It was only after 'a full day's preparation' that a night attack across the river succeeded.

The fighting continued all day, with the machine gunners coming under heavy mortar fire. Several of the Australians were rattled by sniper shots hitting the tops of their tin hats. It took them a while to realise that the snipers had hidden themselves in trees. Occasionally a digger would crawl out to have a crack at one, but it was a risky business: Lieutenant Denny Love tried it and was hit by a mortar, while Sergeant Alex Danger escaped with a scorched neck and a hole in his collar.

It became clear that the Japanese were intent on driving a wedge between the Pioneers and the machine gunners on Blackforce's left flank. Based on the intelligence reports he had received from Malaya, Blackburn had formulated a manoeuvre aimed at neutralising the Japanese tactic of outflanking and enveloping a defensive force. Essentially, he was playing the Japanese at their own game. In his report on the Java campaign, Blackburn wrote:

> The plan which I had ordered all my forces to adopt was to appear to give way in the centre whenever or wherever an enemy attack was delivered and to send out fighting patrols on each flank. The centre then stopped their withdrawal after about 300–400 yards and the flanking troops then swung in swiftly to the original centre of the position, thus encircling not only the enemy's centre but also the outflanking parties which in every case he sent out on one or both flanks to endeavour to encircle my force.

Long-range Japanese artillery failed to dislodge the machine gunners from the hillocks, the shells falling harmlessly short in the surrounding rice paddies, but heavy mortars began to inflict severe casualties, killing a sergeant and fatally wounding another. Lieutenant Brettingham-Moore ordered the men to fix bayonets, but the enemy charge never came, although shooting continued from both sides.

The seriously wounded were sent to the hospital at Buitenzorg and then on to Bandoeng, where Lieutenant Colonel E.E. 'Weary' Dunlop had set up a casualty clearing station in a high school. Like Blackburn, Dunlop had come back from the Middle East on the *Orcades* as part of the returning Australian I Corps. While other units were forced to sail without their equipment, Dunlop had refused to board the ship without 'packs, officers' valises, nurses' trunks, and . . . the first aid pannier'. In the introduction to his wartime diary, Dunlop wrote, 'God help the highly trained I Aust. Corps if Churchill had succeeded in throwing them into collapsing Burma in this scrambled state with essential weapons on other ships!' Thanks to Dunlop's obstinacy at Suez, Blackforce avoided the ignominy of having machine gunners who sailed without machine guns being treated by doctors who came without first-aid equipment.

Among the serious casualties Dunlop saw in those first days of March 1942 was Eric Beverley, a driver from the 105th General Transport Company who found himself attached to the machine gunners only because the battalion's own drivers had been left behind at Port Tewfik. At Leuwiliang, Beverley was driving an armoured car with Corporal Don Doody and an observer, Private Lindsay Arnot, when they saw a wounded Pioneer lying on the road near the demolished bridge. The vehicle came under fire from armour-piercing bullets and Beverley was shot through the neck. While trying to pull him from the driver's seat, Doody was hit and paralysed from the waist down. Arnot did not know how to drive, so Doody had to shout instructions. Somehow they made it back to their own lines, where the two wounded men were dragged from the mangled armoured car and patched up before being sent to Dunlop's hospital at Bandoeng.

Less than three weeks earlier, while they were still on the *Orcades*, Dunlop had taken out Beverley's appendix. Now, in Dunlop's words, the wounded driver was 'near dead, with a great deal of his jaw and carotid artery blown away'. Sergeant Alf Sheppard, in his unpublished memoir, recounts how Beverley, with a hole in his neck, was left to die while Dunlop turned his attention to more hopeful cases. Finding Beverley stubbornly still alive when he returned, Dunlop said, 'Well he's not dead yet, we'd better do something about it.' Dunlop operated, saving his life, but the operation left Beverley's mouth lopsided as a result of a severed facial nerve. The battalion history reports Dunlop telling Beverley, 'I'm sorry, it is not very pretty, come to me after the war and I'll really make it look all right.' In the years ahead the prospect of both men surviving the war would seem increasingly remote, but Dunlop's biographer records that he kept his promise.

By late in the afternoon, it was clear that Blackforce was fighting a losing battle, but events elsewhere on the island were going to determine how and when the battle ended. The capital, Batavia, was about to fall.

Another enemy force was closing on Bandoeng. In the early hours of 4 March the local Dutch commander, General Schilling, told Blackburn that General Ter Poorten had made up his mind to abandon Batavia and concentrate Dutch forces at Bandoeng. Schilling needed Blackforce to tie down the Japanese for another 24 hours at Leuwiliang to enable him to blow up the harbour at Tandjong Priok and withdraw his forces through Buitenzorg to Bandoeng.

In the sodden paddy fields south of Leuwiliang, the endgame was near. The machine gunners were driven off the two hillocks and fell back to a new defensive line on the edge of a coconut plantation. The Japanese moved quickly to occupy the vacated hillocks. The left flank of Blackforce was now in extreme jeopardy. Australians lay face down behind the shallow mudbanks to escape the hail of Japanese machine-gun fire.

'The enemy,' Blackburn wrote, 'were steadily working further and further south and the extension of my front southwards was becoming a very serious worry.' Blackburn's entire defensive strategy hinged on having a strong reserve he could throw at the enemy and use for 'outflanking the outflankers'. The constant need to push his line further south to prevent encirclement now sucked away his best reserve company, A Company of the Pioneers. With all his reserves gone, any further extension of the line could cause it to snap.

Taken to a position several kilometres south of Lieutenant Bretting-ham-Moore's machine gunners, the Pioneers fanned out and went looking for the enemy. A party of around 50 Japanese soldiers was reported to have crossed the river as part of yet another attempt to outflank the machine gunners. The Pioneers were to find and destroy the enemy soldiers before being trucked back to a reserve position.

Things quickly began to go wrong. The rice paddies gave the Australians no cover. Walking in single file along the narrow embankments in heavy rain, the Pioneers made an easy target. Caught in the open, one of Captain Guild's three platoons was pinned down with light machine gun and mortar fire from enemy soldiers dug in on the edge of a kampong (a native village). Lieutenant Ray Allen called out to Guild that he was going to charge with fixed bayonets. Private Byrne jumped up and fired three magazines from his Bren gun, causing the Japanese to run in all directions. Allen then led his bayonet assault. But of the seventeen men who charged out of the sodden rice paddy, three were badly wounded and two more were knocked down by bullets hitting their tin helmets, all for a gain of just 20 metres. As night fell, with Japanese reinforcements gathering and a counterattack imminent, Allen's platoon pulled out, carrying their wounded in groundsheets.

Lieutenant Clifford Lang's platoon also ran into trouble. Two privates were killed and Lang and several others were wounded when the platoon walked into an ambush. 'Lt. Lang was unable to move,' the battalion history records. 'He therefore ordered the platoon to withdraw and abandon him, as he considered he would become an encumbrance. His chance of survival, too, would be greater if he could obtain immediate medical aid from the Japanese.' Lang was never seen again. On the Australian War Memorial's roll of honour, the date of his death is listed as 4 March 1942, the cause of death as 'Presumed'.

At about 4 p.m. Blackburn gave the order to withdraw. All contact with the enemy was to be broken off at 6.30 p.m. Blackforce was pulling back from the river to a narrower front a few miles closer to Buitenzorg. The order came in the nick of time, with the Japanese preparing to complete their encirclement. Rain was still falling and sporadic flashes of sheet lightning lit up the area. Corporal Jackson recalled, 'During the lightning flashes we could see Japanese troops massing and moving towards us 400 or 500 yards away.' Jackson sent a runner to inform Brettingham-Moore, and the message came back, 'Run for your lives.' They got back as the last truck was pulling out.

Oblivious to the general order, the Pioneers of A Company, the reserve unit Blackburn had sent down to help the machine gunners on the left flank, were fighting a desperate battle for their lives among the rice paddies south of Leuwiliang and could not be reached. The battalion's commanding officer, Colonel Williams, took an armoured car and went looking for the three missing platoons. Another armoured car joined the search, but to no avail.

During the fighting some men from A Company had become cut off from the rest. Neil MacPherson recalls being caught in an ambush. 'We were sent to stop them infiltrating round the back. My section was overwhelmed and separated from the platoon. We had a corporal in charge. We managed to extract ourselves from the ambush and got back to the highway in time to get the last truck in the convoy.'

One company of machine gunners, a squadron of British tanks and some Texan artillerymen were to form the rearguard. But withdrawing a large force under the gaze of a watchful enemy was, in the words of the Pioneers' historian, an 'extremely hazardous' operation. Companies not in contact with the Japanese began a process of 'thinning out' one section at a time in order to mask the withdrawal. Heavy rain muffled the sound of troop movement.

By 9 p.m. the pull-back was largely complete, but the danger was not over. As the Australians boarded their trucks, enemy troops could be seen massing on the west bank of the river. As a final trick, Blackburn ordered his men to stop shooting at 10.45 p.m. and then to resume firing half an hour later, as if in preparation for an attack. Initially the Japanese appeared to fall for it, shooting off burst after burst into the darkness.

The last of the trucks reached Sukabumi, about 40 kilometres southeast of Buitenzorg, in the early hours of 5 March. Blackburn's report on the campaign stated that his men were 'still as full of fight and as confident as when they first met the enemy. The spirit shown was not enthusiastic bravado. A number of them wanted to know why we were withdrawing when we had licked the Japanese, licked them badly.'

Between them, the Pioneers and machine gunners who formed the bulk of Blackforce reckoned they had killed around 500 Japanese soldiers. The Pioneers' historian records that the battalion lost 44 dead and wounded. C Company of the Machine Gun Battalion, which saw some of the heaviest fighting at Leuwiliang, lost three missing, seven killed and 28 wounded. The official Australian history records that '[t]he total Australian casualties in Java up to the time of the formal surrender were estimated at 36 killed and 60 wounded'. Japanese commanders believed they had confronted a much bigger adversary at Leuwiliang than the roughly 2500 men of Blackforce. The Australians put up a hell of a fight, but the battalion histories may have exaggerated the enemy's losses.

Jack Thomas remembers being pinned down close to the spot where the Texas artillerymen had their guns. 'The Texans were banging away,' he says. 'We came under heavy mortar fire but most of it was bursting in the palm trees. None of us was wounded. At one stage I crossed the river at dawn. It was very exposed. But there were no Japanese around. I crossed the river and came back again.' Seventy-five years later, Thomas says he remains 'very cynical about the kill rate'.

The official Japanese history of the invasion puts the number of Japanese soldiers killed in Java between 1 and 5 March at 255. Of those, the majority were killed during the initial invasion. Just 85 Japanese soldiers were reported to have been killed during the four days that covered the fighting at Leuwiliang—a long way short of the 500 the Australians claimed to have killed. It seems unlikely the discrepancy will ever be resolved. In every war both sides are prone to overestimate enemy casualties while underestimating their own. Whatever the true figures, Blackburn's improvised battalions did everything that was asked of them. The battle at Leuwiliang was conceived from the outset as a holding action by the Australians to enable the safe withdrawal of the much larger Dutch force, and to buy time for the demolition of Tandjong Priok harbour.

General Schilling would confirm in his report that both objectives were met.

In the weeks to come Blackburn would be harshly interrogated by Japanese commanders, who refused to accept that two Australian battalions could have obstructed the Japanese advance and demanded to know where the rest of the division was hiding. Writing afterwards in his hometown newspaper, the Adelaide *Advertiser*, Blackburn described the Japanese as 'veterans, experienced soldiers from previous jungle fighting' whose aim was

> to brush Blackforce aside and seize the road and railway leading from Batavia to Bandoeng. For 72 hours they never ceased hammering at our positions. Day and night the fighting continued. Effort after effort was made to outflank Blackforce ... There were no other troops to support us ... We were on our own. But through the sheer courage and fighting ability of the men under my command their attacks were beaten off: every effort to get round us was stopped and the whole of the Dutch forces in Batavia were able to withdraw by road and rail and reach Bandoeng.

But while the bulk of Blackforce escaped the Japanese net at Leuwiliang, the fate of the 118 officers and men of A Company remained a mystery.

The move to Sukabumi was no more than a stopgap before a strategic withdrawal to Bandoeng, where Blackforce was to join the other Allied forces in a defensive ring around the city. These troops represented the entire Allied strength in West Java. The Allies' failure to hold onto the airfields, and the consequent lack of air cover, left their ground forces dangerously exposed. Japanese bombers had attacked the oil tanks of a refinery near Bandoeng, and from Sukabumi the Australians, camped in a large rubber plantation, could see the oil fires burning. Narrow roads choked with military and civilian traffic made an easy target for enemy planes flying over the area, but there were no attacks.

As far as Blackburn was concerned, this was to be the site of a last stand by the combined Allied forces, in keeping with military assurances given by Dutch officials over the years. Those assurances had been renewed just hours earlier by General Schilling himself, who, according to Weary Dunlop's biographer, promised a group of Blackburn's machine gunners that the Dutch would fight with the Australians 'to the last man and the last bullet'. However, their reputation as flaky allies was confirmed, at least in Australian eyes, when a party of machine gunners entered Bandoeng ahead of the main force in order to make contact with Dutch army headquarters. 'It was night by this time,' the battalion historian wrote. 'Bandoeng was blacked out and, seeking directions, the party entered a big hotel to find Dutch officers in dress uniform dancing with ladies in evening dress. An officer who spoke reasonable English did not believe any Japanese were on the island, let alone that Australian troops had been in action!'

Another machine gunner, Corporal Peter Webster, stumbled across an identical scene at a hotel in Buitenzorg, and was met with similar disbelief by the dancing Dutch officers.

The Dutch guarantee to fight 'to the last man' was abandoned within hours. Senior Allied officers gathered for a conference at 6 p.m. in Bandoeng, where they heard a series of strangely contradictory statements from General Ter Poorten: Bandoeng could not be defended for long, yet the Dutch high command had to have its headquarters in Bandoeng; Dutch troops had been instructed to disregard any order he might give to surrender; and guerrilla warfare against the Japanese was impossible due to the extreme hostility of the Indonesians towards the Dutch. It looked as if Ter Poorten was preparing to give up.

In *Allies in a Bind*, Jack Ford argues that Ter Poorten 'was under increasing pressure from the Governor-General to spare the population by abandoning Bandoeng' and that Dutch troops were 'under constant air attacks and probing attacks from the Japanese army'.

While the Dutch were ready to surrender, they were not prepared to be made scapegoats for the defeat in Java. In an assessment entitled 'Why Java Fell', the Dutch news agency ANEP-ANETA identified two main reasons for the catastrophe: the lack of air cover and the failure of the Allied command to honour a 'well-grounded expectation' of reinforcement by 'large concentrations of troops'. Dated 7 March 1942 and melodramatically described as a 'final dispatch . . . transmitted just prior to the cutting off of Bandung's communications with the outside world', the bulletin glorified the Dutch troops counterattacking on the Bandung plains, 'incessantly harassed by murderous dive-bombing. Their morale remained high, and history will tell of many individual deeds of heroism. Protection was not possible against this inferno . . . It was always the same story—without sufficient protection in the air the troops were practically powerless . . . The Netherlands East Indies army is now writing history. Against fierce air attacks and greatly superior forces on the ground, the Dutch troops fought . . . for two days without resting for a single moment until the position could no longer be held.'

Jack Ford concludes that with 'minimal support' from their major allies, the Dutch 'fought a series of battles against the Japanese for nearly three months'. Dutch forces, he writes, 'bore the brunt of the fighting in the NEI and their horrendous losses were irreplaceable. The Dutch lost nearly all their navy (85 ships), nearly all their 300 planes and the entire KNIL. Thus for the Dutch, only the Australians put in a strong effort to support the NEI.'

Ford enlists a surprising backer in support of his claim that the Dutch were sold out by their allies: the commander of the Japanese invasion force, General Imamura. According to Imamura, the Dutch government's biggest mistake was to have transferred supreme command in the Dutch East Indies from the Governor-General to General Wavell of Britain, who commanded only 10,000 British and Australian forces altogether. In fact, General Wavell flew to India by air when the Japanese troops began to land and move forward in East and West Java, leaving the Allied forces behind. As a result, the remaining Allied forces did not follow the lead of Commander ter Poorten at all, making it very difficult for him to carry out his strategy. I think it was natural that the commander lost the will to fight. Had the Allied forces in Java been commanded by the Governor-General, the Japanese army would have had to face a tough battle.

It is doubtful that Blackburn's men would have shared General Imamura's opinion that the problem lay primarily with leadership. Numerically at least, the Netherlands East Indies Army was stronger than all the other Allied forces on Java combined, but as far as the Australian rank and file was concerned, the Dutch simply didn't have the stomach for the fight. The Australians were especially scornful of the Dutch officers. 'We were pulled right back to Bandoeng,' Max McGee recalled, 'to see all the Dutch in dress uniform, boozing in the cafes and restaurants.'

According to Private Neil MacPherson, all the Australians felt let down by the Dutch, but especially those who had been part of the fighting in Syria. Many suspected that the Dutch, desperate to hold onto their colony 'in one piece' after the war was over, never had any intention of fighting the Japanese. In the words of Private Jack Thomas, 'it was well known and well felt that the Dutch did nothing'.

In his memoir, *Behind Bamboo*, the captured Australian journalist Rohan Rivett conceded that the Dutch forces on Java 'were up against hopeless odds' and that their units 'contained only a leavening of trained troops'. However,

[t]he unfortunate thing was not that they failed to fight, but that they failed to maintain any liaison or adequate communication with the Allied units stranded in their midst. The bravery displayed by the small Dutch Navy and Air Force at the beginning of the Pacific war, did not serve to maintain Dutch prestige with the Indonesian population in view of the debacle of the army which took place under their eyes.

In December 1941 Rivett had left his job at the Melbourne *Argus* to work for Singapore Radio, countering waves of Japanese propaganda being broadcast from all over Southeast Asia. After escaping to Java he was captured and imprisoned, first at Serang Jail in Batavia and then at a prisoner-of-war camp that became known as Bicycle Camp. Rivett believed that senior Australian and American commanders 'were not, at any stage, given any indication that the Dutch had no intention of fighting'. Rivett was convinced that they acted 'in the belief that the Dutch troops ahead, on their flanks and in the rear, were ready to enter a serious conflict with the invader. In fact, at the first hint of an enemy landing, many of the Dutch units melted away like mists before the sun.'

While the official Japanese account of the invasion records some fierce encounters with KNIL forces, the Dutch never matched the tenacity shown by the Australians at Leuwiliang.

Japanese advance units had advanced into Central Java at break-neck speed. The official Japanese history records two units covering 170 kilometres and 220 kilometres in a day. The first of these had averaged 100 kilometres every day since landing. The drivers 'alternately stood and sat behind the wheel', and some were so tired that they crashed their vehicles on a straight road. Many drivers 'got sweat rashes because they gripped their steering wheels too tightly to wipe off their sweat'. When a Japanese unit attacked the Central Javanese town of Magelang, Dutch troops initially 'fought back with fierce gunfire'. Since Magelang was a garrison town, the Japanese were anticipating a hard battle. However, 'before long, the gunfire of the Allied unit ceased abruptly. From a precedent at Tarakan, Staff Officer Yano judged that it meant surrender, and headed for the town of Magelang with three men in a single captured armoured vehicle.' Rain began to fall, and the four Japanese were driving through a heavy squall when they noticed a Dutch officer approaching them holding a white flag. The lieutenant colonel 'asked them to stop the attack because the garrison army was surrendering'. They put him in the armoured car and entered Magelang, where the garrison commander offered the surrender not just of the Magelang garrison but of Dutch units in nearby areas, despite the fact that there were no Japanese troops heading for those areas. The Japanese commander 'hurriedly sent one platoon to those areas along with an officer of the Dutch East Indies Army. In this way, [the detachment commander] was able to have within that night 1700 officers and men including Colonel Fleischer of the Dutch East Indies Army in the city of Magelang, 600 in Semarang, 200 in Salatiga, 160 in Ambarawa, and 70 in Temanggung surrender.'

In their personal accounts of the failed defence of Java, the Allied commanders showed varying degrees of tact, candour, disingenuousness and wishful thinking. Blackburn declared that throughout the Java campaign he had 'received the utmost assistance from the Officers, NCOs and men of the NEI army. Maj-Gen Schilling and his Staff did everything in their power to assist Blackforce in obtaining equipment and accommodation, in becoming accustomed to the conditions of jungle warfare, and in the actual operations against the enemy. Other branches of the NEI army both in Batavia and Bandoeng cooperated with equal loyalty with myself and my officers and men and the relations between my troops and the NEI army and the civil population were at all times most cordial.' The British General Sitwell was less diplomatic. While insisting that 'the Dutch and ourselves were bound to be hopelessly outnumbered both in numbers and material', Sitwell criticised 'Dutch communications', which, he said, 'did not work well'. The Dutch HQ in Bandoeng, he noted, was 'usually very ill-informed as to what was happening'. In his own 'Report on operations Western Java 1942', Schilling reiterated a stubborn but perhaps delusional belief that 'had not events in other parts of western Java interfered, the offensive operations which we had the opportunity of planning together would have been successful'.

The tensions and disagreements within the American-British-Dutch-Australian coalition were a gift to the Japanese, which continued to exploit them after the capitulation. Blackburn's personal diary includes an indignant entry for 9 June 1942: 'Ascertained today that in broadcasting our names to Australia, it has been prefaced by a statement that we did not fight, but left the fighting to be done by the Dutch & Indonesians!'

In the circumstances, it was little wonder that Blackburn's men lost faith in their Dutch allies. Built on flimsy military foundations and undermined by mutual mistrust, political opportunism and competing strategic priorities, the ABDA alliance was supposed to defend Malaya, Sumatra and Java but in the end could not hold onto any of them. The unified ABDA command became a textbook example of how not to manage a military coalition, lasting a mere six weeks before Wavell signalled its dissolution by leaving for India.

In his Masters thesis, 'American, British, Dutch and Australian coalition: Unsuccessful band of brothers', US Navy Lieutenant-Commander Sam Shepard wrote:

> The brief lifespan of ABDA lends credence to a belief that its existence was ineffective . . . For a house to be in unity, its members must agree. ABDA was never able to agree on strategy until it agreed the NEI was lost.

After General Sitwell and Air Vice-Marshal Maltby indicated that the British were prepared to fight on, Ter Poorten assigned them an area in the mountains south of Bandoeng, within easy reach of the south coast. When Blackburn was told of the arrangement, he made the decision to join the British and take Blackforce south. In his report on Java, he outlined his plan to 'continue resistance against the Japanese in the hope that it might be possible to evacuate my troops from the south coast of Java or elsewhere'.

Blackburn spent the next two days scouring the mountains south of Bandoeng for good defensive positions and organising rations dumps. On the night of 7–8 March, Blackforce linked up with around 1800 RAF men at a location in the mountains. By early evening on 7 March, Blackburn was told that Japanese soldiers had already entered the northern suburbs of Bandoeng.

Both the British and Australians believed that Dutch capitulation was imminent. They were right. At 8.30 p.m., under a flag of truce, the Dutch offered to surrender. Japanese commanders arranged to meet the Dutch Governor-General, Tjarda van Starkenborgh Stachouwer, together with General Ter Poorten and his staff officers, the next day at the Isola Hotel in Bandoeng at 8 a.m. The venue was then changed to Kalidjati airfield and the time pushed back to noon.

The official Japanese history of the invasion confirms that the initial Dutch offer to surrender was confined to the forces defending Bandoeng. This did not satisfy the Japanese.

Army Commander Imamura planned to steer the offer of surrender from the commander of the Bandoeng sector to the surrender of all the allied forces in the Dutch East Indies. He gave a direct order to Staff Officer Saiki to depart and convey to 2d Division Commander Maruyama the message that 'the enemy is starting to lose its fighting spirit,' and that 'the shift of the 2d Division needs to be carried out as quickly as possible in order to take advantage of this opportunity'.

By moving the surrender meeting to Kalidjati airfield, the Japanese forced the Dutch to witness the strength of its air force. When the governor-general arrived he was told by Air Division Commander Endō,

We have accepted your offer of a cease-fire in conformity with the Japanese code of the warrior. The commander of our ground forces is due to arrive later. After conferring with him, we probably will make demands. If you accept them, we will agree to a cease-fire; otherwise, we will probably bomb Bandoeng right away with our aircraft, which are ready to be launched, as you can see.

The meeting eventually started at 4 p.m., but the negotiators immediately struck a problem: when Imamura asked the governor-general whether he had the authority 'to declare surrender or continuation of the war', Tjarda said he had lost that authority when General Wavell became supreme commander of the Allied forces. Imamura then asked Ter Poorten, who said he did not have the authority either.

'In that case,' said Imamura, 'why on earth did you gentlemen come here?'

The governor-general replied, 'We did not come of ourselves; you invited us.'

Losing his temper, Imamura then 'sent all non-military persons out of the room' and asked Ter Poorten whether he would surrender in spite of the governor-general's disapproval. Ter Poorten replied, 'The state of Bandoeng and vicinity is too pitiful to look at. Bandoeng has become completely defenceless and the army has as good as disbanded. It is utterly unbearable to force the citizens into the horrors of war any further.'

Ter Poorten's concern for the civilian population of Bandoeng contrasted sharply with General Wavell's unconcern for the population of Singapore less than a month earlier. With the city encircled by Japanese forces, Wavell had written a letter to his officers:

It is certain that our troops in Singapore heavily outnumber any Japanese who have crossed the Straits. We must destroy them, our whole fighting reputation is at stake, and the honour of the B.E.F. [British Expeditionary Force] ... It will be disgraceful if we yield our boasted fortress of Singapore to inferior forces.

There must be no question of surrender. Every unit must fight it out to the end in close contact with the enemy. Please see that the above is brought to the notice of our senior officers and to our troops. I look to you and your men to fight it out to the end to prove the fighting spirit that won the empire, and still insists to defend it. There must be no thought of sparing troops, or the civilian population, and no mercy must be shown in any shape or form. Commanders and senior officers must lead their men, and if necessary die with them.

Singapore was already in ruins by the time Wavell issued his command for there to be 'no thought of sparing ... the civilian population'. The following morning he made a timely personal withdrawal to Java, where no Japanese soldier had yet landed. In *Ghosts in Khaki*, the history of the 2/4th Machine Gun Battalion, Acting Sergeant Les Cody recalled the plight of Singapore's civilian population as

pitiful in the extreme ... With one million people within a radius of 3 miles and Japanese artillery within 5000 yards of the sea front, heavy shell fire was added to the trauma of the constant bombing and machine gunning. Casualties were already reaching huge proportions with unburied bodies lying in the streets. Fires were burning everywhere, expanding the enormous pall of smoke from the burning oil tanks then blanketing the city. Food deliveries and water supplies had broken down and devastated families were wandering the streets.

Wavell's 'exhortation' to fight to the last man steeled General Percival, commander of Commonwealth forces in Malaya, to order a doomed counterattack. While making 'allowances for the enormous strain placed on the Commanders trying to plug ever widening holes in a defence already at breaking point', Cody concluded that 'nothing could justify' the order to fight on. The decision was 'based on fantasy figures on a map with little relationship to the troops on the ground'. Cody described the ultimately futile counterattack as a 'costly fiasco'.

The Australian General Gordon Bennett (who invidiously fled to safety while ordering his officers to remain with their men) described 'devastation everywhere. Holes in the road, churned up rubble all around, tangled masses of telephone, telegraph and electric cables strewn across the street . . . smashed cars, trucks, electric trams and buses.'

Another Australian officer, closer to the action than Wavell or Bennett, left a grim account of a Japanese bombing raid:

> Buildings on both sides of the road went up in smoke . . . soldiers and civilians suddenly appeared staggering through clouds of debris; some got on the road, others stumbled and dropped in their tracks, others shrieked as they ran for safety . . . we pulled up near a building which had collapsed onto the road—it looked like a caved-in slaughterhouse. Blood splashed what was left of the lower rooms; chunks of human beings—men, women and children—littered the place. Everywhere bits of steaming flesh, smoldering rags, clouds of dust—and the shriek and groan of those who still survived.

Safely holed up in his Java headquarters, General Wavell had been prepared to countenance the savagery of house-to-house fighting in the streets of Singapore while the island was bombed to rubble by Japanese planes. Faced with the same prospect in Bandoeng, General Ter Poorten decided to spare the civilian population what would have been a pointless sacrifice.

Assuring Ter Poorten that seizing Bandoeng would be 'quite easy for the elite troops of the Japanese Army', Imamura demanded total and unconditional surrender; otherwise, the Japanese army would 'reopen hostilities and resort to force until the Dutch East Indies Army is destroyed'. Ter Poorten was commanded to broadcast the surrender over the radio the following morning. '[I]f we cannot hear your radio address from Bandoeng here at [10 a.m.],' Imamura warned him, 'it will mean that the Japanese Army will resume the attacks and the bombardments by the air units will also be resumed.' He then arranged for Ter Poorten to be led safely back to the Dutch lines.

The next morning, the sky over Bandoeng was full of Japanese planes—'intimidatory flights' intended to remind the Dutch what would happen to the city if they fought on. Ter Poorten got the message. At midday he broadcast a list of Japanese demands beginning with general surrender; the prompt discontinuance of all hostilities; the raising of white flags as a proof of surrender; and the disarming of all forces.

At 12.50 p.m., Ter Poorten was driven to Kalidjati airfield, where he signed the instruments of surrender. Imamura allowed him to keep wearing his sword.

Bandoeng was declared an open city. Although the Dutch would attempt to turn back the imperial clock after the war, three centuries of colonial rule in the Netherlands East Indies had come to an end.

The Japanese campaign in Java unfolded exactly as Japanese military commanders had predicted. In his advice to the Emperor, Chief of the Army General Staff Sugiyama promised that

> our side will be able to defeat our enemies one by one by using our
> concentrated fighting power in a sudden offensive ... We believe
> that we have definitely all the odds in our favour for the operations

after landing, considering the organisation, equipment, potential and strength of the enemy and our side. After roughly wrapping up the invasion operations ... every effort is to be made to take the fight out of the enemy through both political and military strategy and to conclude the war as quickly as possible ... we can strategically maintain an undefeatable position by occupying and securing the military bases and air bases of the enemy, and by securing sea traffic.

A sentence in Japanese Monograph No. 66—'The Army ordered the 2nd Division to change its course and to march to the north of Bandoeng and take the town by storm'—leaves no doubt that Ter Poorten's decision saved many civilian lives.

The boundaries of the 'open city' zone included the Garoet area where Blackforce had gathered, obliging Blackburn to keep moving south towards the British positions. Relations with local Dutch officials, already strained, were not improved by the Australian engineers' habit of blowing bridges behind them.

The British and Australians were now under extreme pressure from the Dutch civil administration to stop fighting. According to General Sitwell's report, the Assistant Resident (a provincial official) at Garoet was 'obsessed with the idea that a revolution was imminent by the native population and a massacre of all whites would inevitably follow if we attempted to fight in this area'. Sitwell had 'no means of telling whether this was true or not' but was worried that if it was, 'we should undoubtedly suffer ourselves at the hands of the natives in the later stages of the fight when troops were exhausted and food was running short. There were large numbers of native coolies living in the area working on the tea plantations and no means, so far as I could see, of getting rid of them.' An order came from the Dutch high command to stop destroying bridges.

With Dutch forces surrendering in droves, Maltby decided further resistance was useless and ordered all British troops to lay down their weapons.

That left only the Australians. Moving in heavy rain along a narrow and treacherous mountain track through tea plantations, Blackburn's men tried to establish radio contact with Australia. The Japanese had not yet moved to intercept the retreating Australians, who were making for a small port west of Tjilatjap on the south coast in the forlorn hope that evacuation by ship to Australia might still be possible. But Blackforce's radio equipment was not powerful enough to get a message through to Australia. Faced with the realisation that there could be no evacuation, Blackburn considered fighting on. He still had weapons and ammunition. Enough food had been stashed in the mountains for Blackforce to hold out for a month. But food and weapons were not enough. The wet season still had a couple of months to run, and there would be no shelter for his troops in the mountains.

As for the Javanese, nobody knew how they would behave towards the Australians now that the Japanese were in charge. Not all were unfriendly, but helping Allied soldiers carried the risk of savage punishment by the Japanese. An unnamed American prisoner reported that in the village of Sampang, near Tjilatjap, 'some Allied soldiers were fed and clothed by the natives. Betrayed by a spy, the villagers were murdered and soldiers were taken prisoner.'

Sailors from the USS *Houston* who managed to reach shore after the ship sank were quickly handed over to the Japanese. Their experiences, along with those of other prisoners of war and civilian internees, were recorded in a detailed study compiled in New Delhi in the months after the war. Many of the American POWs had fought alongside Blackburn's Pioneers and machine gunners in Java and went into captivity with them after the Allied surrender. A postwar report on POWs by SEAC (South East Asian Command) confirmed that Japanese officers paid cash for

Javanese villagers to hand over Allied sailors and that 'ten guilders per head was the fee'. Before being given up to the Japanese, captured sailors were sometimes 'beaten, stripped of clothing, and robbed of money, jewelry and other valuables', although 'in most cases . . . the Japanese appear to have taken control very promptly'. The sailors were then put to work unloading supplies from Japanese transports.

The Javanese in the mountains were no more friendly than those on the coast. In the SEAC POW report, they were described as 'universally hostile'. One group of survivors from the *Houston* 'was held bound to posts overnight . . . In all cases, discovery of their presence by the natives resulted in the appearance of Japanese troops within eight hours—which gave the natives ample time for a preliminary beating and robbing of their own'.

Such information might have prompted some Allied soldiers to reconsider their plans to escape captivity by making for the coast. The commander of the Texan artillery battalion, Lieutenant Colonel Blucher S. Tharp, told his men that 'any who wished to try to reach the sea coast to evade capture should do so', although he did not 'advise such procedure or recommend it'.

The SEAC POW report notes that

> several groups made the attempt, including . . . several American enlisted men and a group of Australian troops numbering, in one report, about 300. These men arrived on the south coast around 2100 hours 9 March, and maintained a constant watch along approximately 15 miles of coastland for five days, living off what food could be procured locally, including chicken, goat, potatoes and tea. Reconnaissance parties were sent out over 30 miles of the coast, without success. On 14 March word was received that personnel not back by the 16th would be shot, and thus, after one more futile reconnaissance, the men returned.

In the end, Blackburn was forced to concede that fighting on was impossible. His medical officer, Lieutenant Colonel Eadie, warned that without drugs 50 per cent of his men might fall sick from diseases such as malaria and pneumonia. Eadie, Blackburn wrote in his Java report,

> informed me that he could not accept responsibility for the health of the troops if we took to the mountains as proposed . . . I therefore reluctantly decided that in the best interests of my troops and their lives I must capitulate. Despite the fact that my troops all desired to continue resistance until compelled by force of arms or shortages of food and munitions to surrender, I informed Major-General Sitwell that I would join in the surrender.

Japanese Monograph No. 66 states:

> Approximately 11,000 men of the British–American forces who had escaped to southeastern Java, as well as other enemy units on the island, surrendered in accordance with the terms accepted by the Netherland East Indies commander.
> The invasion of Java was completed.

For the men of Blackforce, the fight was over. A journey that had begun in the sandhills of Palestine ended less than six weeks later with surrender in the mountains of Java. Private Jack Thomas, who had fought hard in Syria, did not fire a single shot in Java. 'I was shot at plenty of times,' he says, 'but I did not see the enemy.' Thomas's experience was not unusual. As a private soldier he was told where to go and what to do but otherwise given no information beyond what he needed to do his job. 'We didn't know much,' Neil MacPherson recalls. 'We were just moved from point A to point B.' Brief periods of shooting and being shot at punctuated long spells of waiting and watching and listening. At Leuwiliang, Jack Thomas remembers watching an armourer sergeant struggling with a .303 rifle that was 'cocked and had a round up the spout. The sergeant couldn't undo the bolt and didn't know what to do with it. He had to pull the thing to bits to get the round out.' Detached from the bigger picture, ordinary soldiers like Thomas could only interpret the war through their own eyes. 'The gun I knew about because I saw it. Other things—like whether there were Japanese nearby or not—we didn't know about. I heard no shots.'

The order to surrender came as a bitter blow to the men of Blackforce, the final betrayal in a campaign that had been doomed from the start. 'It was not a good feeling,' Thomas recalls. 'The most difficult time for a soldier is being told to lay down his arms in time of war. We were lost to the world. We were prisoners of war. We threw down our rifles and waited for something to happen. But nothing happened. We didn't see a Jap for some days, not until they came to take us to Leles [about 50 kilometres from Bandoeng].'

Like Thomas, Private Bill Haskell was forced to surrender without having fired a shot. 'I don't know when you get more angry men than when you're told you've got to lay down your arms and ... you hadn't even been eye to eye with [the] Japs,' Haskell recalled in an interview for the Australians at War Film Archive.

For Des Jackson the surrender was 'a terrible, humiliating and despairing moment ... everyone felt angry and betrayed ... If the abominable Egyptian train had not broken down at El Kantara on 31 January, the 2/3rd Machine Gun Battalion would have been on the *Mauretania*, which steamed straight back to Australia.'

Fate had played a dirty trick on the men of Blackforce, but the worst was yet to come.

Chapter 5

THEY GOT NOTHING FROM ME

————⬧————

Corporal Harry Walker remembered the Pioneers becoming 'very hostile' when told they had to surrender. There was 'much discussion and much confusion' while the Pioneers and machine gunners weighed up their options.

'Blackburn said, "Well, you've just got to wear it", Bill Haskell recalled. 'Even then we thought, "It's only for a short while . . . We won't be in this situation for long" . . . We always reckoned that [escape] was just around the corner and it wouldn't be long before we were picked up.'

Private MacPherson remembers plenty of talk about making for the south coast. 'We thought the *Perth* and *Houston* were going to evacuate us,' he says. 'We didn't realise they'd both been sunk.'

Corporal Walker recalled some of the men wanting to fight on as guerrillas, and the odd group slipping away into the mountains. But when the Japanese put a price on their heads—'so many guilders for

any one captured'—the risk of being caught and handed over forced the
absconders back into camp. Even there, Walker remembered the Pioneers
having to 'guard ourselves' against the Javanese.

Not everyone resented the order to surrender. Neil MacPherson recalls
'some chaps felt relief. But we didn't know the Japs were going to treat
prisoners a bit differently to the Germans.'

The machine gunners' historian noted that 'local Indonesians were
mostly hostile ... their hostility towards all white people increased in
direct proportion to the increasing domination of the island by Nippon'.
Together with an Indonesian-speaking Dutch officer, Brettingham-Moore
gained permission for himself and five others to make for the coast.

After obtaining food and shelter from a reluctant village headman,
the party reached the coast, where they joined other groups of British
and Australian soldiers scouring the beaches for fishing boats. But after
finding boats destroyed and villages deserted, Brettingham-Moore and
his companions gave up and headed back to the mountains.

Before surrendering their arms, the Australians made them useless.
Walker took his machine gun to pieces and 'threw the bolts into the
river'. Private 'Chook' Fowler and his mates stuffed acid-soaked 'pull-
throughs' into the barrels of their rifles. Tanks and other vehicles were
run off mountainsides, and ammunition was ruined by being left out in
the rain. The British did the same to their weapons. According to General
Sitwell, the Japanese became 'very annoyed and told me we were bad
soldiers to have destroyed our equipment in this fashion ... I replied that
it was a point of honour with British soldiers not to let any guns fall
undamaged into enemy hands—a reply which curiously enough appeared
to satisfy them.'

The discarded munitions would take an unforeseen toll on the civilian
population. Private MacPherson recalls, 'We were on a narrow road above
a cliff when they told us we had to surrender our weapons. A lot of chaps
threw their hand grenades over the cliff into the river. The local women

found them and some of them pulled the pin and a lot of those women lost a hand or were blinded.'

The day after Blackforce surrendered, 10 March 1942, was Private Des Jackson's 21st birthday. He spent much of it lying on a ground-sheet beside a muddy track, shaking from dengue fever, having lost his blanket and nearly everything else in the fighting at Leuwiliang. Like most prisoners of the Japanese, Jackson was not issued with blankets or clothing and had to survive on whatever he could lay his hands on. A friendly lieutenant found him a grey army blanket—the only birthday gift Jackson received and perhaps the most precious he would ever be given.

The next day the British, American and Australian commanders were summoned by phone to Garoet to meet one of General Maruyama's staff officers—a man General Sitwell remembered as 'rude and inclined to be insulting'. After 'a certain amount of cross-questioning and discus-sion', the Allied leaders were ordered to accompany him to Bandoeng, where they spent the night 'on chairs in a waiting room' before the formal signing of surrender terms in the morning.

The machine gunners' history records that when Blackburn entered the room, 'General Maruyama, the Japanese commander, and his staff stood up. Through an interpreter Blackie asked the reason and was informed that they wished to pay a tribute to his troops. They could not understand how so small a force could have held them up for so long.'

It would be the last courtesy Blackburn or his men would receive from the Japanese.

The Allied commanders did all they could to hold Maruyama to the terms of the 1929 Geneva Convention regarding the treatment of prison-ers of war, which had been signed by Japan but not ratified. Blackburn, of course, was a lawyer and was passionately concerned for the welfare of his men. Maruyama would later be chastised by his superiors for letting himself be talked into adding to the surrender document the words 'subject to our rights as prisoners of war *vide* Geneva Convention of 1929'. Not that words would offer any protection.

Although Blackforce had been made to surrender, its leader refused to relax the discipline that had been a hallmark of his command ever since the battalion was formed. According to his biographer, Blackburn gave orders for his men to 'parade in proper disciplined manner' before the Japanese in order to 'show the enemy that we are better trained and disciplined than he is'.

But where were the Japanese? Harry Walker remembered staying in a tea plantation at Arinem for several days before moving to a market place where 'we were able to buy things and do whatever we wanted to do . . . we used to go for fairly long walks to try and keep fit. Still we hadn't seen any Japanese.'

After about a week at the tea plantation, the Australians were told to drive in their own trucks to Leles, 50 kilometres from Bandoeng. '[W]e had to put a white flag up which was most galling,' Bill Haskell recalled. 'There we met the Japs and they took the trucks off us . . . They were a scruffy looking mob and I thought, "How the hell did this mob ever take over?" . . . They had split-toe boots and they were . . . running around at the slightest order . . . They were not impressive and they made you feel all the worse for having been told to lay down your arms.'

Des Jackson was shifted to an aid post that Captain Tim Godlee, the medical officer, had set up in a former Dutch tea factory. But his dengue fever was so bad that Godlee insisted on transferring him by jeep to Colonel 'Weary' Dunlop's hospital at Bandoeng. En route, Jackson and his driver ran into a Japanese roadblock manned by several dozen soldiers wearing 'ill-fitting grey-green uniforms with small puttees and black claw-toed rubber boots. They were heavily armed, small of stature, distinctly unprepossessing and unpleasantly arrogant.'

While the soldiers were 'not particularly aggressive', Jackson found it a 'chilling' experience to be confronted for the first time by his captors.

Prodded by bayonet-wielding soldiers towards a waiting ambulance, Jackson was delivered to the hospital at Bandoeng, where he briefly enjoyed the otherworldly experience of 'lying in a comfortable bed and being looked after by the efficient staff'. In a few days the fever was gone. He would hold onto the comfortable bed for a little longer.

Jackson remembered his time in hospital as 'quite pleasant', with 'reasonable' food rations. The Japanese rarely interfered, and although patients were forbidden to leave the grounds, civilian visitors were allowed to come and go. Behind the scenes, however, Dunlop had seen the first signs of the Japanese soldiers' contempt for their beaten enemy. 'Staff officers, extremely truculent and offensive, began visiting and screaming demands to me using the surname only, rendered DUNROP!' he wrote in his diary. 'They issued a string of unreasonable demands, including the removal or obliteration of Red Cross identification and causing red crosses to be scraped off the walls.'

Preoccupied with subjugating more than 40 million Javanese, the Japanese could afford to bide their time with a few thousand disarmed Allied prisoners. The Pioneers' history describes Leles as 'idyllic ... tropical trees bordered the smooth bitumen road that ran through the village ... familiar vegetables, such as carrots, onions and pumpkins, flourished in the market gardens and provided a welcome addition to the food supplies which continued to arrive from Force Headquarters.'

While at Leles the Australians were encouraged to write home at any length and about any subject at all. The letters were gathered up but never sent, although they were no doubt studied for scraps of useful intelligence, such as the whereabouts of the 'ghost division' that the Japanese were convinced had opposed them at Leuwiliang.

In his report on the Java campaign, General Sitwell described being 'pressed ... to give them the name of the divisional commander' and said his interrogators 'refused to believe that the Australian troops who had surrendered were the total numbers present'. When he refused to answer questions about the rest of I Corps, Sitwell was told it might cost him his life. The general reminded his interrogator that this would be against the Geneva Convention, causing the Japanese officer to scoff that 'Japan only obeyed the convention when it suited her—"the same as England".'

Handed over to the Japanese secret police, Sitwell recalled having 'a very unpleasant time for the next month being, amongst other things, kept with my hands handcuffed behind my back for the next ten days without a break.'

Another British officer, Brigadier Pearson, was 'stood up against a wall and threatened that he would be shot if he did not give information. On refusing to do so he was at once released and congratulated by the Japanese Intelligence officer on his bravery.'

Writing in his hometown newspaper after the war, Blackburn recalled being subjected to similar threats. 'A Japanese colonel said to me . . . Nothing less than a division could possibly have held us up the way we were held up. I must know where you have hidden the rest of your division.'

At Leles Blackburn kept his men fit with sports competitions and route marches. Good hygiene ensured that diseases like dysentery and malaria did not get out of control. Books, card games and a program of lectures and debates helped stave off boredom. There were no barbed-wire fences or armed guards, and the Australians were free to wander. Since no attempt was made by the Japanese to confiscate wireless sets, Blackburn was able to listen to daily bulletins on the BBC and the ABC. The news was never good. The Japanese navy and air force had total control of the sea and sky; escape from Java was impossible.

Some soldiers were not prepared to accept their fate. A handful of machine gunners were caught attempting to escape to the south coast. When the same men absconded a second time, they were captured and beheaded. Fear of betrayal by the Javanese, and the realisation that even if they reached the coast they would never find a boat, deterred others from trying their luck.

But the phony captivity could not last. In response to the escapes, barbed wire went up around the market area where the Australians were camped. Guards were posted. Food rations, which had been sufficient if not plentiful, started to dwindle. Over the coming weeks, the slow process of starvation began. Small amounts of buffalo meat were doled out in addition to rice and vegetables, but many of the men could not stomach it.

At the end of March orders were given for the prisoners to be moved. A large advance party was sent to Batavia by truck and train to organise a camp for the main group. Blackforce was to be split up, with the Pioneers going to Batavia and most of the machine gunners being sent to a former school at Garoet, where they were put to work disarming anti-aircraft guns.

Until now, the Japanese had not bothered to search the prisoners, many of whom were still armed. Private Bill Haskell remembered the day Japanese soldiers under the command of a platoon sergeant burst into the school building:

> [T]hey crowded around and searched us. And of course blokes had revolvers and all sorts of things on them . . . [the Japanese] were going to shoot the place up but [our officers] managed to get through to them that we'd never been searched. So then they said that anything of a military nature had to be discarded . . . We had to hand in our tin helmets and our badges of rank and all that sort of stuff. Really it was only a sort of set-up to let you know you are no longer military, you are just trash . . . We got over that.

At Garoet, Jack Thomas 'got used to the idea of going without sustenance'. He remembers being 'hungry for bloody years'. Another machine gunner, Lance Corporal Adye Rockliff, recalled Garoet being the place where he and his mates 'experienced the first signs of malnutrition ... some of us noticed we had bad balance and co-ordination ... [we had] difficulty standing on one leg and we bumped into doorways and each other.'

The Australians soon picked up the basics of Japanese culture—what Thomas describes as 'the right way and the wrong way of doing things'. If there was a Japanese guard anywhere within sight,

we had to call out and bow to him. If the guard saw you and you didn't bow, he'd call out 'Kura!' As soon as you heard that you'd know you'd been spotted and he was going to approach you and teach you some good manners. If you had caused some offence, the guard would hold his arm straight out in front of him, hand horizontal to the ground, and then with his fingers do the 'come hither' thing. He'd point to the ground straight in front of him and then you could just say goodbye to a pleasant afternoon. You knew what was coming.

Beatings from the guards usually took the form of a slap to the face with the open hand, delivered with all the force they could muster. It happened to everyone at some time or other. It happened to Thomas, 'but not regularly. You had to be very sinful to incur a penalty.' Most of the Australians were larger than their Japanese guards, but as they began to succumb to disease and malnutrition many prisoners were knocked to the ground by a hard slap in the face.

The prisoners also had to put up with relentless Japanese military propaganda, much of which was false. After an Australian RAF pilot, Ronald Ramsay Rae, was captured by locals and handed over to the Japanese, he was taken to Garoet for interrogation. According to Bill Haskell, Rae was dragged before a Japanese major 'and the major said,

"You realise you have lost the war because we are bombing Sydney and we are bombing Melbourne" ... And Ramsay Rae had this little birdie [secret wireless] up in the hills and he knew that [Major Jimmy] Doolittle had bombed Tokyo. He said, "I suppose you know that Tokyo has also been bombed?" That infuriated the Jap [who got] stuck into him with a billiard cue.'

From Leles to Batavia was more than 240 kilometres, and Blackburn was told his men would be marching all the way, at a prescribed speed of 50 kilometres a day. Despite it being the rainy season, no shelter would be provided, and at night his men would have to 'bivouac by the side of the road'. As well as Pioneers and machine gunners, many of whom were incapacitated by malaria or dysentery, the group would include RAF ground staff and artillerymen, who were 'quite unaccustomed to marching'. Attempts by Blackburn and other senior officers to have the order rescinded were at first 'entirely disregarded'. It was only when they submitted a joint letter warning of 'a very large number of deaths' if the march were carried out, and threatening, if they were ever released, to inform 'not only our Government but the world at large', that the march was called off. The prisoners went by train instead.

The Batavia camp was a former Dutch military camp which, owing to the number of bicycles found there, became known as Bicycle Camp. Around 2600 Australian, British, Dutch, American and Indian prisoners would be crammed into barracks that Blackburn estimated had been designed for no more than a thousand. By far the largest contingent were the 2000 Australians. Harry Walker recalled that 'once we marched into that camp we lost all our rights, all our liberties, we were down to nothing and it was very soul destroying to be in that position'.

The Pioneers' history records the presence of men in 'green Dutch uniforms' with 'pale lean faces', mostly bearded. 'It almost looked as if a hospital had emptied out all its patients long before they were ready for discharge.' The men may have looked Dutch, but as soon as they opened their mouths it was clear that they were Australians, survivors of HMAS *Perth*, which had been sunk by the Japanese in the Sunda Strait. Picked up by 'menacing and *parang*-brandishing Indonesians', the 300 survivors had been handed over to the Japanese, who kept them 'cramped and confined in unspeakable conditions' for the next six weeks before transferring them to Bicycle Camp. For the next three and a half years, the Pioneers and the *Perth* survivors would be joined at the hip.

Staff Sergeant Harry Whelan was one of the machine gunners who ended up at Bicycle Camp with the Pioneers. Whelan, who had been one of the advance party, recalled being marched by his captors through Batavia to the former Dutch barracks in order to 'exhibit the captured white men to the local population'. The Javanese, he wrote, 'threw quite a bit of this and that at us and jeered very vocally'.

Perhaps the Javanese held the Australians to blame for what was happening outside the camp. According to an American prisoner, Private Franklin Torp, Japanese troops had 'looted the entire town, taking automobiles, refrigerators, radios and furniture from the homes. These articles were placed upon ships and taken to various Jap camps.'

Another American prisoner in Batavia reported that 'a Madurese was shot by a Japanese but did not die. He was then tied to a pole and bayoneted, but as he still did not die he was buried alive. He was crying for help all the time the Japanese were filling in his grave.'

Similar atrocities were reported from all over Java, often with the Dutch as victims. Declassified records from the office of the judge advocate general of the US Army contain testimony from thousands of witnesses. At a camp outside the port city of Surabaya, two Dutchmen were reported to have been bayoneted to death: 'Victims' hands were tied behind them and they were bayoneted in the stomach.' Another witness recalled a large crowd of Javanese men gathering to watch Japanese troops enter Surabaya. '[A] Dutch police inspector trying to keep the Javanese on the sidewalk was killed by a Japanese soldier with a bayonet for no apparent reason.'

Inside and outside the camps, insubordination was usually met by violence. Rohan Rivett reported that prisoners on a working party 'saw another Dutch woman beaten up by Japanese soldiers because she made the V sign towards the prisoners' truck. Two Japanese rushed at her and struck her several times across the face. These incidents make us black with fury at our own helplessness.'

In some cases, Dutch prisoners were singled out for especially vicious interrogation techniques. In *Ghosts in Khaki*, Les Cody describes the punishment of Dutch prisoners at a camp on the Burmese coast:

> About 8 Dutch prisoners were tied around a tree with one long rope looped around each man's knees with a slip knot around his neck. The tree was infested with large green jumping ants which were swarming over and biting the prisoners. They were continually bashed and as one man collapsed it would tighten the knot on the next man's neck. A Japanese officer was present.

The American SEAC POW report describes the treatment of a Dutch prisoner at Serang Jail 'sitting in a chair, bound, with a metal band about his hand, which was apparently being tightened by some sort of thumb-screw'. According to the report, 'this was the only case of actual use of torture devices as a part of interrogation reported by this group, and was apparently not applied to any American personnel.'

Torture by the Japanese during interrogation was commonplace, whether or not 'devices' were used. Wally Summons recalled seeing 'some of our officers [return] from the Japanese Gestapo headquarters, after their intelligence people had endeavoured to extract information by torture methods. Finger twisting, burning and beatings were among the persuasions used. These officers, Handasyde, Winning and Ross, had been away some time, and we had been most anxious about them.'

On entering Bicycle Camp, Harry Whelan was asked by other prisoners for the name of his unit. Hearing that he belonged to C Company of the 2/3rd Machine Gun Battalion, the prisoner told him that three of C Company's officers were in the camp. Whelan recalled 'running up the centre of the camp and meeting John Kennedy, John Hayne and John Redward, much to our delight, as they were all very highly regarded.'

It was more than two months since Captain Kennedy and Lieutenants Hayne and Redward had vanished along a jungle track at Leuwiliang after setting out on a reconaissance mission in an armoured car. The story of what happened to the three officers in that time is contained in testimony given by Blackburn and by the three officers themselves in war crimes trials and in evidence to the War Crimes Board of Inquiry held in Australia after the war.

The three officers had been ambushed at Leuwiliang, but they were too valuable to be killed. Convinced that a much larger Australian force must be on Java, the Japanese demanded to know the whereabouts of the 7th Division.

With their hands tied behind their backs, the captured officers were forced to stand in the rain and were beaten by a guard with a bamboo pole if they moved a muscle. A Japanese officer in Javanese dress (was he the 'Japanese clad in native attire' who had been spotted near the demolished bridge by a police patrol before the battle of Leuwiliang?) claimed that he had been on the island for six months. All three Australians were interrogated and beaten with fists and bamboo poles when they refused to give any information. Captain Kennedy was then separated from his companions and, in Redward's words, 'he was struck heavy blows with a rifle butt. He was gravely bruised from some 20 blows. He was then kicked to the ground, stamped on, particularly about the head . . . this

Japanese and the guard with the bamboo then administered a severe kicking.' When they had finished with Kennedy, they subjected Redward and Hayne to the same treatment.

Over the next three days, the punishment for not talking became progressively worse: the Australians were flogged 'with an improvised cat-o'-nine-tails; hung up by the wrists and forced to stand all night in the rain; tied to posts and kicked, had pen nibs driven under their finger nails, and were forced to lie face down in deep mud while Japanese soldiers stood on their heads 'apparently in an endeavour to smother us'.

A correspondent for the Adelaide *Advertiser* who spoke to the three men in Bangkok in September 1945 wrote: 'While Hayne and Kennedy were being flogged, Redward was threatened with a big knife placed against his lower stomach and drawn over the surface of his skin towards his neck. The Japanese then intimated that the Australians would be killed if they did not tell. A party of soldiers came up with rifles and went through loading preparations. The three were lined up against a wall to be shot, and waited several minutes for death which did not come.'

When the three Australian officers were taken by truck to another location, a Japanese war correspondent took their pictures 'for propaganda purposes'. For another six weeks the trio languished in prison. The interrogations and bashings continued, but by now the officers were confident they would not be killed. The story as told by the *Advertiser* had a bizarre postscript:

On Easter Sunday, 1942, they were taken before a Japanese camp commander, who talked to them and showed them his sword. He then told them of the Japanese method of committing hari-kiri, and offered the sword to them. The boys refused the offer. He then treated them to lunch, with beer, fitted them out with clothing and sent them back to gaol. The three were taken to Batavia with others, and then to Singapore.

The machine gunners' history records simply that 'the three men were brutally tortured, but their torturers were given no information of any kind at all'.

For the men at Bicycle Camp, food was a constant preoccupation. The Pioneers' history records that 'rations were poor; only rice, and a small quantity of green vegetables in a thin stew just barely flavoured with pork'. At great personal risk Blackburn began keeping a personal diary, in which he described the meat allowance as 'so small that it can only be used to strengthen the soup'. In his memoir, *Twice their Prisoner*, Wally Summons recalled that the 'ration of meat was so small you considered yourself lucky if you received a piece larger than a shilling'. For a while the camp diet was boosted by a weekly distribution of rations—dried potatoes and tinned sausages—that Blackburn had stockpiled as part of his plan for the Australians to fight on as a guerrilla force.

Eventually the army rations ran out, forcing the prisoners to rely on whatever they could scrounge to supplement the meagre allowance supplied by the Japanese. According to Wally Summons, 'The American personel were eating cats. They killed them and then fried them, and they were reported to be quite edible.'

Some of the Australians managed to trade their possessions with the civilian population for food, or for money to buy food. Nineteen-year-old Private MacPherson sold the watch his mother had given him before he left Australia. He recalls, 'A few chaps were brave enough to sneak out at night to the edge of the camp to trade with the Javanese. You could get a few guilders for a pair of army shorts and turn that into a bit of food.' Constant hunger was now giving way to malnutrition, which would quickly strip the prisoners of their resistance to tropical diseases such as malaria and dysentery.

In a corner of the camp, high-ranking military and civilian prisoners, including Major General Sitwell, Air Vice-Marshal Maltby and the governor-general of the Netherlands East Indies, were held incommunicado behind barbed wire in an enclosure that was out of bounds to other inmates.

Blackburn, meanwhile, did all he could to keep his men fed, healthy and occupied. Prisoners were allowed out of the camp on work parties and many leapt at the chance to spend a day roaming outside the wire filling petrol drums and collecting vehicle spare parts for shipping back to Japan. 'Half full drums of petrol had been left by the Dutch in various locations and these had to be rolled into heaps,' Corporal Walker recalled. 'Nobody was allowed to have a car. Nobody was allowed to use petrol.'

Lieutenant Colonel Lyneham of the 2/3rd machine gunners recalled that 'Dutch women while passing working parties would throw cigarettes and food to our troops. At first the Japanese guards would only slap and beat them if they caught them, but later . . . the guards were provided with hide whips, with which . . . they slashed such women across the face.'

Exempt from joining the work parties, Brigadier Blackburn did his best to protect the Australians from casual beatings by the guards. Protesting after the event was largely futile. '[A]ny complaint made was treated with an intimation that it was the Japanese method and we must adapt to it,' Blackburn wrote in his evidence to the war crimes inquiry.

The camp commander, Lieutenant Suzuki, while not regarded as 'one of the vicious types of Japanese', was considered to be untrustworthy. The hardening of the camp regime—and in particular the 'unprovoked bashings' by guards—took place on Suzuki's watch. The Pioneers' history records, 'To Brig. Blackburn's protests aginst this harsh treatment, Suzuki would silkily reply that perhaps the prisoners were not saluting the guards properly (Japanese style) or standing properly to attention (Japanese style), and he would proceed to demonstrate the correct manner of carrying out these formalities. But the bashings continued.'

Suzuki gave orders to all sentries to 'slap the face of any man seen not saluting'. Harry Walker was one of those caught. 'Once I was washing a few clothes out under a wash tap,' Walker recalled. 'I never saw the sentry walking up to me. He started to slap me around the face. I didn't have a clue as to why I was slapped. I knew I had done nothing wrong. I just stood there to attention and after he had made about half a dozen swipes he walked away.'

Others remember Bicycle Camp differently. Neil MacPherson recalls that 'apart from starting to feel a bit hungry after our own rations were used up, we weren't treated that badly. We didn't have much contact with Jap guards because most of the time they stayed around the perimeter, outside the main camp. Inside the camp we were under the control of our own officers. At night there were Jap guards on sentry duty. A prisoner had to be on duty in each hut. The guard would come round and ask a question in Japanese. We knew what the answer had to be—we had to tell the guard how many men were in the hut and how many had left to go to the toilet.' MacPherson witnessed little violence personally.

One by one, Australian officers were taken away for interrogation, during which they were beaten, burnt with cigarettes and had bamboo slivers pushed under their fingernails. The Pioneers' commanding officer, Lieutenant Colonel Williams, suffered the worst of it. Held at night in a cell with '16 native prisoners', forbidden to shave and barely allowed to wash, subsisting on a daily diet of a plate of rice and a fish head, Williams was interrogated for a month at the headquarters of the miltary police, or *Kempeitai*. As well as being lashed to a chair and kicked and dragged around the room, he was forced to drink water in order to fill up his lungs. 'At the end,' Williams recalled, 'they took me outside, blindfolded me and told me that if I did not answer the questions they would shoot me ... They also promised me a house in Batavia and a servant if I would answer their questions, but they got nothing from me.'

After several weeks of interrogation and torture, Colonel Williams was returned to Bicycle Camp, where Neil MacPherson remembers seeing him 'with his hands all bandaged'.

Life inside Bicycle Camp took a more sinister turn when the order came for every prisoner in the camp to sign a declaration promising to obey the Japanese army and 'not to resist it'. The order, according to the Pioneers' history, was 'treated with the contempt it deserved' and returned unsigned. As a result 'the screws were turned'. Orders were given to close the canteen and one of the kitchens; church services, concerts, lectures and classes were banned, and Lieutenant Suzuki warned that 'those who did not sign would not be guaranteed their lives'. Singing, whistling and all other forms of music were forbidden. Half a dozen officers and at least 40 men were bashed by guards 'for no apparent reason'.

Australian, American and British prisoners still refused to sign. Suzuki was ropable. On 2 July Blackburn wrote in his diary, 'Atmosphere at once became very frigid.' Two days later Blackburn was warned that not only food but medical supplies would be withheld if the form was not signed. Unmoved by Blackburn's efforts to convince him that the men's defiance was worthy of his respect, Suzuki brought in more guards and set up machine guns inside the camp.

Blackburn and his senior officers were thrown in the guardhouse and other officers removed from the camp. While the Australians were still holding out, the camp's American prisoners agreed to sign. Further refusal now seemed pointless. Blackburn urged his men to comply with the order, reasuring them that the oath was not valid because 'their signatures were being obtained under duress'.

Four Australian officers, however, refused to sign without a direct order from Blackburn. An American survivor from the *Houston* described their punishment. At about 5 p.m. the four were 'taken down to the guardhouse. They were forced to kneel on a gravel walk with a stick inserted across their legs behind their knees . . . until about 11 o'clock p.m.' Every 15 to 20 minutes the men were

beaten with bamboo sticks and rifle butts by about six guards and the Camp Commander, Suzuki. Several times the Japanese officers also placed his entire weight on the shoulders of the men so that the sticks would bite deeper into the legs. He also beat each of the men across the head and face with the flat side of the saber in its scabbard.

According to the sailor, the prisoners 'were in obvious pain, but bore the torture with great fortitude. The men were black and blue all over, and so remained for several days. They did not lose consciousness during the torture.'

It was only when Blackburn personally intervened to persuade the men to sign that the torture ended.

Having got the signatures he was after, Suzuki gave back most of what he had taken away, but failure to bow or salute still resulted in a beating. 'We were not allowed to straighten our backs until the person taking the salute allowed us to stand at ease,' Lieutenant Colonel Williams recalled. 'If a cook came through the camp we had to salute him. The whole compound bowed or stood up to him. Brigadier Blackburn and Major General Sitwell were compelled to salute privates and Korean guards.'

The American sailor recalled the difficulty of giving a satisfactory salute 'from the standpoint of the position of the eyes, arms, hands and feet. We were not instructed in the rules. When a Japanese was not satisfied with our salute, he usually proceeded to slap us.'

Not every Japanese revelled in humiliating the prisoners. The Pioneers' history concedes that 'no black mark can be recorded' against the name of Lieutenant Suzuki's adjutant, Lieutenant Kataguri. In his POW diary

Blackburn described having meals with Kataguri and receiving presents of whisky, beer or fruit to share with his comrades. Sometimes Kataguri even took him out shopping. But even in the early months of their confinement, such humane treatment was the exception.

So far, little serious attempt had been made by the Japanese to exploit Allied prisoners for labour. They made a concerted effort, however, to extract information that could be used for military or propaganda purposes. On 10 July a notice was issued by Lieutenant Suzuki to all prisoners in Bicycle Camp. It said:

1. Reply honestly to what the Japanese ask you. If the answer is incorrect you will be punished seriously. Examples—(A) If you know that a certain part of Australia cannot be passed by motor car or on foot on account of forest or marsh and you answer that it can be passed we go to the place and suffer hardships believing your answer. (B) In spite of knowing there is a traffic organisation believing your answer 'There is none' we find the traffic organisation in the district.

2. But for the lying propaganda of the senior men of your countries you would not have met with hardships as prisoners of war.
   Because you believed them:—
   You came here to fight against us
   You surrendered
   You are prisoners of war
   I am sorry for that.

3. Dai Nippon is a just country and does not use lying propaganda. Do everything honestly and be well repaid.

The claim that Japan did not use lying propaganda was a lie, as many prisoners found out when their names were broadcast to

Australia together with what Lieutenant Wally Summons described as 'very uncomplimentary remarks and implications as to the bravery of the Australians'.

After Blackburn and other prisoners refused to take part in any broadcasts to Australia, Blackburn noticed 'the whole atmosphere of the camp has changed for some reason and everything is now absolutely tense and difficult.'

In Bandoeng, Japanese propaganda officers asked Dunlop for the names of prisoners suited to broadcasting. 'I kept out of the way as I don't want to be involved in radio publicity or propaganda,' Dunlop wrote in his diary. 'They wanted to know of professional actors . . . someone with a typical English voice . . . and an "Oxford" voice . The propaganda laddy spoke excellent English.'

The Japanese found what they were looking for in a prisoner named Clephan 'Tinkle' Bell, a former professional actor on the London stage whose 'booming theatrical "Old Vic" voice' could be heard in Australia broadcasting news of prisoners from Batavia. Dunlop warned the star-struck actor to beware of the 'intolerable pressures' he would be under from the Japanese when he was 'all alone' in front of the microphone. In the end the pressures caught up with Bell, and he cut his own throat with a razor blade. 'Poor Tinkle,' Dunlop wrote after hearing the news. '[T]he devil that took him up into high places and showed him the earth got him quickly enough. I suppose he just could not go on with their propaganda line.'

On 26 August 1942 three wasted figures arrived at Bicycle Camp: Lieutenant Allen, Private Vin McCrae and Private Stan Baade. All were survivors of Captain Guild's missing A Company, the Pioneer company that had been lost during the fighting at Leuwiliang. The trio had been left behind in the mountains when Guild set off with another party for a final attempt to escape by boat from the south coast.

As soon as they entered the camp, the three prisoners were put in the cells. Worried that they would soon be moved somewhere else, and eager to hear news about the 118 officers and men of A Company, Blackburn quickly slapped his trusty batman, Private 'Mick' Webster, with a charge of using insulting language, which gave Webster four days in the cells to debrief Lieutenant Allen and his two companions. The account Webster was able to give Blackburn on his release from the cells was remarkable enough, but not even Allen knew the full story of what had happened to Captain Guild and his men.

Chapter 6

SPECIAL MISSION 43

———◆———

The survivors of A Company reached the river at midnight on the night
of 4–5 March 1942, having dragged their wounded three miles across the
paddy fields in groundsheets. One of the injured men, Corporal Rolly
Galloway, died during the move.

The badly wounded Lieutenant Clifford Lang had insisted on being left
behind. Without their leader, the remaining members of Lang's platoon
became separated overnight. Three privates were swept away while crossing
a fast-flowing river. Another Pioneer was killed and several more seriously
wounded after Sergeant Terry Croft's platoon ran into a party of Japanese
in a kampong. Croft divided his men into groups of six under an NCO
and told them to head for the south coast, but one by one the groups were
rounded up by enemy patrols. Seven wounded men who could no longer
keep up were left in the care of Private Garbutt at the village of Babakan,
but they were ambushed by a Japanese patrol and all were presumed killed.

Captain Guild's party continued moving south along the bank of a river. Towards evening, a Javanese man approached and handed Guild a handwritten message. It read: 'To the Australian commanding the Australians from the Australian commanding the Australian Forces. Your position is south-west of Buitenzorg. Cannot supply further information. May fall into enemy hands.' The message was signed in barely legible script 'Capt. Hans' and time given as '1000 hours'. Guild was sceptical. There was a Pioneer named Richard Hands, but he was a private, not a captain. And the convoluted heading did not sound genuine. He decided, however, to risk following the Javanese across the river and in the direction of Buitenzorg, which they reached soon after dark. They found the town had already been evacuated. Fearing he had been led into a trap, Guild withdrew his men to a nearby kampong for the night.

Since escaping from Leuwiliang, A Company had been whittled down to just 67 men of all ranks. Still unaware that the Allies had capitulated, Guild's party managed to evade Japanese patrols as they made for the prearranged Allied rendezvous at Sukabumi. It was only when they hit the main road from Buitenzorg that Guild heard news of the surrender. The large number of Japanese troops in the area made it impossible to go on, so Guild headed instead for the south coast in the hope of escaping by boat. Hunting for food at a tea plantation, the Pioneers spotted a Japanese officer and were able to slip away unseen.

The near miss convinced Guild that it was too dangerous to continue in a large group, so he split his men into small parties and arranged for them to meet on the coast at a place west of Tjilatjap. On the night of 12–13 March, Guild's men found their rendezvous. It seemed they were in luck. A ship, the SS *Sea Bird*, was in the harbour. Two men were rumoured to have slipped away in one of the *Sea Bird*'s lifeboats. Guild tracked down the captain, who told him that his ship had enough fuel to last ten days but that the crew was refusing to put to sea. The captain made him an offer: if Guild could lay his hands on a crew—including three marine engineers—the *Sea Bird* would sail. Guild might as well have been asked to supply a marching band. The escape plan came to nothing.

In his account of what happened next, Lieutenant Ray Allen wrote that Dutch army patrols 'helped us with rations' and acted as interpreters in dealings with the Javanese. After hearing that a group of British officers were hiding out in a disused gold mine in the mountains of South Bantam, Guild decided to make contact. One of the officers was a Japanese-speaking commando, Lieutenant Colonel Laurens van der Post, who had orders to coordinate a guerrilla campaign. As well as a wireless transmitter and receiver, Van der Post had rations, arms and ammunition. Guild decided to join forces.

After sleeping rough and marching for hours in heavy rain, many of the Australians were suffering badly from dysentery and malaria. During the next few days, Lieutenant Allen wrote, 'the men rested and regaled themselves on water-buffalo, poultry and native fruits' before dividing into groups of ten, each group led by an officer and with its own food caches and emergency escape routes. Rations, according to Allen, were 'still very good—rice, bully beef, biscuits, tinned milk and beans', but the Australians were growing sicker and they had no medicines. Sodden clothes, added to the debilitating effect of physical and mental exhaustion, wore down their resistance to tropical diseases. Within a period of ten days four men died, probably of typhus. Guild decided that the only chance of survival for men already sick was to surrender in the hope of receiving medical care from the Japanese.

Another problem for the Australians was the hostility—real and perceived—of the local population. In his secret POW diary, which somehow managed to survive 'over a hundred Japanese searches', Rohan Rivett commented, 'It isn't the Japanese guards who keep us prisoners, it's the fact that every one of these teeming millions of Sundanese and Javanese acts today as a Japanese agent.' Referring to the Javanese who captured himself and his comrades and handed them over to the

Soldiers of the 2/3rd Machine Gun Battalion march through Adelaide on 15 January 1941. (State Library of South Australia)

Puckapunyal camp in Victoria, where the 2/2nd Pioneer Battalion was formed in 1940. Bitterly cold in winter, unbearably dusty in summer, 'Pucka' was not the ideal training ground for jungle warfare. (State Library of Victoria)

Australian troops on the *Orcades* wait to disembark at Batavia. A soldier of the Netherlands East Indies Army stands guard at the end of the gangplank. (AWM 011779/21)

Captain Guild and Captain Handasyde of the 2/2nd Pioneer Battalion grab a few minutes' rest during the fighting at Leuwiliang. Shortly after the picture was taken, Guild was caught in an ambush. He died trying to reach the Java coast. (AWM 030390/09)

In February 1942 Weary Dunlop established a hospital in this former girls' school in Bandoeng, Java. After the Allied surrender, the Japanese ordered the obliteration of all Red Cross signs. (State Library of Victoria)

Australian prisoners of war at work on the Siam-Burma Railway. After their clothes rotted away, many wore only a loincloth or 'Jap Happy'. (State Library of Victoria)

Tamuan POW camp, 26 kilometres from the Siamese end of the death railway, served as a transit camp and hospital for prisoners. (State Library of Victoria)

Prisoners laying rails on the death railway c. 1943. The track-layers were constantly on the move from camp to camp. (AWM P00406/031)

Native labourers work on a bridge at Ronshii, 60 kilometres from the Burmese end of the railway c. 1943. As many as 90,000 'coolie' labourers died building the railway. (AWM P00406/036)

Ronshii, Burma c. 1943. The funeral of a prisoner of war who died during construction of the railway. By the time it was finished, the railway had cost the lives of more than 12,000 POWs, including 2646 Australians. (AWM P00406/031)

Saraburi, Siam, September 1945. Japanese Sergeant Seiichi Okada, known as 'Doctor Death', forced sick prisoners to work and was responsible for many POW deaths in the Konyu area. (AWM P00634/005)

Allied prisoners swarm over the bamboo scaffolding used to build a bridge on the Siam-Burma railway. (State Library of Victoria)

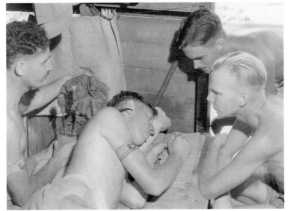

Changi prison camp, 1945. A wireless set hidden in the head of a broom. Secret radios brought precious news from the outside world, but being caught with a 'dicky bird' could get a prisoner killed. (State Library of Victoria)

Lieutenant Colonel EE 'Weary' Dunlop amputates a prisoner's left thigh in the 'operating theatre' at Tha Sao, near Hintok in Siam. (State Library of Victoria)

An emaciated prisoner of war lying on a stretcher in Siam. (State Library of Victoria)

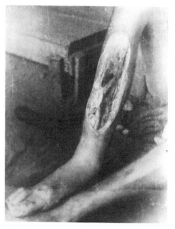 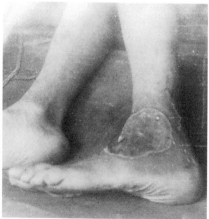

Tha Sao Hospital, Siam. The right leg of an unidentified POW has a deep tropical ulcer on the shin exposing the bone. The ulcer ward at Tha Sao appalled even Dunlop. (State Library of Victoria)

Tha Sao Hospital. Prisoners working in bare feet lived in mortal fear of tropical ulcers but sometimes (as in this case) they healed. (State Library of Victoria)

Prisoners wearing artificial limbs at Changi in 1945. Amputation was often the only treatment for deep tropical ulcers. (State Library of Victoria)

Allied POWs in a camp near Tokyo wave at a low-flying plane of the US Third Fleet. Inmates had been told that if the Allies invaded Japan, all prisoners would be shot. (State Library of Victoria)

Neil MacPherson was 19 when he joined the 2/2nd Pioneer Battalion. His parents lost their land during the Great Depression. One of five brothers, Neil knew what it was like to go hungry.

Neil MacPherson as a prisoner of war.

Jack Thomas had been earning 15 shillings a week as an office boy in Broken Hill when he enlisted in the 2/3rd Machine Gun Battalion.

Japanese, Rivett wrote, 'I suppose we were lucky they didn't cut our heads off. Some of the *Perth* and *Houston* boys saw other shipwrecked mates decapitated as soon as they washed up on the beach.' Not every Javanese villager was hostile to the Allies, let alone murderous, but enough were to make the Australians constantly fearful of betrayal or attack.

One day a 'native' approached Guild's men with a message warning them to surrender as they were surrounded, but the Australians refused. The following weeks saw a game of cat and mouse as the guerrillas succeeded in dodging large Japanese patrols, but in late April one group was ambushed and overrun. Among the men captured was Van der Post, whose leadership and organisational skill had been inspirational. His loss would prove devastating.

The rest split up into small groups, sometimes bumping into one another on remote jungle tracks. At one of these chance meetings, Captain Guild made a fateful decision: together with Lieutenant Alister Stewart, Corporal Tom Hynes and Private Alf Murray, Guild decided to make a final attempt to escape from the south coast, either by small boat or perhaps by submarine (Van der Post had raised the possibility of Allied troops being evacuated by submarine). The four Australians were never seen again. In his own secret report about the guerrilla mission, Van der Post described the south coast of Java as 'wild and inhospitable' and noted that 'the beaches that could be used for possible evacuation were very few'. The prevailing ocean conditions in May would have made an escape by sea especially dangerous. As it turned out, the Australians did not even make it as far as the coast.

The extraordinary story of what happened to Guild and his companions was told more than half a century later by David Kriek in a report entitled 'Special Mission 43'. A Dutch expatriate, Kriek was manager of the gold mine where Van der Post later established his guerrilla headquarters in the mountains of South Bantam. Along with other Dutch civilians, Kriek had been given military training. Even after the Japanese occupied the mine, he helped guide stragglers to find Van der Post. The Pioneers' history, referring to him as 'Sgt Krick' and describing him as a 'Dutch patrol leader', recounts that Kriek 'offered every assistance' to Guild and his men.

Kriek's account largely tallies with Lieutenant Allen's, describing the arrival of 'some forty Australian soldiers ... exhausted and starving, asking for help. Their instructions had been to go to the gold mines ... but [they] were too poorly clad and shod to walk.' According to Kriek, many of them 'had no weapons'. They were glad when Kriek offered to have them delivered by truck to the gold mine where Van der Post had set up his headquarters.

By now the Japanese were aware that there were Allied soldiers in the mountains and had tasked a British officer, who introduced himself to Kriek as 'Captain MacDonald', with bringing them in. In order to do this, they had issued a *passe partout*—a sort of transit pass—for MacDonald and his driver, which MacDonald was using for the opposite purpose, namely to help important Allied officers avoid capture by enabling them to join Van der Post.

Kriek painted a far more dramatic and incident-filled picture than Lieutenant Allen of their time in the mountains. At one point Allen and Kriek, on horseback,

> encountered a gang of robbers on the narrow mountain path just before Lembak Sembada, and managed to frighten them off with a few shots. Further on, as we were crossing the wide Tjimadja river, Allen's horse suddenly went down, and the Australian vanished under the water. For a split second, I thought he had been shot, but there was no sound of gunfire and I realized his horse had merely tripped. Man and horse suffered no worse than a thorough soaking.

'Robbers', in Kriek's account, were a constant menace to the Dutch civilians and reservists left behind in South Bantam after the capitulation. Van der Post claimed in his secret report that immediately after the senior Allied command left Java, the local inhabitants had 'thrown away the traditional headdress of their country and had all donned the new fangled black fez of the extreme native nationalist and anti-Dutch movement'. Arms caches in the mountains, which had been intended to be used by guerrillas against the Japanese, were soon found and plundered by locals. Well-armed and often hostile, the Javanese represented a more dangerous—and certainly more imminent—threat to the Austalians than the Japanese.

The Japanese extended their patrols to search for guns, petrol, secret radio transmitters and the fugitive British and Australian soldiers reported by locals to be hiding out at the mine.

Kriek's successor as manager of the gold mine, a man called Tauw, was 'taken up the mountain by some Japanese soldiers and told to lead the way to Van der Post's party. They failed to make any contact, and the Japanese officer decided that further pursuit was too dangerous, given the impenetrable nature of the terrain. On the way down, they had come across the bodies of two Australian soldiers at Tjirotan, their throats slashed.'

According to Kriek, the Japanese were in no hurry to capture Van der Post; they knew he was trapped in his mountain hideaway and were content to starve him out. In order to avoid Japanese patrols, Van der Post's group retreated deeper into the jungle, making contact and resupply more and more difficult. After Van der Post was captured in April, it seemed only a matter of time before the weakened, sick and desperate Australians would be caught. Kriek was repeatedly interrogated but he stuck to his story of never having seen an Australian or British officer at the mine, and the Japanese appeared to believe him.

In mid-September a group of 'guerrillas' surrendered and were taken to a prisoner-of-war camp at Serang. According to Kriek, five British and three Australians gave themselves up 'when they discovered that the Japanese were planning to revenge themselves on the population of Bantam in general and the Europeans of Tjikotok in particular'.

The camp at Serang was a former jail that still housed a number of ordinary criminals. Another Australian inmate, Rohan Rivett, described these 'native convicts' as a 'wretched gang' who were 'very amused at the fact that they are fed about five times as well as we are'. In his book *Behind Bamboo*, Rivett recalled the month he spent as a prisoner in Serang 'lying on your back, watching the big bluebottles crawling over the filthy bandages of your legs'.

An American sailor who wound up in Serang after surviving the sinking of the *Houston* reported:

> [A]t least 50 % of the prisoners had no clothing other than shorts or a 'loin cloth'. There were no beds. We were forced to sleep on the wooden floor. In the other cells, the men were forced to sleep on sloping concrete floors; no bedding was furnished to any of us. We were fed twice a day. We were given an extremely inferior type of rice, badly prepared by native prisoners. Most of the men became ill with dysentery.

Another witness, Johann Feldscher, said that at Serang prisoners 'were made to sit straight up, Japanese fashion, from 8 a.m. until 10 p.m. They had only three five-gallon cans of water each day for about 200 men.'

The mystery of what happened to Captain Guild, Lieutenant Stewart, Corporal Hynes and Private Murray was solved by Paul Vogt, a Swiss geologist employed by the gold-mining company. Vogt was among the group who surrendered to the Japanese in mid-September. He wrote:

> Three Australian officers decided to return to Australia, as we had a chance to direct a submarine to Wijnkoops Bay. With the consent of

our commander I offered to guide the Australians to the coast, through a very deep canyon. They thought this too big a sacrifice, considering the important tasks I had to fulfil for those who stayed behind. So I provided them with maps and taught them, in a canyon, how to manage dangerous descents with the aid of a bamboo stick. I warned them several times, while other officers were listening, never under any circumstances to follow a road or hill ridge as I was certain they would be seen, followed and killed, not out of sympathy for the Japs, but only in order to rob them. They went—and three days later I got the sorry proof of their death. They had chosen a guard house in a rice field to spend the night, were surrounded, spent all their ammunition without wounding anyone but for some light leg and arm wounds, and all three Australians were robbed and hacked to pieces.

It is not clear who the 'three Australian officers' mentioned by Vogt were, since Lieutenant Allen was not with Captain Guild and Lieutenant Stewart on their final journey to the coast. Nor is it possible to conclusively identify the two Australian soldiers found at Tjirotan with their throats cut. Kriek named the following Pioneers as having died in the mountains: Captain Guild, Lieutenant Stewart, Sergeant Smith, Corporals T. Hynes and L.H. Dunstan, and Privates A.C. Murray, N.R.C. Gibson, E. Marshall and M.G. Byrne. The battalion roll of honour lists all the above except Sergeant Smith. Some are reported to have been 'killed in action' and some as having died of 'illness'.

According to the Pioneers' history, Lieutenant Allen 'had been left in the mountains with the very sick [and] avoided capture until 2 August, when at last, very weak and suffering from prolonged exposure, he with Privates Vin McCrae and Stan Baade were surprised by an enemy patrol and captured.'

Three and a half weeks later, the three bedraggled survivors were delivered to Bicycle Camp.

Chapter 7

JAVA RABBLE

<hr>

After being captured in the mountains, Colonel Van der Post was taken to Bandoeng, where he joined the Australians imprisoned with Weary Dunlop. 'Weary's Thousand' now included Jack Thomas and the machine gunners transferred from Garoet at the end of June.

Compared with what was to come, the regime at Bandoeng was relatively benign. Food was short and random slappings common, but the battalion history mentions 'a well-stocked library, a canteen for those who still had money and even a pawnbroker's shop. Buying parties were sometimes allowed out.' Education inside the camp continued through the so-called 'University of Bandoeng', which taught everything from basic literacy to arts degrees. The role of senior education officer was filled by the polymath Van der Post, who wrote in *The Night of the New Moon* that 'We created a vast prison organisation for the re-education of ourselves, a sort of prison kindergarten, school, high school, technical college and University rolled in one.'

According to Dunlop's diary, 'The British and American officers seem to be very confident and are settling down to an easy-going life of gardening, reading, bridge playing and making marmalade jam. Col. Van der Post in particular turns out to be a good marmalade cook.'

Below the surface, however, tensions existed between the many different nationality groups. As well as Australians, British, Americans and Dutch, there were Canadians, Portuguese, New Zealanders, Ambonese, and Menadonese from northern Sulawesi. Most of the arguments concerned accommodation and the allocation (and price) of food sold at the canteen. After the Australians moved into huts previously used by the Dutch, a squabble erupted over a box claimed by the Australians but wanted by the Dutch. 'Dutch officer rudely seized this [box] from [Major Morris] . . . I gave [the Dutch officer] the full blast of my wrath, comparing his officers to carrion birds and refused to speak to him any more in the presence of other ranks.'

In July 1942, for no obvious reason, the guards at Bandoeng turned more aggressive. 'Slapping is rather in vogue again,' Dunlop wrote in his diary. In one attack the victims suffered 'a ruptured eardrum, a broken tooth plate and a tooth knocked out'. In September—again, without explanation—Dunlop noted 'slapping much improved' but complained about the 'extreme annoyance' of constant patrols by Japanese officers demanding 'full compliments' from prisoners.

At Bicycle Camp, Lieutenant Sonai took over as commandant from the sabre-wielding Lieutenant Suzuki. Sonai proved to be scrupulous in his concern for the prisoners' property, instigating a thorough search of the camp to discover a watch and a lighter said to have been stolen by sentries. The missing items were returned to their owners and Sonai apologised personally to Blackburn, who wrote in his diary, 'This is an illustration of the care which is taken by the Jap authorities to see that the prisoners' private property is respected and of the honesty and integrity of the authorities in respect to stealing.'

Blackburn found Sonai pleasant company. After being invited to lunch with Sonai and one of his sergeants, the Australian noted in his diary, 'Very much enjoyed interesting talk.' He protested, however, about the harsh treatment of a prisoner who was 'made to kneel for 30 minutes and then taken to the guardhouse'. Sonai conducted a 'full and searching inquiry and found that the man's story to me was inaccurate'.

Blackburn's diary paints Sonai as a capricious martinet: returning a confiscated piano but banning music except for an hour in the morning; donating beer but forbidding drunkenness; investigating some abuses while ignoring others. Other ranks remembered Sonai as a vicious brute.

In September, the camp's Japanese guards were replaced with Koreans, who appeared to delight in attacking the prisoners. Dunlop believed the Koreans had not seen active service and were taking out their frustrations on the inmates. Sonai did nothing to discourage the violence; sometimes he joined in. In the words of an American prisoner, Stanley Gorski, Sonai was

probably the worst human I have ever had the misfortune to come in contact with . . . an out and out sadist. It was nothing for him to line up ten or fifteen men, strip to the waist and proceed to knock them all unconscious . . . I've seen this man single handed demolish a whole hospital barracks with a crowbar. He threw microscopes into the . . . street, tore down shelves of the few medicines we were fortunate enough to have and in general made life miserable for everyone.

After the war, numerous American POWs testified to the savage beatings inflicted by a Korean guard they nicknamed the 'brown bomber'. Among the victims was a soldier named McCone, who was bashed nearly unconscious for '[having] a bottle of whiskey in his haversack when he returned from a work detail'.

The growing violence put further stress on prisoners already demoralised by boredom. In late September 1942, word went around that some prisoners at Bicycle Camp were to be sent overseas to work. The news aroused curiosity and even a sense of relief. 'Like all Japanese moves,' the Pioneers' historian wrote, 'it was to be to a better land, where food would be plentiful and work would be available so that prisoners could earn money to buy those extras that would make life just one big dream of paradise.'

In the first week of October, Blackburn was told that more than a thousand prisoners—including nearly all the Pioneers—would be moved out. Among them was Corporal Harry Walker. Blackburn himself would stay with the rest of the Australians at Bicycle Camp, where every couple of days brought another death from disease—dysentery, mainly, but sometimes typhus.

The Pioneers had brought a large quantity of tinned rations with them to Bicycle Camp. Carrying these to their as-yet unknown destination was impractical, so the food had to be eaten. On 6 October they sat down to a feast: tinned pork sausages and rice followed by condensed milk and white sugar. The next day all their gear had to be laid out for inspection by the guards. At 2 a.m. on 8 October, the departing prisoners, newly inoculated against typhoid, typhus and plague, were herded out of the camp gates. Many of them were ill with fever, but the sick had to march with the rest. From Koenigsplein railway station, they were delivered to the docks at Tandjong Priok.

After six months behind the wire at Bicycle Camp, most of the men were relieved to be going. Few would have been sorry to see the last of the sadistic Lieutenant Sonai.

Tandjong Priok was scarcely recognisable as the bustling port where they had disembarked from the *Orcades* in February. Wharves were deserted and cranes lay idle. Waterfront buildings stood blackened and scarred from bombing. The masts and funnels of sunken ships protruded from the oily water. 'When I thought of Tanjon Pryok as I had seen it at the beginning of January en route for Singapore, bristling with ships of all nations, with naval launches, submarines and flying boats arriving or departing amid the shoals of freighters and liners, it seemed as if the port itself had died,' wrote Rohan Rivett.

Twelve hundred Allied POWs were pushed aboard a small Japanese steamer, the *Kinkon Maru*. The hold was already packed with Bren-gun carriers captured from the Allies and waiting to be used against them. The prisoners were allowed between and underneath them but could not sit on them. The Bren carriers were not secured, and the men were scared of being crushed if the vehicles moved in heavy seas. 'It was nine o'clock in the morning when we clambered down into the hold,' Rivett wrote. 'We remained there for the next ninety-six hours. Well before midday the heat at the bottom of the hold became almost intolerable . . . Three times a day buckets containing rice and soya soup with a little radish floating in it were lowered to us.'

The *Kinkon Maru* took three and a half days to reach Singapore. During that time the prisoners were issued with a pint and a half of tea per man per day. Orders for the prisoners to be kept on board were countermanded, and they were taken by truck to Changi, on the north-eastern tip of the island, where around 15,000 Australian POWs were incarcerated at Britain's former Selarang army barracks. Driving through Singapore, Rivett felt that 'an indefinable shadow seemed to lurk over the city even in the more crowded thoroughfares'.

Despite its later notoriety, conditions at Changi were far better than at most other POW camps. As befitted a former British barracks, the buildings were large and sturdy, but they could not cope with the influx of prisoners. Des Jackson recalled, '[t]he food . . . was bad and there was little to be bought', but Changi had a decent camp hospital and by mid-1943 many prisoners had access to electric lighting and running water. Rivett found the few days he spent at Changi 'like a holiday'. In the official Australian history, the camp is described as having 'a pleasant suburban atmosphere'. Weary Dunlop was more lyrical: 'This is a delightful spot,' he wrote, 'with the sparkling sea of the straits stretching across to the green jungle of the mainland and the perfume of frangipani and hibiscus.' The one thing missing was enough food. '[A]ll the time one feels ravenously hungry and rice is very inadequate.' While rations were short, there was a library of 20,000 books to feed the mind.

The POWs at Changi were still nominally under the control of their own officers. Only senior Allied officers dealt directly with the Japanese. Neil MacPherson, who passed through in October 1942 en route to Burma, remembers being 'very impressed' with the discipline enforced by British officers. But submitting to it was another matter. MacPherson recalls a sharp encounter with a British lance corporal. 'The lance corporal looked at the two of us and said, "Don't you know to stand to attention when you talk to a lance corporal?" We looked at each other and told him, "Not in the Australian army!"'

The Pioneers' arrival at Changi coincided with the delivery of a large food consignment from the British Red Cross, of which they received a share. Another welcome surprise was the distribution of cards on which prisoners were allowed to write a few words to their families at home. They would be the first letters to reach Australia since the surrender. By then the Japanese had begun broadcasting information about prisoners through Singapore Radio.

Towards the end of October, Harry Walker's father, Thomas, found a letter waiting for him at the Alma Post Office. The letter, from the Victorian records office in Melbourne, informed Mr Walker that 'a broadcast over Tokyo radio intimates that your son VX22708 Cpl. H. E. Walker 2/2 Pioneer Battalion, A.I.F. is claimed as being held a Prisoner of War by the Japanese.' The writer warned Mr Walker that 'taking into consideration the circumstances of its receipt and that it originates from enemy sources', the information 'may not be authentic'. It was authentic all right, but it did not begin to tell the true story of Harry Walker's captivity.

The prisoners who had arrived on the *Kinkon Maru* stayed at Changi for less than three days before being loaded onto another ship, the *Maebisi Maru*, where conditions were 'even worse'. The original party was supplemented by another 200 prisoners who had left Batavia five days earlier, and a hundred Dutchmen. Some of the sickest prisoners had been left in the hospital at Changi. That left around 1500 men to be packed into the two holds of the *Maebisi Maru*.

To reach the forward hold, the prisoners had to climb down a 40-foot (12-metre) ladder to an area piled high with Japanese equipment, boxes, bed rolls and machinery, including a tractor. Rohan Rivett and some others clambered on top of the tallest pile of gear, 20 feet above the bottom of the hold, where they could be 'at least a little nearer to fresh air'. Nothing, Rivett wrote, 'could convey the depression which seemed to settle on us in the depths of that pit'. But the Australians refused to be cowed.

Suddenly, a lad from Wagga, Micky Cavanagh, called out in a ringing voice, 'Don't let them get you down, chaps. We can take it! Are we down-hearted?' The Japanese, crowded along the rail of the tiers above, like visitors at a zoo peering down into the animals' pit, must have been amazed at the vigour of our response. The spell had been broken. The boys were not going to be licked, however grim things might become.

Cavanagh is not an uncommon name, and Rivett might have misspelt his name, but there was a Cavanagh—Private Clifford Cavanagh—among the 2/2nd Pioneers who were sent to work on the Siam–Burma railway. At the age of 41, he died of 'illness' on 31 July 1945 and was buried at Kanchanaburi War Cemetery in Siam.

For two and a half days the *Maebisi Maru* lay at anchor in Singapore's Keppel Harbour. There was so little room for the 650 prisoners packed into the forward hold that some men slept on top of others. After the anchors were finally pulled up, the *Maebisi Maru* steamed up the coast of Malaya and Siam en route to its final destination: Burma. Rumours of a railway being built between Siam and Burma had been circulating while the Australians were in Changi; some prisoners had even been sent up there earlier in the year.

Many men became sick with dysentery. As they became weaker, they found it harder and harder to climb the ladder to the latrine on deck. The Japanese eventually allowed the worst cases to be placed on top of the hatch so they could be near the latrine. Occasionally the guards indulged in one of their arbitrary 'orgies of bashing'. Prisoners were driven back into the hold with rifle butts and 'sometimes, for hours on end, even the sick were not allowed access to the latrine'. Harry Walker remembers bodies being buried at sea.

Luckily for the Australians stewing at the bottom of the holds, the British submarines known to be prowling the Malayan coast did not attack the *Maebisi Maru*, although a Dutch POW ship was torpedoed a week later. Nine days after leaving Singapore, the ship reached the mouth of the Irrawaddy and moved slowly up the muddy river to anchor at Rangoon docks.

Meanwhile, conditions for the prisoners left behind in Java were worsening. Men weakened by malnutrition were falling sick with beri-beri, pellagra and scrotal dermatitis. At Tandjong Priok camp, a Japanese guard nicknamed 'Charlie Chaplin' found a prisoner called Moss sleeping under a tree and beat him mercilessly for not coming to attention quickly enough. A witness reported, 'He beat Moss with his rifle about the face and head and his forearm was badly swollen.' Prisoners at a camp in Surabaya, on the north coast, 'were made to drink the water from spittoons, this invariably produced terrible vomiting'.

In November, Dunlop and his men were moved by train to a camp in a former coconut plantation on the outskirts of Batavia. More crowded and more basic than Bandoeng, the Makasura camp was described by Lieutenant Brettingham-Moore as 'flat and frequently waterlogged'. The prisoners lived in bamboo huts.

Conditions in the Makasura hospital were primitive, with a desperate shortage of drugs and ointments to treat rampant skin complaints. 'Patients lie on the universal "bed", wrote Dunlop, 'the bug-ridden, iron-hard, slippery structure common to all huts.'

Accustomed to the 'wide open spaces' of the camp at Bandoeng, Private Jackson found the cramped conditions at Makasura depressing, although he adjusted soon enough. Food was better than it had been at Bandoeng, with soya beans added to the prisoners' rations and the occasional 'beefsteak porridge' replacing the standard breakfast fare, described by Jackson as 'thin gruel: 90 per cent water, saltless but made more bearable on every second day by a spoonful of sugar'. Lunch was more substantial—'a reasonable serve of steamed rice, occasionally accompanied by a boiled egg or a piece of dried fish'—while dinner consisted of rice and 'half a pint of good vegetable soup, frequently improved by a small ration of meat'.

At Makasura, camp discipline began to break down. While this was a predictable consequence of men from so many different units and different services being thrown together, it was also a reflection of the demoralising conditions of their captivity. The machine gunners' history notes ruefully that 'Colonel Lyneham realised that it was no longer possible for him to have any control of his men'.

Terrified of contagious disease breaking out in the unhealthy conditions at Makasura, the Japanese inoculated prisoners against typhoid, dysentery, cholera and plague. On 22 November, inmates were ordered to start catching flies. Dunlop reported being told that 'anyone who cannot produce 4 tonight will be in for trouble'. Men roamed the camp with 'fly swotters', but officers exempted themselves from the hunt.

Three days later Blackburn celebrated his 50th birthday in Bicycle Camp. A band was allowed to play. Guests included the governor-general of Java and assorted American, British, Dutch and Australian officers. Thanks to the fifteen bottles of beer donated by Lieutenant Sonai, they had 'a very pleasant evening'—a rare case of harmonious collaboration between ABDA forces.

The purchase of 100 ducks from Javanese vendors outside the camp enabled Blackburn to lay on a slap-up Christmas dinner for everyone: 'Soup, sardine rissoles, roast duck, potatoes, mixed vegetables, fruit salad, Christmas pudding, custard, a cigar each and half a pint of wine.' The officers treated themselves to a formal mess dinner.

The decision had now been made to move Blackburn and other high-ranking officers to another camp. They left Bicycle Camp on 28 December. 'His quiet dignity,' the Pioneer's historian wrote, 'masking an unquenchable spirit of protest against Japanese injustices, earned him the admiration of the officers and men who shared with him the humiliation of captivity.'

Makasura was the next camp to be emptied out. The first sign that the Japanese were up to something was an improvement in rations. 'Every now and then,' Des Jackson recalled, 'as a treat, the cooks were able to produce a rice cake which was called a doover, containing a little meat or an egg or a piece of fish. Also, we received a cup of weak tea with every meal—a real luxury.' Some guessed correctly that they were being 'fattened' for some 'unpleasant purpose connected with the Japanese war effort'.

On 30 December, two days after Brigadier Blackburn was driven away from Bicycle Camp, the men left behind were 'issued with a small piece of clear cellophane paper and instructed to use it on the following morning as a wrapper for a faeces sample . . . at 9 o'clock we were ordered to go to the parade ground, armed with our samples. The *tenko* [roll call] which followed was impossibly hilarious, for the spectacle of 1000 men lined up in open formation in five ranks, each clutching a small package of cellophaned faeces, was ludicrous in the extreme.'

A major from the Japanese medical corps walked along the line, occasionally banishing a prisoner to the opposite side of the parade ground. While Dunlop, who was then in reasonable health, passed over the incident in a few lines, Jackson recalled how 'the numbers of banished men slowly increased and the mystery deepened'. Eventually about 125 men were weeded out, leaving 875, including Jackson, in their original lines. After the major had made his selection, Dunlop addressed his troops: 'the purpose of this unusual parade has been to ascertain who will be sent away on a working party and who will remain here. Only fit men are to go and the test of your fitness or otherwise has rested on the state of your stools.'

The incident was remembered afterwards as the 'turd parade', but only the 125 rejected men were laughing. Where the rest were bound, nobody knew. More inoculations were given, as well as the uncomfortable 'glass rod test' for dysentery, which led to a few more men being ordered to fall out. Mosquito nets were issued.

At 1.30 a.m., Dunlop Force, as it was now called, marched out of the gates of Makasura camp en route for the Meester Cornelius railway station. A train was waiting, but it was almost dawn before it pulled out. A half-hour ride through the suburbs of Batavia ended at Tandjong Priok, where most of the men had disembarked eleven months earlier from the *Orcades*. An 'ancient three-island tramp steamer', the *Usu Maru*, was waiting for them. At the top of the gangplank, two 'white-coated gauze-masked Japanese' hosed each prisoner with disinfectant from 44-gallon drums. 'We had to move through clouds of suffocating white vapour,' Des Jackson recalled. Counted and fumigated, the men and officers—including Colonel Dunlop—were herded into the rear hold to join the rats and cockroaches.

'We were loaded onboard cattle style,' Jack Thomas remembers, 'in very much the same style, I should think, that the Japanese transported their own troops. We probed and pushed and made our way in. There was no room so we had to make our own room. We couldn't lie down. We were given very little to eat.'

Des Jackson recalled spending the next five nights 'lying on our backs with knees up and feet under the head of the man in front'. Peace was interrupted by minor arguments as feet slipped, knocking heads and leading to 'the occasional skirmish'.

The *Usu Maru* had another hold, but the Japanese tried to prevent contact between the two groups of prisoners. Nevertheless, a visit to the latrines—ramshackle wooden structures hanging precariously over the ship's edge—offered an opportunity to swap stories. The inmates in the other hold were mostly Tasmanians from the 2/40th Infantry Battalion, captured after a short but bitter fight on Timor. After surviving sickness and starvation as prisoners on Timor, they had endured three months of bashings and abuse in a POW camp at Tandjong Priok. None knew what lay ahead, but few were sorry to leave Java.

After picking its way through the sunken ships in Tjandong Priok harbour, the *Usu Maru* followed the Sumatran coast before crossing the open sea to Singapore. On the morning of 7 January 1943 the nearly 900 officers and men of Dunlop Force were taken on trucks to Changi. Jack Thomas remembers being unloaded from the ship and paraded through the streets for the locals to gawk at. 'The Japanese had machine guns mounted for a bit of show,' he says, 'but they didn't shoot anyone.'

Dressed in rags, their hair cropped, wearing broken-down boots or none at all, Dunlop's men were dubbed the 'Java Rabble'. Thomas does not dispute the description. 'We were a rabble,' he says, 'a pretty untidy looking lot.' The name stuck and in future would be worn (the machine gunners' historian wrote) 'like a badge of honour'.

Since leaving Suez with no weapons—but full knapsacks—the machine gunners had been gradually shedding their gear. Much equipment had been lost or cast off when they moved camps in Java. By the time they arrived at Bandoeng, Thomas and his mates had 'weaned ourselves of anything superfluous'. Most now reached Singapore with nothing more than the clothes they were wearing and, if they were lucky, a spare shirt in their backpack (underwear 'wasn't much in fashion'). Unlike many of his comrades, Jack Thomas still had a serviceable pair of boots, possessions that would become more precious in the months ahead.

At Changi the machine gunners were reunited with their commanding officer. Blackburn had arrived in the camp a few days earlier with Generals Ter Poorten and Sitwell, Air Vice-Marshal Maltby and the US artillery commander Colonel Albert Searle, en route for Taiwan. Blackburn, Dunlop wrote, was 'extremely thin and wasted, but his skin remains clear and his eye keen'.

Changi already had a sizeable contingent from Major-General Gordon Bennett's 8th Division, captured at Singapore. It was 8th Division headquarters staff who had come up with the name for the new arrivals. The fleet-footed Bennett had slipped away to Australia, leaving Lieutenant Colonel 'Black Jack' Galleghan in charge of the Changi prisoners, who were well equipped and in reasonably good shape. Private Russell Braddon, a gunner in the Australian 2/15th Regiment, remembered Galleghan as 'conceited and vain', an 'egomaniacal' man who 'became quite hysterical if he were denied by anyone, even officers, the military courtesies'. Not everyone agreed with this assessment. Lieutenant Colonel Glyn White, the senior Australian doctor in Changi, found him 'a truly remarkable man and an outstanding character, hard as nails but basically so kind'.

Dunlop and Galleghan locked horns from the outset. Black Jack took grave offence when Dunlop and his men were slow to salute him on their arrival at the camp. Galleghan's mania for neatness and saluting drove Weary mad. 'He insists on a proper dress and a smart turn out,' he wrote, 'and has lashed verbally all Australian troops into smartness and saluting—a praiseworthy achievement.'

Although a surgeon with a colonel's rank, Dunlop was not strictly a 'combatant' officer. Galleghan wanted to replace him as commander of Dunlop Force with Major Bill Wearne, a staff officer at ABDA headquarters who had stayed behind in Java after the rest were withdrawn. He advised Dunlop of his intention by memo, asking rhetorically, 'Is there any reason for not making change?'

Blackburn, who knew exactly how much Dunlop's men owed to his inspirational leadership, was having none of it. Galleghan had been left in command of all AIF forces in Singapore, but as a colonel he was outranked by Brigadier Blackburn. In a carefully worded note, Blackburn told Galleghan that having 'considered this matter' he wanted Lieutenant Colonel Dunlop to 'retain command for administrative and disciplinary purposes so long as the troops brought over by him remain together as one body'. Weary tucked the note away for future use.

As well as soldiers, the Java Rabble included sailors like Ray Parkin, a survivor from HMAS *Perth*. Although an outsider, Parkin understood the tension between the two groups. 'The Machine-Gunners and Pioneers of the Seventh,' he wrote in his POW memoir, *Into the Smother*, 'have Syria and a victory to their credit, which has softened this final defeat a little; but the Eighth have faced a defeat, it seems, ordered by Fate from the start.'

Les Cody was one of the Australians left feeling 'dazed and vulnerable' by the 'instant transition from a fighting soldier in the middle of a war to [a state] of total submission to the enemy'. The defeated troops of the 8th Division 'felt betrayed, their losses during the whole campaign in Malaya and on Singapore a pointless and wasted sacrifice. Stripped of all purpose and the capacity to do something about it, their anger turned into bitterness and recrimination ... [a] general resistance to discipline began to develop as the power of the officers to retain control came into question—petty or badly delivered orders were ignored or actively opposed.' These attitudes, which emerged in the immediate aftermath of surrender, 'extended well into the early days of captivity'.

Fuelling the antagonism inside Changi was a sour rumour, put about by embittered Dutch prisoners, that rather than two Australian battalions in Java, there were two *divisions*, which did not fight.

The Java rabble were a nuisance ('an irritating flea crawling over a large, well-fed body', in Parkin's words) and they knew it. They wore their disreputableness 'with pride', scorning Galleghan's pomp and fastidiousness.

'There is a high standard here which is taken by their officers to be synonymous with morale,' Parkin wrote. '[Galleghan] is preserving an élite corps which is being trained with broomsticks . . . We must appear to him as a deliberate affront. In our rags and with our close-cropped heads, we have suffered his wrath . . . [he] deplores that men should have fallen to such a low state.'

When Galleghan asked what he could do for the men from Java, Dunlop told him they were 'badly off for clothing . . . he promised help, though there was little on the island'. Some prisoners from the 8th Division willingly handed clothing to the ragged machine gunners, but the well-stocked British and Australian stores were kept firmly shut.

'Black Jack' Galleghan was reputed to have a fierce temper, and Dunlop's 'repeated requests' for boots and clothing riled him. There was also the small matter of Weary and his men having been slow to salute him on the first day. When the time came for Galleghan to make his move and strip Dunlop of his command, Weary 'produced Brig. Blackburn's note very casually'. A furious Galleghan then 'dragged off' Wearne and demanded an explanation, only to be told that neither Wearne nor any other officer in Dunlop Force would take over from Weary.

Galleghan continued to seethe, chastising Dunlop's men for 'straggling on the march, irregular movements etc'. Weary conceded (at least to his diary) that the men looked 'pretty dreadful' but it was 'hard to put up a good show in rags'.

Worse still was the lack of boots: 178 men had none at all, and another 204 had boots Dunlop considered 'unserviceable'. The problem, Weary was assured, was the Dutch, who jealously guarded their share of the communal stores and were on the lookout for anything that smacked of favouritism. Dunlop didn't buy it: he blamed Galleghan.

The antagonism between the Australians boiled over at a formal dinner where 'someone ill-advisedly referred to the Java Rabble and Weary shot to his feet in defence of the men under his command'. A furious Dunlop recited a list of battles and campaigns—the Battle of Britain, the Atlantic, the Mediterranean, the Western Desert, Greece, Crete, Syria, Java—in which his men had fought, ending with a sardonic toast, 'And now we, the Java Rabble, salute you, the 8th Division, who have fought so gallantly here in Malaysia.'

Parkin's parting shot was more ominous: 'We tell the well-dressed that they have much to learn about this P.O.W. business: their day will come, we say.'

Before leaving Changi, the Rabble were issued a grand total of '6 pairs of boots size 11, 150 pairs of socks, 20 Glengarry caps'. Parkin quotes Dunlop writing to Galleghan on the day before they marched out of Changi:

Two weeks ago my men arrived in a pitiful condition in this camp from Java. You have done nothing to alleviate their needs. Tomorrow at 8.30 they leave in the same pitiable condition, bootless and in rags. You have done nothing.

The men knew it, too. 'They could have given us so much in the way of medical supplies and what have you,' Private Bill Haskell recalled bitterly, 'but they didn't. The only thing we got of substance when we left were rice polishings and nothing else.'

Blackburn had already gone. With his fellow senior officers, Sitwell, Ter Poorten, Maltby and Searle, the machine gunners' commanding officer was on board a ship to the Japanese port of Moji. It was now the middle of the Japanese winter. After a few 'extremely uncomfortable' days at a barracks filled with American and Indian prisoners, they boarded another ship for the island of Formosa (now Taiwan).

Paraded at night before the camp commandant, the officers— several of them veterans of the First World War—were told to sign an oath promising not to escape. The American Colonel Searle signed. Blackburn said he would only sign 'under protest and duress'. Asked twice what the penalty was for not signing, the commandant shrieked, 'You will see what the penalty is!' and had Blackburn dragged off to the guardhouse.

Blackburn described what happened next in his POW diary and, after the war, in his evidence to the International Military Tribunal for the Far East in Tokyo.

'Suspecting what was coming,' Blackburn wrote, 'I ripped off my spectacles and put them on the table at my side. I had just got them off when the officer stepped up to me and struck me a violent blow on the jaw with his clenched fist. He repeated this several times forcing me gradually back until I stumbled over some boxes.'

After the officer had given him a kicking, the guards picked him up and stripped him to his underpants and socks. Blackburn was then locked in a bare cell with a hole in the concrete floor for a toilet, and ordered to sit. The freezing winter weather aggravated the heavy cold he was already suffering from and before long Blackburn was 'coughing almost incessantly and . . . shivering violently'.

A torch was shone in his eyes every ten minutes to force him to stay awake. Throughout that night and the following day he was ordered alternately to sit or stand. Apart from a mug of water he was given nothing but a ball of rice. 'I remained in the cell all day,' he told the tribunal. 'With my bad cough I began by evening to feel very feverish. At 9 p.m. I was at last allowed to lie down.'

In *The Knights of Bushido: A short history of Japanese war crimes*, Edward Russell notes that the policy of forcing prisoners to sign forms undertaking not to escape was 'quite common'. The Japanese war ministry had issued clear instructions that '[a]s soon as prisoners of war have been imprisoned, they will be administered an oath forbidding them to make an escape. Prisoners of war who refuse to take the oath . . . shall be deemed to have intentions of escaping, and shall be placed under strict surveillance.'

Strict surveillance in such cases meant more than close observation. It was 'a euphemism for being confined on reduced rations and subject to torture until the oath was taken'. At Selarang in Singapore, 16,000 prisoners who refused the pledge not to escape were 'herded into a barrack square . . . and kept there without food or latrine facilities for four days'.

After a night shivering in his cell, Blackburn was given back his clothes and found '[a]ll the buttons had been cut off'. The same officer who had bashed and kicked him in the guardhouse offered him a cigarette. He was then invited, again, to sign the oath. Blackburn signed, as he had always indicated he would, 'under duress'.

Blackburn's British superior, General Sitwell, endured similar treatment for objecting to the oath. General Percival, who led the Commonwealth forces to disaster in Malaya, was 'severely beaten up' after being accused of having 'a speck of dirt under one of his nails'.

It was a savage initiation for the commanders, but the men left behind were to suffer much worse, and for much longer.

Chapter 8
A HELL OF A TEMPER

Between October 1942 and January 1943, the machine gunners and Pioneers of Blackforce were among thousands of Australian prisoners who passed through Changi. Many had already witnessed Japanese brutality or been victims of it, but some—like Private Neil MacPherson—had not. Hungry and weak, but not yet starving, MacPherson could have been forgiven for hoping that things would get better.

The *Maebisi Maru*, with its cargo of nearly 1500 prisoners, anchored at Rangoon on 23 October. Harry Walker recalled it being late at night when they tied up on a fast-flowing branch of the Irrawaddy River. Rohan Rivett remembered being allowed on deck to enjoy a vibrant Burmese sunset until 'the guards decided that we seemed too happy' and pushed them back down below. Both remember the mosquitoes, whose 'droning buzz ... beat against one's eardrums relentlessly'. Walker reckoned 'every mosquito [in Burma] was there to welcome us and nobody slept.

Perspiration was just pouring out of us and the mosquitos really liked it. One fellow, a baritone, sang *The Road to Mandalay*.' The singing cheered up the prisoners, and for once the Japanese guards made no attempt to stop it.

The next day the prisoners were transferred to a smaller ship, the *Yinagata Maru*, for the trip to Moulmein. In the daylight they could see the damage caused by British bombers. The masts of sunken ships poked out of the oily water, and around them floated the splintered wreckage of warehouses.

Gangs of handcuffed Burmese and Tamil labourers could be seen hauling rails on the wharves under the eye of Japanese overseers. The way they were treated convinced Rivett that 'the Jap was not likely to make himself any more popular in Rangoon than in Singapore or Batavia'. From the docks, the prisoners had a clear view of the city, which seemed as lifeless and inert as Singapore—perhaps even more so, since there were no motor vehicles in Rangoon. The sense of unreality enveloping the city was heightened by the cartoon figures that adorned the façade of the Hollywood Hotel; the beaming faces of Mickey Mouse and Donald Duck gazed across the water at the browbeaten coolies.

The *Yinagata Maru* was carrying a cargo of gravel, which was flat if not exactly soft. It was, Rivett wrote, 'by far the most comfortable billet I had yet found in a Japanese ship'. The *Yinagata Maru* reached Moulmein at around 10.30 p.m. Under a full moon the prisoners were taken off by pontoon. The whole operation took some hours. Walker remembered the moon being so bright that it felt almost like daylight.

Although some prisoners died, there had been no epidemics on any of the ships carrying the Pioneers. The 1500 Dutch POWs who set off from Batavia a week after them were not so fortunate. During the 22 days the journey lasted, they were not allowed to leave the ship. At Penang they were kept aboard in the stifling heat for nine days. An outbreak of dysentery took the lives of fourteen prisoners and left many more close to death. Marched to Rangoon jail, they were thrown into bare stone cells and left all night 'without food, water, pans, buckets or anything else'. Afterwards they they were given nothing but rice to eat. 'The Japanese provided nothing whatever for the dying men except tools for their comrades to bury them,' Rivett wrote. When, five days before Christmas, the Dutch prisoners capable of physical labour were taken away to work on the railway, they were forced to leave behind '200 dead and 450 more incapable of movement'. The final death toll was 260. 'All things considered,' Rivett wrote, 'we were tremendously lucky.'

Herded along the moonlit streets, the men from the *Yinagata Maru* sometimes caught sight of faces watching them from balconies or squinting through half-open shutters. The streets themselves were deserted. Eventually they came to a halt outside the stone walls of Moulmein district jail. Another day, another country, another jail, but this one was better than most. 'Compared to Serang,' Rivett remarked, 'this was a jail *de luxe*. You could even roll over without touching the man next to you.'

The jail was crowded with Burmese prisoners, segregated according to the diseases they suffered from. Many were in a wretched state. Walker was shocked to see some dragging chains connected to heavy steel balls. A few looked 'hardly human'. On the hill behind the jail stood a large golden pagoda whose softly tinkling bells, brushed by the wind, were clearly audible to prisoners in the jail.

The food wasn't much to write home about, if they had been allowed to write home: rice and melons, sometimes with a few meat scraps tossed in. One man, Vaudan Heggaton, a driver from the 2/3rd Motor Reserve Transport Company, died of dysentery picked up on the Japanese hell-ships. His death affected everyone. To Rivett, it seemed like a portent of what lay ahead.

After four nights in Moulmein jail, the POWs were marched out through the colonial part of town, past houses with quintessentially

English names—'Lyndhurst', 'Rosehill'– to a local market district where, according to the battalion history, the Burmese 'ran out with hands and arms filled with bundles of bananas, cigars and anything else that the sparsely stocked shelves of their shops would yield'.

This generosity from the Burmese was startlingly different from the scorn and hostility they had encountered from the local population in West Java. Having borne the brunt of Javanese resentment towards Dutch colonial rule, the Australians now found themselves swamped by a 'spontaneous ... demonstration of sympathy and friendliness'. The prisoners, marching to a fate crueller than any of them could imagine, were deeply affected by it. Corporal Walker recalled 'native Burmese ... running backwards with all sorts of rice cakes, cigarettes, sugar and salt'. Rivett described 'many women and girls standing crying' and others running out of their houses with trays of hot biscuits they had been baking.

According to Sergeant Harry Whelan, 'The Japs screamed and started to kick and bash the Burmese but they continued to force their goods upon us.' Private Neil MacPherson also remembers the guards 'knocking them about with rifle butts'. Corporal Walker remembered the scene differently, with the Japanese guards making no attempt to stop the Burmese from showering the departing prisoners with gifts. It is possible both versions of the incident are accurate and that some guards tried to stop the Burmese giving food to the POWs while others turned a blind eye. Whelan and Walker agreed that the incident 'made us think a bit and ... lifted our morale.' After the war, the Pioneers showed their appreciation by sending gifts from Australia.

From South Moulmein railway station the prisoners were taken by train to Thanbyuzayat, a base camp consisting of long bamboo and attap huts. Huts like these were often far too small for the number of men expected to sleep in them. According to evidence given to the Tokyo war crimes tribunal, 23 POW officers and 23 other ranks were forced to sleep in the space occupied by three Japanese soldiers. Inside the huts at Thanbyuzayat were notices urging the inmates to 'Work Cheerfully'.

Under their battalion CO, Lieutenant Colonel Williams, most of the Pioneers found themselves assigned to Lieutenant Colonel Nagatomo, who would be their Japanese commandant until the Siam–Burma railway was finished at the end of 1943. The prisoners comprising Williams Force were organised into work units of 50; each man was given a small wooden tag bearing his prisoner number, which was attached to his belt for easy identification.

On the afternoon of 27 October, Nagatomo summoned the men of Williams Force for a lecture. Nagatomo did not speak English but was evidently proud of the French he had picked up while studying at a French military academy. Standing on a dais, he addressed the Australians in French, which was translated into English by a Dutch prisoner. Acording to the battalion history, the gist of his remarks was that the men standing before him were 'but a rabble—the skeleton of a broken army'. The Emperor had graciously spared their lives, but in return the prisoners would now have to work. Idleness would not be tolerated and slackers would be punished.

The Pioneers had to fight back laughter as the pompous comman-dant rambled on in French about Japan's mission to bring happiness and civilisation to the oppressed people of Southeast Asia. But beneath the careless exterior, the Australians were genuinely worried about what lay ahead. Rivett felt that 'in Nagatomo we had struck the extreme type of Japanese military fanatic' and that 'prospects for the thousands of white men now going forth to labour in the jungle, under the worst coolie conditions, were forbidding to the extreme'. The Emperor had spared their lives so far, but for how long?

Leaving a few sick prisoners at the base camp, Colonel Williams and his men travelled in trucks to Tanyin, 35 kilometres along a new railway line that was going to link Thanbyuzayat in Burma with Bampong in Siam, a total distance of nearly 420 kilometres. According to railway historian

Rod Beattie, the job of building the Siam–Burma railway involved shifting three million cubic metres of soil and rock, building four million cubic metres of embankments and building fourteen kilometres of bridges, all without the aid of heavy machinery. In the wet season the roads would be impassable even to trucks, and all materials and every piece of equipment would have to be dragged up the line by hand.

The purpose of the railway was to supply the large Japanese army in Burma, which otherwise depended on the long and exposed sea route to Rangoon via Singapore and the Malacca Strait; and on a road into southern Burma that was unfit for continuous military traffic.

The Japanese intention was for the railway to be built by prisoners of war and coolies under the supervision of Japanese railway engineers. The work would be coordinated by two army regiments working from opposite ends of the line towards the centre at Konkoita, where the two sections would meet. Basic materials and equipment were to be sourced locally, while steel rails, rolling stock and construction materials for the many bridges would have to be brought from Japan.

More than half of the Pioneers taken prisoner in Java were now with Colonel Williams in Burma, but others had been left behind in Singapore and a few were still in camps in Java. When the war ended nearly three years later, Pioneers would be freed from POW camps in Siam, Japan, Indochina, Java, Sumatra, Singapore and Borneo.

For some families it would be months, for others years, before they discovered what had happened to the soldiers who had surrendered on Java. Japan did not allow the Red Cross any access to its prisoners. However, Japanese propaganda broadcasts from Java often included the names of a small number of Australians who had been taken prisoner. One day in late 1942, Private Neil MacPherson's name was among those read out at the end of a propaganda announcement. The broadcast was picked up by the stationmaster at Victoria Park railway station, a keen radio ham, who jumped on his bicycle and rode over to the MacPherson family home to report the news. During the next eighteen months, Neil MacPherson would receive two batches of letters, mainly from his mother (he still has the letters), and be able to send three or four pre-printed 'prisoner of war' cards to Australia, all of which got through. Not everyone was so fortunate.

It was still the dry season when Williams Force arrived at Tanyin, better known as 35 Kilo camp after its distance from the terminus at Thanbyuzayat. Harry Walker recalled:

Our work was to carry dirt for the embankments. Everybody had to carry around a cubic metre a day, probably had to walk 40 or 50 yards for it. The only way we could transport the dirt was in a cane basket that held 3 or 4 shovels full. We had to dig it, put it in a basket then walk up the embankment, tip it, and go back. It wasn't too bad. The harder we worked the quicker we were able to knock off . . . We always looked on Tanyin as the best camp we had.

Neil MacPherson also remembers the conditions being bearable in the early days at Tanyin. But things would change as work began to fall behind schedule. When he suffered a severe case of conjunctivitis, MacPherson was transferred to the base hospital at Thanbyuzayat. The doctors had very few drugs, but rations were better and being in hospital saved a patient from having to work. At mealtimes, MacPherson was pushed to the front of the rice queue along with other prisoners who had lost their sight. Shuffling around with a handkerchief over his eyes to protect them from the sun, he stayed at Thanbyuzayat for six weeks before being sent back up the line. His bed was quickly taken by someone else.

Life in the camps was dictated by the Japanese commandant, and the commandant at 35 Kilo camp was unusually humane. While his appearance was remembered as 'grim and forbidding, especially after leaving his razor untouched for a week', Lieutenant Yamada ran the camp with 'intelligence and tolerance'. Unlike other commandants, and contrary to the rules of the Imperial Japanese Army, Yamada went out of his way to ensure that Colonel Williams was treated in keeping with his rank, and did not demand to be saluted himself as he moved about the camp. According to Harry Walker, Yamada 'had been educated in England and he did not allow harsh punishment'.

Near the camp was a Burmese village. Since the camp had no fence, prisoners were able to slip out and bargain for fruit and chickens. Yamada found out and ordered the visits to stop, but when a snap parade found two dozen men missing he sent out armed guards to bring them back. 'An hour or two later,' the battalion history records, 'they marched into camp under escort, shirt fronts bulging with trussed-up fowls, pomeloes and other good things'. Yamada confiscated the merchandise and had it sent to the guards' hut. That evening he announced that the owners could retrieve their property, but it had to be done after dark, 'as Yamada did not wish to witness the illegal act'.

Around this time, the prisoners were allowed to send a printed card home. Under the heading 'Imperial Japanese Army', it read,

I am still in a P.O.W. Camp near Moulmein, Burma. There are 20,000 Prisoners, being Australian, Dutch, English, and Americans. There are several camps of 2/3000 prisoners who work at settled labour daily.

We are quartered in very plain huts. The climate is good. Our life is now easier with regard to food, medicine and clothes. The Japanese Commander sincerely endeavours to treat prisoners kindly.

Officers' salary is based on salary of Japanese Officers of the same rank and every prisoner who performs labour or duty is given wages from 25 cents (minimum) to 45 cents, according to rank and work.

Canteens are established where we can buy some extra foods and smokes. By courtesy of the Japanese Commander we conduct concerts in the camps, and a limited number go to a picture show about once per month.

Beneath the printed sentences Harry Walker wrote carefully in ink, 'HOPING ALL WELL AT HOME. I AM WELL. LONGING TO BE WITH YOU. CHEER UP. LOVE TO ALL. HARRY.'

Many such cards never reached their destination. Those that did must have been read with scepticism—not least the suggestion that Japanese commanders endeavoured to treat prisoners 'kindly'. Real wages for the prisoners were also significantly less than advertised. According to the official Australian war history, payment was at the rate of 25 cents a day for working warrant officers, 15 cents for NCOs and 10 cents for privates. Since money was deducted for board and lodgings, officers might receive as little as a quarter of their entitlement, but this was still more than a private soldier could earn. In February 1943 wages privates were increased to 25 cents a day. Crucially, however, those too sick to work received nothing.

As well as building earth embankments, the Australians had to build bridges, driving in wooden piles with muscle power alone. 'Although strenuous enough in the heat, the work at this stage was not really arduous,' the Pioneers' history records. Rohan Rivett's memoir tells a different story:

> Gangs of men, straining on ropes, raised the heavy 'monkey', or iron weight, then let it thud down on the top of the pile, repeating the process endlessly until at last the great beam stood securely in the river-bed. Some men . . . spent many hours each day for months on end standing waist-deep and sometimes shoulder-deep in the rivers. All work was carried out under an incessant barrage of shouting and screaming . . . from guards and engineers. Men were struck with pick-handles, with bamboo rods, with anything the guards found to hand.

Officers who tried to protect their men from bashings by the guards were themselves bashed, while the Japanese engineer in charge stood on the bridge raining 'iron spikes and tools' on the heads of the prisoners labouring below.

Acting bombardier Tom Uren and a north Queensland cane cutter named Harry Baker were partners in a 'hammer-and-tap' crew. Interviewed in 1996 for the Australian Biography project, Uren explained:

> [T]hey'd set a darg first of all. The darg is the contract, of 80 centimetres a hole and you could go home, and then they built it from 80 centimetres up to a metre then a metre 20, then a metre 50, two metres, two metres 50, three metres a day, and then ultimately they made them work all day . . . some of the show-offs really got stuck into it and got home early and that was that . . . the weak had to pick up the blast rock and put it into embankments, and some of those people would work from 16 to 20 hours a day. If you talk about the . . . six or seven kilometres they had to walk and work and then get home again, it was just hell for the sick and the weak . . . the great thing about Harry Baker was, he said, 'Look Tom, just take your time, let the hammer do the work'—an eight-pound plumb hammer—'let the hammer do the work. Don't bust yourself, those blokes are busting their guts.' And of course, they did. They got sick and when they got sick they went down and they were the same as anybody else . . . Harry's guidance . . . the science of an intelligent worker . . . helped me survive.

'The first disease that showed was pellagra,' Harry Walker recalled. 'We lost the skin off our mouth and lips and also down below. It was very painful . . . the lack of vitamin B caused burning soles of the feet at night. It was all right when walking around but at night the burning pain was just unbearable. Many times you would see fellows standing on one foot trying to sleep . . . it got the better of a few of them and they gave up.' Beri-beri, caused by lack of vitamin B, led to grotesque swelling of the legs and feet. 'A bad case was virtually the end because the body would retain all fluids and blow up to three times the normal size.' As a last resort, doctors could try to extract fluid by tapping the spine, but Walker 'never heard of any success'.

Malnutrition and vitamin deficiency could affect eyesight; some men went almost totally blind. Unable to see the approach of guards, they were bashed without mercy for failing to bow and salute. Exasperated medical officers made affected prisoners carry signs with Japanese symbols indicating their blindness.

Dysentery reduced soldiers to skeletons. Private William Tollett, a driver in 105 General Transport Company, contracted the disease on one of the hell-ships that carried prisoners to Burma. Two months of suffering reduced Tollett from his normal weight of around ten stone (63 kilograms) to a mere three stone thirteen pounds (25 kilograms). He was given three days to live at most when another driver from the 105 General Transport Company, his friend Sergeant Geoffrey McCaulay (or Macaulay), was sent to be with him. Tollett came back from the brink. He started eating again. Fourteen eggs were reportedly fed to him in a day. Somehow Tollett kept them down. After two months he was considered to be out of danger, although his comrades estimated that he weighed no more than five stone. His chances of surviving the war must have seemed bleak, but the Australian ex-prisoners of war memorial at Ballarat records Private Tollett as having been repatriated to Australia after the war ended.

Outbreaks of dysentery triggered an all-out assault on flies. '[T]he Japs set each man a daily fly quota which had to be delivered to the "chief fly catcher", Les Cody recalled. 'Weird and wonderful were the many fly traps in operation, supplemented by an assortment of crude fly swats. It didn't take long for the smart boys to come up with a recycling programme by substituting each day's catch for the next day's quota.'

Not all ailments were life-threatening. While at 35 Kilo camp Walker suffered from toothache. Captain Goding, who had been the Pioneers' medical officer since the battalion's formation at Puckapunyal, told Walker his infected tooth would have to come out. As Goding could not give him an anaesthetic, he advised Walker to 'bring someone big and strong to hold me down'. The next day Walker returned with a survivor from the sunken *Perth* called Freddie Spicer, 'a very solid sort of a fellow, no taller than I, but much heavier'. The tooth came out. Petty Officer Spicer and Walker had only known each other for a few days, but they would become 'railway mates', forging the kind of bond that for thousands of Australian prisoners of war would be the difference between living and dying.

With the death toll rising, Brigadier Arthur Varley, a battalion commander in Malaya who was now in charge of several thousand Allied POWs at Thanbyuzayat, took the radical step of ordering the sale of personal effects to raise money to buy food for the sick. Watches, fountain pens and other items that under normal circumstances would have been kept and forwarded to the next of kin were unsentimentally sold off; only wallets and photographs were exempt.

When the Japanese demanded all prisoners in Burma sign a pledge not to try to escape, senior Allied officers again refused. Major Charles Green, of the 2/4th machine gunners, although sick, was told he would be kept in a small cell with only rice and salt to eat until he signed the oath. Green eventually signed under duress. Prisoner escapes had been a nuisance to the Japanese since the capitulation, despite the minuscule chance of success and despite the prescribed punishment of death for anyone caught trying. In June a group of eight Australians led by Warrant Officer Quittendon of the 2/4th Anti-Tank Regiment were recaptured after escaping from the Burmese coastal town of Tavoy. Despite the protests of senior Allied officers, all eight were executed without trial. They were not the last. A few days later two more Australians were executed after being found outside the wire at Mergui; at the end of July another prisoner was shot for trading with a local outside the camp.

Declassified US Army records describe the punishment of three British soldiers who attempted to escape to India from a POW camp in southern

Siam. 'Each man was forced to dig a hole and put into it a stake to which they were later tied and a fire was lighted under them. At the same time they were bayoneted from behind the back by Japanese soldiers.'

The pledge the prisoners in Burma were required to sign stated: 'I the undersigned hereby swear on my honour that I will not under any circumstances attempt to escape.'

As in other cases, the fact that it was being signed under duress rendered the pledge meaningless, and Brigadier Varley eventually ordered all the Australians to sign.

The following month Korean soldiers arrived to take over as camp guards throughout Burma. Those who had witnessed the bastardry of Korean guards at Bicycle Camp and elsewhere had a fair idea of what to expect. 'We are not looking forward to this,' Varley wrote in his diary, 'as our guards here are the best we have had.'

Varley's forebodings soon proved correct. One of the victims was Private Sidney Barry, an assistant driver and labourer in the workshop at 63 Kilo camp. Born in 1900 in Manchester, Barry had enlisted at the age of 40 in Caulfield, Victoria. After joining the Pioneers, he fought in the Middle East and was captured in Java. Corporal John Roberts of the 2/3rd Motor Reserve Transport Company gave evidence after the war about Barry's treatment at the hands of a Korean guard. Barry had been suffering from chronic malaria and dysentery. Unable to get out of bed and running a fever of 104°F (40°C), he had been declared unfit to work by a Dutch medical orderly. According to Roberts's testimony, 'a Korean guard named Masaki Fumio entered the sleeping hut, dragged Barry out and severely beat him about the head and body with a bamboo'. Roberts tried to intervene and explain that Barry was very sick, but Fumio ignored him. 'Barry was knocked unconscious a number of times and each time he was felled he was kicked by Masaki Fumio. He was then forced to go to work and owing to the severe rains was working in quite deep water. He collapsed after a time and was again taken to his quarters by me and two [prisoners]. When Masaki Fumio discovered that he had gone off duty he dragged Barry out again and sent him off in a truck to 85 Kilo station. During the afternoon after his return ... Masaki Fumio again brutally beat him and kicked him into unconsciousness, forcing his head into a nearby mud pool. Barry was evacuated to hospital at 80 Kilo camp. He died the following day.'

After the war Masaki Fumio was tried in Singapore for war crimes. In the precis of evidence, Fumio was alleged to have 'made a habit of beating prisoners of war including those who were sick'. The allegation was supported by several witnesses. An American sailor from the USS *Houston*, Ross Glover, testified to having seen Masaki 'kick a sick Aussie named Jock Mackenzie on his ulcer sore a number of times. Masaki beat me repeatedly and on many occasions he beat sick men. I saw him beat men who had high fevers.' (Glover also accused Masaki of stealing medicines meant for the treatment of POWs.)

Another American witness, Corporal Thomas Whitehead, saw Masaki beat a prisoner named Harris and force him to 'stand at attention and hold a heavy truck spring which ... weighed about 40 pounds, over his head for three hours. He fell to the ground 3 or 4 times and was beaten and kicked until he got to his feet again.' After beating him, Masaki would 'make Harris hold the spring overhead again. From then on Harris could do nothing to please [Masaki] and he was beaten almost daily for the next 1½ or 2 months.'

A character witness for Masaki Fumio described him as a 'gentle' man who used to buy bananas and other gifts for POWs, and Masaki's defence counsel argued that the bashing of Private Barry either never happened or was done by someone else. The court did not believe them. Masaki was found guilty and sentenced to fifteen years' imprisonment.

In the Australian War Memorial's roll of honour, the cause of Private Sidney Roy Barry's death is given as 'murdered'.

The Australians had a theory about why the Korean guards were so vicious. Korea had been occupied by the Japanese for decades; even in Burma, the Japanese still lorded it over the Koreans. Private Wal Williams told author Peter Brune that the Korean guards were 'downtrodden bastards ... and the only retaliation [they] could get was to take it out on us, because we were the lowest of the low ... they were brutal bastards.'

War crimes trials like that of Masaki Fumio offered insights into the second-class status of Koreans in the Japanese military hierarchy. Cross-examined over allegations that Masaki had hit a prisoner with a leather belt, a Japanese sergeant was asked whether Koreans 'could have [a leather belt] the same way as Japanese NCOs or Japanese soldiers'. The sergeant told the court that 'as a rule Koreans were not allowed to wear leather belts'.

While working at 18 Kilo camp in Burma, an RAAF officer, Leonard Shore, was given permission by one of the Japanese railway engineers to fetch some water from a nearby river. Returning from the river, he was stopped by the Korean guard in charge of his section. When the guard, nicknamed 'Muckin', started to abuse Shore in Korean, Shore indicated that he would need a Japanese officer to translate for him. 'After several attempts he understood what I had been getting at and then proceeded to bash me,' wrote Shore. While this was going on, a Japanese standing nearby tried 'to persuade "Muckin" to let me go and stop wasting time'. Eventually 'Muckin' let Shore go and sent him back to his work gang, but by then a Japanese engineer had been told about the fuss. 'I happened to look back,' wrote Shore, 'and could see the Jap officer reprimand "Muckin", who must have done something to annoy the officer, who then proceeded to bash him.'

The prisoners soon got to know which guards were the most dangerous and they did their best to stay out of the way, but it did not always work. Williams recalled:

[T]hey'd go round looking for bloody trouble; they'd pick on some poor bastard for anything really. And they'd work themselves up into this bloody frenzy, they all seemed to do that ... a hell of a temper ... they'd do a bloke over, they start slapping him across the dial ... and then work themselves up and put the boot in ... they'd go for your bloody crutch and if you avoided it well that'd make them more determined than ever. They'd belt you till you couldn't take any more—you'd have to drop.

If the Korean guards could not find a prisoner to beat, they would beat an animal. Sergeant Jim Forbes told Brune about 'the sadism ... the joy and pleasure they got from kicking a dog around'. It was not just the Koreans, and they did not stop at kicking. Rivett observed the 'Japanese delight in torturing and tormenting animals ... this form of sadism was not confined to a few perverts but was general through all ranks of the army. Not even the bashings dealt out to ourselves infuriated us so much as the deliberate cruelties to helpless beasts.' Blackburn's diary describes a sentry at Bicycle Camp walking into the officers' compound and breaking up a game of cards. After speaking 'very rudely' to the officers and ordering them all to salute him, the sentry 'kicked up their cards, threw them away and then bayonetted a fox terrier puppy which had attached itself to us and was lying down alongside them'. Rivett saw 'trussed pigs tortured for an hour before execution, by having boiling water poured down their ears ... fowls packed helplessly in a crate had their eyes gouged out by gloating guards using pointed slivers of bamboo ... Any prisoner can add endlessly to the list.'

Jim Forbes said that over time prisoners developed a 'sixth sense' for danger; they could tell by the attitude of the guards that 'trouble was brewing, that something was going on ... that you were going to move, that there was going to be a search'.

There was no consistency to the scale of violence in the camps; it depended on the individual personalities of guards and camp commandants as well as on other factors, such as whether or not they had been drinking. 'I could never tell when a guard was drunk,' recalls Jack Thomas.

They could all put on an act. Some of them could be almost civil—not friendly, but civil. If they were bad-tempered or drunk or under some other influence they just made it their business to be difficult. But they would always stop short of doing some ultimate damage. They knew we were under their complete control and that we had no way of protecting ourselves. They could take advantage of that, and they did.

In January 1943 Colonel Williams saw a prisoner being beaten up by two guards. 'He already had had one lot ... The guard said he adopted a threatening attitude when hit on the job (same old tale) so they kept beating him until he kept his hands to his sides.'

The violence might have been arbitrary, but it was not mindless. Its purpose was to enforce total subjugation; sooner or later most prisoners understood that. In his memoir, Max McGee quoted an unnamed fellow POW:

One of the first lessons in survival that we learned was not to show any resentment, no resistance, and to hide all expressions of anger and disapproval. We learned to be docile in the face of extreme provocation. Where the normal response to a blow is to strike back, we learned not only to repress that reaction, but also to repress the emotion that would prompt such a response ... we found ourselves enduring pain, discomfort and physical punishment without displaying any emotion of any kind.

The American SEAC POW report found little difference between the conduct of Korean and Japanese guards, describing both as 'illiterate and low-grade personnel' whose 'sudden rise to a position of command, directing the lives and labors of large groups of men, developed a latent and infractious cruel streak in their characters.' The abuses they inflicted on prisoners of war replicated the abuses inflicted on them as soldiers of the Imperial Japanese Army.

Domination over men of races which had, in their eyes, traditionally asserted a superiority over them was a new and wonderful thing; it led to an unrelieved display of arrogance, cruelty and bestiality. They spoke no English, and made no apparent effort to learn it. Being largely treated as animals by their own superiors, they bettered their instructors, and showed an inspired skill in humiliating, degrading, and torturing those in their charge.

Not every humiliation involved physical violence. At certain times of the year bamboo clumps secreted a fine powder that was as irritating to the skin as itching powder. 'If a man upset the Japs for any reason,' Max McGee recalled in his memoir, 'they would make him stand underneath, while they stirred the clump with a long pole. If he moved then he would get a second lot.'

The SEAC report found that camp commanders did nothing to discourage abuses by the guards but rather gave their approval, 'either tacit or expressed, in almost all cases'.

Bashings from the guards were something that most prisoners could avoid most of the time, but the climate affected everyone all the time. During November the weather became cooler. The temperature at night plummeted, and few of the prisoners had blankets to keep out the cold. Every night scores of men would sacrifice sleep in order to stay warm in front of the open fires allowed in the huts. 'All of us went to bed wearing every scrap of clothing or wrapping on which we could lay our hands,' wrote Rohan Rivett. 'Even when wrapped in my entire wardrobe, consisting of two aged shirts, a pair of shorts, a pair of slacks, a sarong, plus woollen socks and a thin blanket, I found that I often awoke long before dawn and lay shivering, too miserable to be able to get to sleep again.'

Most did not have as much as Rivett. Colds and bronchial complaints, exacerbated by malnutrition, made men susceptible to more serious tropical diseases. Over the next three months, numerous prisoners had to be evacuated to the hospital at Thanbyuzayat suffering from pellagra, dysentery, beri-beri and infected sores. So far, few prisoners had fallen victim to tropical ulcers; that was a nightmare waiting to begin. Records from the office of the US Army's judge advocate general contain references to prisoners 'dying like flies of a virulent type of rat plague'.

While it was close to impossible to smuggle information out of the camps, underground wireless sets enabled the Australians to pick up news from outside. The sets had accompanied the Pioneers from Java and Singapore, their components hidden inside packs and waterbottles, concealed under belts or sewn inside items of clothing. (The machine gunners' history mentions an American prisoner named Buchanan at Bicycle Camp who 'had a radio set built into his tin leg'.) A death sentence awaited any prisoner caught in possession of a wireless set. Warrant Officer Arch Caswell kept his radio set operating for fourteen months under the noses of camp guards. Caswell's son-in-law, the parliament-arian Warren Truss, told how the set was '[c]onstructed from an array of pilfered parts and hidden in the leg of a stool . . . As the war drew to an end and the presence of the radio became too dangerous, it was buried beneath the kitchen at his final camp at Tamarkan—and who knows, it still may be there.'

Bulletins were distributed through the camps at regular intervals. As well as providing antidotes to Japanese propaganda, they enabled prisoners to follow the progress of the war in Europe and in the Pacific. Hidden radios—known as 'dicky-birds'—brought news of Montgomery's victory at El Alamein, the recapture of Tobruk, the Soviet counter-offensive at Stalingrad and the American victory on Guadalcanal. 'The effect of this news on us all was incalculable,' wrote Rivett.

> The good news from the world, which seemed incredibly remote to those toiling day long in the dust and heat on cuttings and embankments, came like a great light to pierce our darkness. It brought hope and comfort to weary men, exposed daily to the brutalities and incomprehensible whims of brutal guards; it helped to stiffen morale when we were overwhelmed with the hopelessness of our conditions and the calculated inhumanity of our captors.

One night in early December, a message for Lieutenant Wally Summons came through on a hidden wireless. The message was from his mother in Australia. In his memoir, Summons described how he could 'remember clearly the joy with which I received my first message from home'. Many prisoners, however, did not receive a message or a letter for the entire duration of their captivity.

On 12 February 1943 three Australians, a captain and two privates, tried to escape from Burma to India, a distance of more than 1200 kilometres. All three had experience of the jungle; the officer had served in Burma with the regular army and had a brother in Burma who was a planter; one of the privates was a surveyor, and the other had worked in Malaya as a mining engineer. The escape went wrong from the start, with the men getting lost in the mountains as they made for the Siamese border. Dickinson, the surveyor, had malaria and had to be left behind; he was caught by Burmese villagers and handed to the Japanese, who dragged him to a cemetery, forced him to sit and shot him in the back of the head. The other two were ambushed by Burmese police: Captain Mull was shot and killed (the war memorial's roll of honour records him as being executed), while Private Bell was taken away and handed to the

Japanese military police. Captain Thomas of the 2/4th Machine Gun Battalion wrote in his diary:

Last night [Bell] was visited by Padre Bashford, Brigadier Varley and [Surgeon] Allan Hobbs, who dressed his wound. He refused morphia for the wound saying that as it was in short supply, it should not be wasted on him. He died as a man should, declined a bandage for his eyes and asked that his hands be left untied. He received the volley standing to attention. We were advised officially of this by the Japanese Lieutenant, who added 'it was a pity one so brave should be so foolish'.

The deaths of Mull, Dickinson and Bell brought to eighteen the number of prisoners executed in Burma for trying to escape. By the last day of March, three Pioneers had died of sickness at Thanbyuzayat. Before long those ratios would be reversed.

Chapter 9

HUNDREDS OF WHORES
AND WICKED BASTARDS

————◆————

On 20 January 1943 Weary Dunlop led the 900 men of Dunlop Force out of Changi. Among them were the machine gunners from Blackforce. Many of the prisoners had no boots, but thanks to 'Black Jack' Galleghan, 150 men sported new socks. After three hours waiting at a railway station, they were packed into closed vans for the four-day journey to Siam. There were 28 prisoners to each van. They were given two meals a day and warned to be careful of the 'natives' in Siam, who, they were told, would try to rob them.

'The guards,' Tim Brettingham-Moore recalled, 'were fairly tolerant and we were able to buy produce from native merchants at most stops.' Conditions inside the van, however, were 'cramped, sticky and uncom-fortable'. The doors were shut from dusk until daylight, and the men found it impossible to sleep. 'They had 30-odd men to a carriage and they had a Korean at the door,' Bill Haskell recalled. 'It was stinking hot of the day time and freezing cold at night.'

After four days the train pulled into Bampong, around 70 kilometres west of Bangkok. This was the junction for the new railway being built from Burma. Colonel Williams and his Pioneers were at the other end. The survivors—the prisoners not killed by work or disease or shot trying to escape or beaten to death by guards—were destined to meet in the middle. Even in loincloths and handmade clogs, the soldiers of the 2/2nd Pioneers and the 2/3rd machine gunners remained inseparable.

On the second day the train reached Kuala Lumpur. The prisoners were allowed to leave the cars and stretch their legs on the platform. Des Jackson found a tap and was washing his face when a voice screamed '*Kura! Kura!*' Prisoners, he discovered, were forbidden to touch the taps. After a long rant from a 'bespectacled little guard', Jackson received the customary Japanese face-slapping—his first since becoming a prisoner. After a meal of rice and curried water, they resumed their slow journey up the Malay peninsula and across the border into Siam.

It was cold at Bampong. After getting out of the train, Jack Thomas was given a banana to eat. The Australians were ordered out of the cattle cars and into trucks. Further on, after a night in a camp beside a river, the jungle road was so steep that the prisoners had to get out and push. Some of the mountains were more than 1000 metres high, covered with dense, thorny bamboo. Dunlop's diary describes 'tough vines winding python-like about great stout trees rather like ironbarks'. Along the way they passed ramshackle camps holding British POWs, exhausted souls who resembled 'wild-eyed madmen'.

Three-quarters of a century later, Jack Thomas is still haunted by memories of the journey from Bampong.

There was a lot in that trip. You are in a new country. You're feeling very apprehensive. You're under the authority of people who do not have a friendly disposition towards you. You realise you've lost the war. That's not a good feeling. There is a tendency to feel overwhelmed. I felt overwhelmed from time to time.

At Tarsau they stopped for the night at a small camp fenced with bamboo. There was a river down below, but Thomas didn't see it; he didn't even know the river was there. Dunlop commented in his diary, 'Trench latrines (filthy) are in use.' Thomas's description is more visceral. 'It was our first look at the open latrines,' he says. 'They were pretty disgusting, a stinking reeking mass of maggots.'

The Australians were commanded to stay inside the camp and not to speak to the British who were already there. The order was impossible to enforce. Dunlop soon found himself talking to a 'tow-haired, fresh, beefy-faced, brainless type of Englishman with no particular thought for the tiredness and dirtiness of the troops'. He was able to talk the Englishman into giving his party water to drink, but not for washing.

The camp at Tarsau was not the worst Dunlop Force would see, but it was bad enough. Food was short and many of the inmates were suffering badly from dysentery and malaria. Around 300 men were reported to have died in the surrounding area during the previous three months. After dark the temperature fell rapidly, and at night the Japanese ordered big fires to be kept burning throughout the camp. The prisoners called them tiger fires.

That night Des Jackson 'lay wondering what was in store for us. My feelings of foreboding were acute.' Although weakened, like everyone else, by lack of food, Jackson was confident that youth and stamina would see him through. Had he known the horrors that lay ahead, 'perhaps my courage might have failed me there and then'.

In one respect, at least, Jackson was lucky: while in Java he had picked up a mosquito net, which he was determined to (and did) hold onto for the duration. Others, less fortunate or less far-sighted, had to sleep out in the open, prey to every passing mosquito. Few of them would escape the agonies of malaria and dengue fever.

Acting bombardier Tom Uren, a future parliamentarian, recalled having 'well over a hundred attacks of malaria. In fact, the last six months of the war, I had malaria like clockwork every 10 days. It was four days malaria, six days off, four days on, six days off. And generally when you get malaria you get the rigor [severe shivering], the strong rigor on the first day and then the next day you're weaker but then the third day you get the rigor again then the fourth day you seem to be all right.'

For Corporal Harry Walker, the attacks came every eighteen days.

The shivering would last for two or three hours no matter what was done to keep warm. A lot of people sat near or stood near fires with whatever they had—a rug or a blanket or a canvas. Their legs would get too hot from the fire and they would peel and get ulcers . . . Then after the shivers there would be hot sweats. That lasted for about two or three hours and then back to normal but no appetite. This would normally go on for about three to four days in a row and then it would seem to pass. There would be about a fortnight's break before it would all happen again.

Neil MacPherson's mate Bluey Rowe always knew when MacPherson's malaria had come back because he would start hallucinating. 'I kept accusing people of talking about me,' MacPherson recalls. 'That was the sign. They knew my mind was going.'

Men were ground down by recurring malaria, and by the drugs they took for it. '[W]e are never really free of it,' Ray Parkin, the sailor from the *Perth*, wrote. '[W]e are just hanging on with ringing heads full of quinine. My head rings all the time like the high-pitched humming of telegraph wires on a hot summer's day . . . Many say that their heads ring all day against cotton-wool walls inside. They don't want to think;

they don't want to listen: just go where they have to go, do what they have to do and, at last, get back to camp and fall onto their bamboo slats.'

On 25 January 1943 Dunlop's men were on the move again. The morning air was 'very keen and cool', Weary wrote, and the road 'terribly rough'. Again there were times when the prisoners had to get out of the lorries and push, but compared with groups that came later, Dunlop Force was lucky: in future prisoners would be forced to walk all the way from Bampong on foot.

Just before midday, after travelling a mere 25 kilometres, the trucks stopped and the prisoners were ordered out. The new campsite lay further down the mountain, hidden in the jungle. To reach it from the road, Dunlop's men had to scramble a mile down rough steps cut into the mountainside and then walk half a mile along a jungle track. The place was called Konyu.

For Private Jack Thomas, the arrival at Konyu was a moment of truth. Thomas has never forgotten the trepidation he felt as he reached the bottom of that 'bloody steep hill'.

I had no idea what tomorrow was going to bring. I had no idea we were going to build a railway, no idea that before the year was over there would be a railway line traversing that hill, no idea what the future would hold for us. We were going into the jungle, away from civilisation. There did not seem to be anyone around for a million miles . . . I was worried.

Ray Parkin recalled being harangued by a 'young, sleek, Japanese officer who looked us over like a schoolmaster receiving a new crowd'. This was the camp commandant, Lieutenant Osuki. According to Parkin, 'He was affable; he spoke of fine things like honour. He cut quite a good figure up there on the mound of earth.' Speaking through an interpreter, Osuki told the prisoners he was 'glad to see us and . . . gratified that we had come such a long way to help him. He respected our character. His orders must be obeyed ... He was sorry there was so little food, but he would try to improve it.'

Weary Dunlop was less impressed, describing him as a 'one-pip beardless little youngster ... Perhaps an alcoholic ... he mixes rather vulgarly with his men and drinks like a fish.' As well as forcing sick men to work on the railway, Osuki would demand 'commissions' from Thai bargemen, pushing up the prices they charged to prisoners. Dunlop later accused him of forcing prisoners to buy 5794 packets of cigarettes for him to use in a 'private trading venture'.

Not only was there no food at Konyu; there was no camp either. Dunlop's men were told they would have to build one. They were allocated a small area beside the river bank, a few hundred metres beyond the British camp. 'We spent the first day just sitting around,' Jack Thomas recalls. 'It was January and the teak trees were losing their leaves. They were big leaves and they rocked from side to side as they fell. A fellow lying beside me with his hands behind his head looked up at the falling leaves and called out, "Tobacco issue now on!" It was a still day and we sat there watching those big teak leaves floating down. I don't know if anyone tried smoking them.'

The Thai jungle was all bamboo and teak and creepers. Jack Thomas and his mates were soon put to work pulling out the bamboo. Before long smouldering mounds of cut bamboo surrounded the site where the camp was to be established.

Bamboo grows in great thickets. These were old man bamboos, they had not been harvested for many years. They were thick and hard and very thorny. We didn't have any machinery. We had to attack one bamboo stem, attach a rope to it and pull it clear, then trim it and strip the brambles. Underneath the bark you strip off fibrous material and use it to bind one piece of bamboo to another. When we had laid out sufficient bamboo we built huts of it. Boats coming up the river brought attap for the roof.

After just five days at Konyu, Ray Parkin was already suffering from the sore throat and tongue that were the first symptoms of vitamin deficiency. Those suffering from the condition received one egg a day from the regimental fund and had to buy another for seven cents. Bad cases were given two eggs. The eggs were gathered from the paddy fields, where ducks foraged for insects. Some had lain there for a long time before being found. Parkin remembered eating eggs that, as well as being sun-cooked, were 'quite black in patches' or even 'wholly rotten'. Sometimes a man broke open an egg that was so rotten 'we all have to clear out until he has buried it. But we know that eggs might save our lives and that is why we face the blackness.'

According to Des Jackson, privates were now being paid wages of 20 cents a day and NCOs 25 cents. A proportion of the money earned by both officers and men went into a fund to buy food and medicines. 'Money was administered by the work battalion,' Jack Thomas recalls. 'We became a kind of socialist society.' Food could be bought from the Thai boats that came up the river bringing building materials for the huts and the railway. Eggs were vital. Cooking oil was always welcome. Thomas never saw any of the money he earnt as a prisoner but 'now and again' was given a duck egg. Sometimes the rations included something more nourishing than rice. Thomas remembers eating 'little dried beans, like split peas'. Occasionally there was a watery stew with scraps of meat. Mostly it was just slivers of white radish. But food alone was not enough to keep up morale. According to Ray Parkin, a shortage of tobacco at Konyu caused 'bad temper and . . . bickering'. Jack Thomas was not a smoker, but he remembers men queuing up to buy local tobacco from the Thai boats: it was coarse, gingery stuff, and the men called it 'hag's bush'.

Work on the huts ground to a halt after a fortnight when Dunlop's men ran out of ties to bind the bamboo. By then, stark differences were emerging between the mental and physical state of the Australian prisoners and that of the British and Dutch in neighbouring camps. On 4 February Dunlop reported that 'only about 12–15' men were in the Australian hospital each day, mostly thanks to the effectiveness of sulfa drugs against dysentery. On the same day Dunlop noticed '[s]omething ... terribly wrong with the British camp; all the barracks have a terribly sick smell and it is appalling to see the mess of the dirty, gaunt bodies and unmade beds all hours of the day.'

Signs of indiscipline among the Australians were quickly dealt with; NCOs were instructed to 'squash insubordination on the spot'. But while insubordination could be squashed, it could not be stopped.

Jack Thomas remembers having 'the highest respect for our officers' and believed 'most' Australian soldiers felt the same way. 'The troops will always be agin the officers—it's become a sort of mantra, but it's not necessarily true.' Compared with the British, the Australians 'had a more laid back attitude to the officers. Behind their backs we'd tell them to get stuffed but upfront they were pretty decent people.' According to Thomas, 'Most of our junior officers never left Java. The Japs were not interested in having junior officers on the work forces—they knew the troops would respect senior officers more than they would lieutenants. We were commanded mostly by captains and majors.' The machine gunners' history lists five captains and thirteen lieutenants who 'remained in Java for the whole term of their imprisonment'.

According to Neil MacPherson, the Japanese left most of the officers behind because they feared that any mutiny among POWs on the death railway would be led by officers. After the campaign against the Vichy French, a number of officers were seconded to the Pioneer Training Battalion and missed the debacle in Java. Several of the junior officers in Williams Force had been sergeants in Syria. As former sergeants, they already had a strong bond with their men. MacPherson remembers having a deep respect for them.

British officers repeatedly came in for harsh criticism, both from Australian officers and from other ranks. But as conditions in the camps worsened and the work schedule became more punishing, tensions broke out between Australian soldiers and their own officers. Not only were officers able to avoid heavy work; some were taking extra food at the expense of the men.

Sunday, at least for now, was a rest day. One Sunday, Dunlop's men were furious to be given only a very small serve of plain rice for breakfast; Ray Parkin watched 'a *full* bucket of rice and a bucket of tea going over to the W.O.s [warrant officers]—ten, plus two batmen. This was thirty men's rations. We have also seen a bucket of soup going over—fifty rations. All this in the face of visible malnutrition.' Eggs were rationed to one each per day for the men, but in the officers' canteen fifteen officers were caught treating themselves to 250 eggs.

A sailor among soldiers, Parkin saw and reported the growing animosity between officers and other ranks. '[T]he officers have got out of touch with the men,' he wrote, 'and can only wave the manual of Military Law at them in an endeavour to intimidate. This only produces a violent reaction in the men, who become even more bloody-minded on seeing the officers vaunting privilege and neglecting responsibility.'

Exempt from such criticisms were the doctors, led by Weary himself, both a doctor and their commanding officer. 'The men would do anything for him,' Parkin wrote. 'I am sure it is his presence which holds this body of men from moral decay in bitter circumstances which they can only meet with emotion rather than reason.'

In addition to the courage and authority Dunlop showed as their commanding officer, his skills as a doctor and surgeon sometimes seemed little short of miraculous. With nothing more than the surgical instruments he had carried on his back since leaving Java, working on a makeshift bamboo operating table, Dunlop tended to Private Bert Jones, who was suffering from a perforated peptic ulcer. 'Under the stars at two in the morning with two hurricane lamps and a torch for light, Weary worked until dawn and saved Bert's life,' the machine gunners' historian wrote. 'Among the group watching was a Japanese officer. He fainted.'

But as the workload grew and conditions in the camp deteriorated, not even Weary could keep his men's spirits up. As morale sank, the number of sick began to climb. By the first week of March there were 59 Australians in the hospital at Konyu, almost all suffering from malaria. The condition of the Dutch prisoners was far worse: the Dutch hospital had more than 200 patients, most suffering from dysentery. The Dutch leader, Smits, told Weary, 'We have too many old men; we cannot work like the Australians—we cannot dig the deep latrines—it is too hard for us.'

But just because a soldier was not in hospital did not mean he was well. Only a fraction of the promised meat and vegetable rations ever arrived. The Japanese had already proposed a solution to the food shortage: put the sick men on half rations, thereby hastening their deaths and increasing the amount available for the healthy.

By the beginning of March Dunlop considered only 350 out of a total of 873 men capable of heavy work outside the camp.

Dunlop Force spent six weeks building the camp at Konyu. What would happen next nobody knew. There was talk of the Australians being sent back to Bampong. Ray Parkin heard a rumour that they were to be replaced by Japanese soldiers. When the job of building the camp was finished, Weary gave a speech. Jack Thomas was standing close to him when he spoke.

Weary told us a story about a wise man from the east with an engineering project. The people in charge made it clear there were to be hundreds of hoes and wicker baskets for the engineering project but when the message came down the line it was delivered as 'hundreds of whores and wicked bastards'. Nobody else remembers Weary's story but I remember it very well.

Thomas and his mates had come to build a railway, but they would leave Konyu without seeing it. Thomas would have found it hard to believe that within a few months a railway track would be cut into the side of the steep hill he had struggled to climb down on foot. Dunlop himself described the route as 'astonishing ... It seems to run without much regard to the landscape as though someone had drawn a line on the map!'

Les Cody, who arrived at Konyu a month later with the machine gunners from the 2/4th battalion, described the Konyu section of track as one of the 'major engineering achievements that made up the Burma/ Thailand Railway ... the line snaked its way through innumerable cuttings, literally gouged and blasted out of the rock—along the tops of impossible embankments and over crazy bridges, leaving behind a mass of human wreckage in the lonely graves in the jungles and in the "hospitals" throughout Burma and Thailand.'

Excavation of the Konyu Cutting—soon nicknamed Hellfire Pass— began in April. Within two months, progress would be badly behind and hundreds more Australian and British POWs would have to be brought in. But the Japanese had other plans for Dunlop Force.

On 13 March 1943 the Konyu camp was deluged. '[M]uggy and terribly hot,' Dunlop wrote in his diary, 'then severe thunderstorm which turned the whole area into a lake.' Weary and his officers were still sleeping under canvas in the open. At 2 a.m. their beds were inundated: '[O]ur backs were in the water. All the officers had a most bloody night recalling the Somme.' Four days later, Dunlop Force walked out of Konyu. Ninety men suffering from malaria or dysentery were too sick to accompany them and had to be left behind.

The monsoon season was approaching. Working conditions on the railway would get worse. The prisoners' health would get worse. Everything would get worse. But Des Jackson still had his mosquito net and Jack Thomas still had his boots as they trudged the five kilometres up the road to the so-called 'mountain camp' at Hintok.

Unlike at Konyu, where there was no camp before Dunlop's men arrived, some framework and a few tents already existed at Hintok. But amenities had to be built from scratch: huts were constructed and the camp was fenced off with a bamboo palisade. The cooks had to make do, as usual, without proper receptacles. Jack Thomas remembers sailors from HMAS *Perth* weaving baskets out of grass for storing and carrying rice. Bamboo could be put to a variety of uses. 'It was a creative time,' Thomas recalls. 'One of our officers, Major Woods, did an excellent job of rigging up a shower. Water was brought down the hill using lines of bamboo pipe. Bamboo matting was laid over the mud. It was more a dribble than a shower but it was better than nothing.' A bar of soap was a rarity; Thomas did not have soap for two years. 'Some people had handmade stuff, little cubes about an inch and a half square. It was pink and blue with cinders in it. You could buy it from the Siamese traders. But a lot of us didn't have access to traders.'

Australian resourcefulness was not lost on other Allied prisoners. In his book *Railroad of Death*, the British officer John Coast noted that 'Several things were unusual about Hintok. The latrines were made of wood, were clean and sixteen feet deep; they had made a complete water system out of hollow bamboo pipes and had rigged up showers in a bath place entirely carpentered from bamboo; and they had a silver bugle blown by a first-rate bugler, who made the calls sound more beautiful with the mountain echoes than I'd ever believed a bugle could sound.'

But the Australians were there to build a railway, not a camp. Weary estimated that only 400 of the men he took to Hintok were fit to work. On 19 March Lieutenant Hiroda, the Japanese engineer in charge of the section, demanded 600. In order to provide them, Dunlop had to put a stop to latrine-digging, antimalarial and 'improve water' schemes inside the camp. '[W]orst of all,' Dunlop wrote, 'light duty and no duty men and all men without boots to go [to work] just the same. This is the next thing to murder ... a cold-blooded, merciless crime against mankind, obviously premeditated.'

From now on, Hiroda declared that everything was to be done 'speedo'. The amount of soil that had to be dumped on the embankment went from 1 cubic metre per man per day to 1.5 or 2. A temporary agreement with the senior Japanese engineer for the prisoners not to work beyond 5 p.m. was torn up; the new working day lasted from dawn to dusk. Rest days were abolished. Arbitrary beatings by the guards increased. One day, a sergeant known as 'Molly and Mad Monk' laid into Des Jackson with a crowbar. 'He struck me without warning about twelves times on the legs, buttocks and back ... I do not know why I was hit; perhaps he mistook me for someone else or perhaps he just wanted to demonstrate his power.'

Insatiable demands for labour far outweighed the number of prisoners fit to work. Men supposed to be on 'light duties ' could either join their mates on the railway or go to hospital and lose their pay. Corporal Okada, who was known as 'Doctor Death', was in charge of one work detail. Each day he would demand a certain number of men to work on the railway. 'Okada was never amenable to reason,' Tim Brettingham-Moore recalled. 'He demanded always more men. We told him we could not do this without sending sick men out of the hospital. Okada repeated his number and said, "If not, you die," at the same time producing a dagger and driving it into the table in front of us.'

But the workforce did not consist only of prisoners of war. As well as roughly 70,000 POWs, the Japanese pressed around 180,000 'natives' into labouring on the railway. These 'native' workers, largely Burmese and Tamils, had been softened up with propaganda about the Japanese-sponsored Greater East Asia Co-Prosperity Sphere—a concept motivated, according to a 1945 report by the US Office of Strategic Services, by a combination of 'high idealism and frank opportunism'.

While promising to free colonised populations from 'the yoke of British–American domination', the Japanese had a more selfish imperative: to secure the 'maximum cooperation from the conquered peoples of Greater East Asia'. Railway volunteers were tricked into signing up with guarantees of generous pay and good working conditions. 'When these unfortunates reached the jungles of Burma and Thailand,' Des Jackson wrote, 'they found that all the Japanese had organised for them was work. There were no camps, no administration officers, no arrangements for the provision of supplies and no hospitals or medical facilities. Confronted with a situation of utter hopelessness and despair they died in tens of thousands and as a result . . . contributed virtually nothing to the construction of the railway.'

The OSS report found that

> Japanese officials sent to administer the GEA regions displayed a tendency to disregard the sensibilities of native peoples. Repeated warnings were sent out to these officials 'not to show superiority even when they know they are superior'. Japanese soldiers were even worse in this respect and won a particularly bad reputation in Burma, where they desecrated religious shrines and mistreated Burmese ecclesiastics.

Australian POWs were horrified by the living conditions of the 'Tamil and Burmese coolies' and by the way the Japanese treated them. Rohan Rivett described a sick Indian labourer

> left dying on the side of the road without food or water. Passing natives never turned aside to lend him succour of any kind, and when we asked the Japanese if something could not be done for him, they

forbade us to go near him and said he would soon be dead. Nevertheless, some of the boys kept him supplied with water and rice from their own scanty rations until, after four days of exposure, he died. Even then the Japanese would do nothing about the festering corpse, which was immediately attacked by swarms of maggots and other insects. Finally a party of prisoners was allowed to bury the body.

Weary did his best—often with Japanese rifles pointed at him—to frustrate the engineers' demands for sick prisoners to work, but it was rarely enough. The Japanese high command was desperate to have the railway finished before the monsoon rains came. Men were marched to work without water or food, often without boots, and given only two ten-minute breaks in a day. Poor quality tools, especially 'shoddy' drills, made the work more hazardous. Dunlop complained of 'five or six injuries daily from flying fragments of drills'. Constant blasting with explosives caused more injuries. 'They never, ever gave you fair warning that they were going to set off a charge,' Bill Haskell recalled. 'There would be fractured arms and fractured legs.'

Adye Rockliff was climbing a cliff to cut timber for a bridge when a rock fell and 'wiped me off my perch'. A glass bottle of water in his haversack broke and a shard stabbed him in the shoulder. Rockliff suffered multiple fractures and abrasions and had six stitches, splints to his arm and foot, and a shot of morphine. While he slept, 'a rat found a patch of blood on the back of my shorts and chewed a hole in them'.

With every available man working on the railway, *benjo* (latrine) digging and 'wood and water carrying' were now being done almost entirely by officers, who had effectively become simple labourers.

Morale and discipline among some prisoner groups had virtually collapsed. Dunlop was aghast when his Australians were moved to a hut previously occupied by Dutch prisoners who had 'even dug holes in the floor for defecation'.

Towards the end of March the Siamese section of the railway had reached the 40-kilometre mark, at a cost of nearly 150 British and Dutch lives. Yet the Australians were holding up. 'The Australian resilience is startling,' Dunlop wrote in his diary, 'the men are extremely cheerful and emphatic that the Ns [Nippons] will never get them down and they will all be square one day. Their morale under terribly trying conditions is excellent.'

Opportunities for escape were frequent but illusory. Harry Walker recalled, 'I could have escaped virtually every day I was in Burma.' Camps and work sites were designated with 'imaginary lines' that were easy to cross. The Japanese regarded being outside those lines as an attempt to escape, and POWs could be—and were—executed simply for trying to buy food outside the camp. The real barrier was the Irrawaddy River, which escaping prisoners would have to cross to reach India.

The remote possibility of a successful escape still drove prisoners to make the attempt. Near the end of March, four British POWs tried to escape in a lorry, but when the petrol ran out their Siamese guides gave them up to the Japanese. Dunlop saw the four men 'roped together' on their way to being shot. Three days later he reported two more 'Tommies' going 'back to Rin Tin for execution' and another pair who absconded from Kanchanaburi only to make the deadly mistake of walking straight into Tarsau.

The dry season was nearly over. Rain was falling day and night. Dunlop had injured himself while chopping down a tree; his legs were now 'covered with scabbed, septic sores and a large, raw, septic mess on one thigh'. As the monsoon descended, Weary asked for more tents to keep his men dry, but the Japanese responded by taking away some of the tents they already had. 'Many men get dreadfully wet at night,' he wrote in his diary. 'Things can't go on like this.'

Chapter 10

SPEEDO!

The Pioneers at the Burma end of the railway were being driven as hard as the machine gunners in Siam. As the work fell further behind, coolie labourers were enlisted in ever larger numbers. A riot nearly erupted in one camp after the Australians were kept working long after dark. Harry Walker recalled: '[W]e hadn't had our evening meal. The Japs lit fires for us so we could finish a job on the bridge. It was just about midnight when we were told we could finish. Some of the fellows ... in disgust threw their shovels and picks into the fire.'

At the end of a day's work, prisoners had to return their tools to a designated spot in the camp, where they were checked off by the guards. 'When the shortage was noticed, the officers were called out in the middle of the night,' Walker recalled. 'It looked like there would be repercussions ... but nothing came of it and I don't know why. I felt that the guards realised that they might have been in a difficult position and the matter wasn't taken any further.'

Sabotage was one of the few ways in which prisoners could rebel. Anyone caught in the act faced savage punishment or even death, but the Australians proved to be enterprising saboteurs. The machine gunners' history records that 'If a nest of white ants or wood lice was found in the bush it was re-established alongside the wooden pylons'. Lance Corporal Rockliff was working with a Japanese surveyor at Kinsayok, a Siamese camp, using a measuring device that consisted of thin strips of overlapping bamboo tied with bits of rag. Rockliff and his mates 'found that by loosening the bits of rag we could extend this device and later on by the same method reduce it … this bit of sabotage made the job more interesting'.

Mockery was another form of rebellion. Private Wally Holding remembered Major Bruce Hunt taking the mickey out of a Japanese called Toyama who was in charge of the Korean guards at Nieke camp: 'Major Hunt was giving us a talk. He said, "This little Japanese gentleman alongside me was born out of wedlock" and he carried on. Of course Toyama heard … "Japanese gentleman" and he was bowing and the boys all had great grins on their faces … Toyama was an awful little bastard.'

The Australians' scrounging habits were 'a continual source of annoyance to the Japanese', Wally Summons wrote. 'The prisoners would take anything from Jap stores, either to supplement their own rations or sell for money to buy food essential for life.' Summons remembered a Japanese officer giving the Pioneers a lecture on 'the evils of stealing, and punishments awaiting any offenders caught … During his talk, somebody stole the petrol from his tank and later sold it.' The Japanese lost everything from boots to trucks, Summons recalled, and 'very seldom was anybody caught'.

On rare occasions, prisoners hit back against their tormentors. In his memoir Des Jackson recounts a story he got from a close mate,

Private Ken Linford, about an incident at Lower Kinsayok, in Thailand. Linford and two friends had gone down to the river to wash, an activity that the Japanese had forbidden because of the risk of cholera. The three were spotted by one of the engineers, who started 'bashing the hell out of us', Linford told Jackson.

> He worked himself up into a proper rage and we stood stiff to attention, taking our medicine ... He knew how to hit and it went on and on. He ranted and screamed and we were getting hurt so badly that it seemed he was going to kill us. I suddenly thought I had to do something to save my life, and I lashed out at him. I hit his chin and he fell over backwards. Immediately all three of us knew we were in real trouble. Without a word we attacked him, knocked him unconscious and threw him into the river.

The river was in flood, and the three Australians hoped the engineer's body would be carried far away by the current. Washing the blood off their faces, they made it back to camp in time for roll call. They told no one what had happened. Several days went by and nothing was said about the missing engineer. Just as they were starting to believe they had got away with it, the engineer's body was found not far from the camp. There was 'one hell of a row' and the Japanese asked lots of questions, but the three kept their mouths shut and in the end the Japanese were forced to conclude that the prisoners had had nothing to do with the murder. 'I don't think I'll ever be so frightened again as I was in those few days,' Linford told his mate. 'As far as the Jap was concerned, I don't feel any pity. He was a particularly nasty little brute and what he was doing to us when I hit him was terrible.'

Opportunities for prisoners to take revenge against the guards were scarce, potentially suicidal—but not impossible. The Bull was a big Korean guard more than six feet tall who worked at 105 Kilo camp. His fellow guards included Boofhead, The Snake, Pinhead, and 'the happy twins the BB and the BBC (the Boy Bastard and the Boy Bastard's Cobber)'. According to Les Cody, 'they were all bastards ... they were particularly severe on the men suffering with tropical ulcers, kicking, hitting and even twisting bamboo sticks in open wounds. All were capable of inflicting deadly beatings.' Harry Walker remembered a guard called the Bull 'bashing everybody for no reason at all'.

The 2/4th machine gunners' history records one such beating, after Sapper Iles was caught by the Bull scrounging for scraps in the Japanese kitchen. 'During that night he was beaten at regular intervals by both the Bull and Boofhead and for those in the same hut, divided only by an attap wall, it was a dreadful experience. All night long the sickening sound, the soggy slap of flesh meeting flesh, the ever diminishing moans of the victim until finally silence.' After being left hanging from a post through the following day and night, Sapper Iles was taken to hospital, where he died. The roll of honour at the Australian War Memorial records the death of Sapper Iles at 105 Kilo camp in Burma due to 'injuries'.

One day Corporal Walker and some of his mates decided the Bull's beatings had gone on long enough. It was Walker's job to collect food for the guards and place it in a designated spot near their hut. Together they hatched a plan to collect some mucus from the latrines from a prisoner 'who was bad with dysentery or might have had a touch of cholera'. Like the prisoners, the camp guards each had a dixie—a mess tin—with their name on it. Walker and his mates found out which dixie belonged to the Bull and smeared some of the mucus on his rice. Within a few days, the Bull went missing from the camp. 'He was away for about two or three months,' Walker recalled in his memoir. 'When he came back he had lost about four or five stone and he was much easier to get on with. He stopped a little bit of his bullying.'

After the war the Bull—identified on his charge sheet as 'Korean Guard Kaneshiro Masa'—was prosecuted at the war crimes trials in Singapore.

Accused of 'kicking and torturing' Sapper Iles, Kaneshiro denied the charge but admitted that in August 1943 he had 'slapped a PW across the face for being lazy at his work'. Although identified from photographs, he also denied that he was the Bull. The court did not believe him, and on 2 April 1947 the Bull was sentenced to life in prison.

In the early months of 1943, few gave much thought to the possibility of the Bull or any of his fellow guards being brought to justice for their crimes. March 9 marked a year since the surrender in Java. Colonel John Williams noted the anniversary in his diary. 'Twelve months as prisoners of war today and what a 12 months. I hope we haven't another twelve months to go as we will either all be cuckoo or dead.'

Many prisoners had given up hope of emerging from the jungle alive. 'Our only wish was that somebody would survive to let our families know what had happened to us,' Harry Walker recalled.

The hospital at Thanbyuzayat was now overflowing with men stricken by malaria and dysentery. Older POWs, especially the 40- to 50-year-olds from the motor transport units, were finding it difficult to go on. Hardly a day passed without the sombre notes of the bugle floating through the camp. Under pressure from the Japanese, men who were barely convalescent, let alone fit, were sent back to the jungle to work. Many did not survive. The hospital itself, wrote Rohan Rivett, whose legs were a mass of suppurating sores, was 'a torture chamber . . . thanks to the hordes of bugs that swarm out of every crack in its boards to devour the unknown delicacy of white flesh.'

In late March the sick from Williams Force were evacuated from 35 Kilo camp to a newly built hospital at 30 Kilo, while the rest marched nearly ten kilometres to 26 Kilo camp at Kun Knit Kway. Williams Force and another working party led by Lieutenant Colonel Anderson of the 2/19th Infantry Battalion were now combined as No. 1 Mobile Force. For the next few months it would rain almost nonstop, and No. 1 Mobile Force would be constantly on the move laying rails.

Kun Knit Kway was one of the more notorious camps on the Burmese side. Five months earlier, Rivett had found it in 'a state of filth that defied description'. Burmese and Tamil workers had left the huts strewn with '[e]xcreta and other dirt of every kind'. Cholera had broken out and the Australians discovered two unburied corpses lying in the bushes just a few metres from one of the huts. While they were burying them, another was found further up the hill. Since then, Kun Knit Kway had been occupied by British and American prisoners, but they had done little to improve the camp. '[A]rrived at 26 Kilo camp at dawn—one of the worst camps I've ever seen,' Colonel Williams wrote in his diary. 'No latrine accommodation and no tools to dig any. Water inadequate, huts in a bad state of repair and camp generally dirty and overrun with flies . . . everything was bug-ridden, rats ran everywhere and fleas carried one away . . . a rotten camp.'

The battalion history records that the men in No. 1 Mobile Force were subject to 'very harsh treatment' during their brief stay at Kun Knit Kway. 'Long working hours became the rule rather than the exception; rations, never good, deteriorated further, and medical supplies to treat the increasing numbers of sick practically ceased.' The entry for 18 April in Williams's diary notes '20 men called out to work tonight, returned at 2.30 a.m. . . . men who worked all night still had to work today, the majority of workers returned at 2230 hrs tonight, and they want to know why the men cannot stand up to the work. They can at least only work us 24 hours a day and they now work us seven days each week.'

Williams Force worked at Kun Knit Kway for less than a month before it was shunted by rail to take over from the Dutch prisoners at 45 Kilo camp. 'The force moved to 45 Kilo camp by rail,' the medical officer, Lieutenant Colonel Eadie, noted in his diary. 'Lieutenant Naito [the Japanese commandant] was very drunk and gave a great exhibition as a comedian on this move.'

Barely a quarter of the men had blankets. Some of those without blankets were issued with rice sacks, but these were later taken away when they were needed for rice. The huts were so infested with lice that some men preferred to sleep out in the cold, risking a bashing by the guards if they were caught. Two weeks later they were shifted again, this time to 60 Kilo camp at Taunzun.

Sickness was no longer a justification for not working. The commander of No. 5 Group told prisoners in the camp hospital: 'Any sick man who staggers to the line to lay one sleeper will not have died in vain.' Lieutenant Hochi issued a blunt warning to the sick at 75 Kilo camp: 'No work, no food.'

There was little enough food for the working prisoners, and much of it was rotten. (Rations for coolies could be even worse.) 'We had been brought up to revolt against anything that was sour and anything that was putrid,' Harry Walker recalled. 'It was natural to want to vomit if anything nasty was swallowed ... we had to train ourselves to do the absolute opposite. It didn't matter how stinky it might have been or how rotten it was, the possibility that there might be some vitamins forced us to eat ... Musty rice was pretty common. We ate the weevils or grubs in the rice for the nutritional value.'

Vegetables were scarce. The difficulty of driving cattle up to the railway meant that meat sometimes had to come slaughtered. By the time it reached the prisoners 'it would have gone rotten and become a sort of a jelly. Often the medical officers said it was too dangerous to use.' Anthrax was not uncommon in Burmese cattle. 'It could be passed on to humans but sometimes we had to take the risk,' Walker wrote.

The monsoon had set in. The bright, sunlit jungle became, in Les Cody's words, 'a dark, waterlogged, rank-smelling muddy hell'. As the jungle floor became a bog, Japanese engineers redoubled their demands, working the prisoners twenty-four hours a day—in camp, to and from, or dodging the screaming Japs on the job—with the eternal rain and mud constant companions. And the struggle intensified, on the embankments, in the cuttings and on the bridges as the engineers, driven by an ever-shrinking 'finish time' goaded the men day and night. In the cuttings the drill holes became one metre, two metres, and finally three metres for each two-man team. Turn about on the drill and hammer, aching arms and shoulders swinging the heavy hammer grimly concentrating on the target, aching hands lifting and twisting the drill after each jarring blow. Dreading the mistake, the slip of bare feet in the mud or the tired swing at the end of a fourteen-hour day or the lack of vision in the half light of a bamboo flare that brings the agony of a smashed hand or fingers as the head skids off the top of the drill. And always the Jap, guard or engineer, with only one message: 'Speedo'.

The hats and shorts and shirts possessed by the lucky few were now scarcely more than rags. Thousands of men had to go barefoot, with the perpetual risk of cuts and splinters that could turn into dreaded tropical ulcers. Between violent monsoonal downpours, the tropical sun beat down and men sweltered in the steaming jungle. Before long, 90 per cent had discarded what remained of their clothes in favour of something more basic. '[T]he men's clothing is shocking,' Weary wrote, 'some having sewn the most odd garments about their loins. Many have just a bit of tape around the waist and simply tuck some cloth around the crutch region. This we call a "Jap Happy". One or two have natty garments made out of sacking.'

Trying to stay clean was a constant battle. 'We would get terribly dirty from greasy rails and from working hip deep in slime in the jungle,' an American prisoner recalled.

In one year on Sumatra the only soap I had I stole from the Japs, this amounted to about three bars ... the only way we could get clean was to scour our bodies with sand from the streams we would bathe in. We didn't even have a rag to scrub ourselves with the sand ... Most of us had nothing to wear but a *jawat* (loin cloth). Any cloth material was hoarded for sores and cuts ... a slight scratch invariably turns into a tropical ulcer of the most horrible type.

For the exhausted, half-starved, fever-ridden prisoners, trudging four or five or six kilometres with heavy tools to the railway, there was now a new command: 'No finish, no sleep.'

Amid their own misery, some Australian POWs found a skerrick of sympathy for the columns of Japanese foot soldiers forced to march along the boot-sucking quagmire that had been a road running alongside the projected railway. Weighed down with full packs, the wretched troops had to drag artillery and wooden carts laden with food and ammunition through knee-deep mud that no truck could penetrate. 'Our own men toiling on the railway watched with grim satisfaction that was tinged with pity the ordeal of this Nippon cannon fodder struggling to the front,' Rivett wrote. 'They saw privates, who sank to the ground exhausted, kicked in the face and stomach by officers and NCOs. These front-line troops were plucky and tough, but they were doomed. We felt a certain admiration for their gameness.'

Cholera was now moving up and down the line, spread—according to the official Australian medical history of the war—by 'Asiatic coolies'. Arriving at 60 Kilo camp, Williams Force found the site strewn with the shallow graves of native workers who had died of cholera, while other bodies lay rotting in the sun.

Nothing spread fear through the camps like the approach of cholera. The disease killed indiscriminately, wiping out coolies and white POWs alike. Without the selfless care of medical officers and orderlies, those afflicted with cholera had little chance of surviving.

In his unpublished memoir, Wally Holding recalled how the disease struck his mate Jack Carroll:

[H]e was this big, tall bloke and twice my weight, but we worked together for quite a time at the hammer and tap. One night we came in after dark and we were getting our rice and someone said, 'You had better go and see your mate. He is pretty crook.' Well I walked down to where I knew Jack was camped further down the hut and I could not recognise him. In about two hours since we had knocked off work he had lost probably half his body weight. He had cholera. He never saw that night out.

Cholera became the focus of camp activity; in July 1943 Dunlop reported being 'completely extended' supervising the 'flat-out night and day production of the still [for manufacturing distilled water]' while also organising 'wood and water supply, the digging of graves, and the collection of wood for funeral pyres'.

The men who were too sick to work on the railway were given the job of burning the bodies. 'They would have two poles,' Wally Holding recalled, 'drop a body across the poles and then run in towards the fire and throw the body in, then get back as quick as you could because of the heat of the fire . . . you would throw a body on the fire and all of a sudden you would see his arm come up or a head shift or some other movement. The heat of the fire pulled sinews in the body and caused the movement but it was a shocking thing.'

As far as many Japanese commanders were concerned, the sick were dead already and deserved neither food nor proper shelter. While the Japanese were terrified of cholera and had mobile laboratories capable of diagnosing it, they sometimes refused to acknowledge the presence of cholera in an area despite the evidence of the sick and dying.

'Isolation quarters for cholera . . . were sited in marshy jungle, and only half protected from the rain, which poured through leaky huts and tents on sodden improvised beds,' Allan Walker wrote in the official Australian medical history of the war.

Weary's cholera hospital was located in a 'dreadful quagmire' of pestilential mud and slime that became known as 'cholera gulch'. The cholera area at night, he wrote,

> deserves a circle in Dante's inferno. Extremely low, inferior N tents, all leaking. Patients lie on rough bamboo bedding a few inches off the muddy floor and one works bent almost double. The only light at night is the fitful flicker of crude oil lamps improvised by wicks of fibrous materials suspended in condensed milk tins of oil. Patients vomit in gushing fashion into bamboo containers and indeed often all over the place.

The orderlies manufactured bed pans out of cut-down tins set inside wooden boxes, but these were wholly inadequate to contain the tidal waves of shit that burst from men stricken with cholera. In their primitive bamboo cots, delirious soldiers whittled to a fraction of their former body weight writhed in an agony of cramps and abdominal pains, filling the air with 'groans, cries for relief and curses in weak, husky voices'.

The ravages of cholera changed a man's appearance so drastically that patients had to be marked with an indelible pencil to avoid misidentification. In his POW diary (a book 30 x 20 x 2 centimetres that he managed to hide from the Japanese for three and a half years), Major Bert Saggers described a cholera victim 'completely nude carried back to the bamboo slats that served as a bed, his head hanging down and lips drawn back from his teeth like a snarling dog. His eyes were glassy and stared horribly. Every ounce of flesh had dehydrated from his body.'

The only hope for the worst cases was an intravenous saline drip, and Dunlop and his fellow doctors devised ingenious ways of both producing saline solution and administering it. In a chapter devoted to cholera, Allan Walker's medical history of the war states that distilled water was made 'from improvised stills, stolen petrol pipes being used for the coils and these being cooled with bamboo jackets and circulating water'. Weary's diary records that due to the shortage of rubber tubing his own stethoscope 'has gone into the crude administrative apparatus ... Beer bottles sawn off at the top, bamboo joints to rubber tubing and finally a sawn off needle as a cannula. Of necessity, everything is terribly crude.'

Private Bill Haskell described the process in his audio memoir:

They boiled the water and the water created steam and the steam ran up the copper tubing and ran into this bamboo water jacket and it was hit by a cold jet. When the cold jet hit . . . it condensed the steam and the steam ran off into a sake bottle and they virtually had pure distilled water . . . That was the start. Then they had a Burroughs Wellcome pill they knew the exact weight of and . . . blocks of salt that they used for feeding stock. They would chip off . . . the amount of salt necessary for the quantity of distilled water they had. They would mix it up into a saline and then they'd boil it twice in bottles. Then having boiled it twice . . . they would strain it through a type of muslin that you get on the bottom of a mosquito net and then they had a pure saline solution which was capable of being intravenously fed into patients . . . They were making over 100 pints a day.

If some officers were remembered after the war without much affection, Weary and his medical staff would never be spoken of with anything but reverence and profound gratitude, above all for their treatment of

cholera patients. Many times Haskell returned to camp long after dark
to see Dunlop still working in the cholera compound. 'They had no
lights ... They had a bit of an oil wick in half a coconut or a bit of a
tin ... You would see the silhouette of this giant figure bending over and
changing the drips. This went on day in and day out over a matter of
six weeks.'

Despite the best efforts of the medical officers, three Pioneers died
of cholera at 60 Kilo camp and another died later from the same disease
at the 55 Kilo hospital. The rest were being gradually worked to death:
a bridge-repairing party under Lieutenant Lloyd Burgess was forced to
work for 36 hours straight.

In the first week of June most of Williams Force was sent back to the
malaria-infested 40 Kilo camp to lay ballast. As so often, the hospital hut
was sited in the unhealthiest part of the camp: a gully almost completely
surrounded by water. For more than a month there was no quinine.
Malaria raged through the camp.

Harry Walker became so ill with malaria and dysentery that he had
to be sent back to the hospital camp at Thanbyuzayat. Before leaving, he
spent four nights in the camp medical hut. 'We slept only two feet apart,'
he recalled. 'Each morning I was there I discovered that the fellow on my
right had died in the night.' It was so crowded in the medical hut that
Walker and his fellow patients slept feet to feet. 'I knew the fellow opposite
me. He just sat there, ate very little and never got up to be washed. The
orderlies eventually got him up and washed him ... There was a river
close by. They brought him back [but] the next morning he was dead.'
The man had probably died from cerebral malaria, compounded by
malnutrition. 'Some would be sitting talking to you and they would just
fall over dead.'

By the time Walker made the trip back to Thanbyuzayat he was in
a coma. Afterwards he remembered nothing of the journey, although
prisoners were commonly sent down the line in an open railway truck.

The food at Thanbyuzayat was better than he was used to, but men were still dying. Walker still had the watch given to him by his family before he left Australia. 'I had hung onto this as a last resort,' Walker recalled. 'The Burmese brought food to the camp and there was a well-established black market. I decided I would sell my watch. I think I got four rupees for it. I'm not too sure. But the watch disappeared. I had to trust somebody to handle it, because it would pass through many hands before the money would come to me.' Eventually Harry Walker got his money. He used it to buy peanut oil, sugar and salt, and made sweetened rice cakes by grinding rice into a dough, adding sugar and frying it in peanut oil.

While in the hospital, Walker cooked for other men who were too sick to feed themselves. After the war, Walker's sister was approached in Melbourne by a stranger who stared at her for a while before asking if she had a brother called Harry and whether he had been a POW. When she answered yes, the man said, 'When you see him, tell him he saved my life.' The soldier was not a Pioneer. Walker never even found out his name. Stories like this were not uncommon.

During the monsoon, the paltry supply of fresh vegetables diminished even further. The few cattle being herded along the churned-up roads either died or arrived so emaciated as to be hardly worth butchering. Japanese guards and engineers stole from trucks and from the odd train hauling supplies up the first few kilometres of track. 'Many Japanese and Koreans, under the pretext of building up their own rations, already vastly better than ours, commandeered our rations and sold them to the thousands of natives, uprooted from their homes and normal food supplies to work along the railway,' Rohan Rivett wrote.

The same story, with local variations, was being played out in camps across the entire length of the line. To make matters worse, the Japanese army was falling behind on payments to prisoners, while inflation was making the prices of black market food and medicines unaffordable.

Early on the afternoon of 12 June 1943, six four-engined planes flew over the large hospital camp at Thanbyuzayat before splitting into two groups of three and wheeling around for a second pass. The planes were American-made Liberator bombers. It was not the first time the prisoners had seen Allied planes in the sky over Thanbyuzayat. A few weeks earlier five Liberators had overflown the camp. Rivett remembered every patient who could get out of bed hobbling outside to wave to the pilots. Some nights later, Allied aircraft had done more than simply fly over the camp: they released flares and dropped bombs near a petrol dump.

Their mission this time was more deadly. As the Liberators approached, guards rushed to drive prisoners into the huts. The bomb-aimers' target was not the camp itself but the railway track and some adjacent coolie huts. The Pioneers' history records that Japanese machine gunners fired at the planes and were strafed in return. While the Liberators had carefully avoided bombing the hospital area, eight prisoners who had been sent to fetch water from a well outside the perimeter fence were killed by a direct hit. According to Rivett, the well had been mistaken for a gun position. Two prisoners inside the camp were killed by shrapnel. That night the dead were solemnly laid to rest among their colleagues in the camp cemetery. One Japanese soldier was reported to have died. It was a bitter irony that American, British, Dutch and Australian soldiers were now being killed by Allied air power that had not been available to them when they needed it to fight the Japanese.

The Australian POWs had been afraid of just such an attack for months. The longer they waited for it to happen, the more they tried to convince themselves that British spies in Burma had warned Allied headquarters in India about the concentration of prisoners at Thanbyuzayat. Around 3000 sick POWs were squeezed into fourteen huts that were indistinguishable from the adjacent Japanese barracks and storage sheds. Beyond the cemetery was an ammunition store. For anyone unaware of the prisoners inside, the tight geometric layout of the huts could indicate only one thing: a Japanese military camp.

Allied officers begged the Japanese commandant, the pompous, French-speaking Nagatomo, for permission to daub red cross signs and the letters 'POW' on the roofs. The side of the camp furthest from the railway was already marked with a red cross, but Rivett noted that without the white background it probably looked from the air 'like two intersecting red paths'. The allied officers also protested about guards firing at the planes from within the perimeter, in violation of the camp's non-military status. Dismissing the pleas for identifying signs, Nagatomo instead gave his approval for the prisoners to dig more slit trenches outside the huts. He also took action to bolster the camp's defences.

A request by Brigadier Varley for the chief medical officer, Lieutenant Colonel Tom Hamilton, to broadcast the location of the Thanbyuzayat hospital camp over the radio from Rangoon was also rebuffed by the Japanese.

Three days after the first raid, the prisoners at Thanbyuzayat heard the telltale drone of aircraft engines. By the time six Liberators appeared overhead, the freshly dug slit trenches were packed with men. Their target this time was the camp itself. Three planes, descending to as little as 2000 feet, took turns to bomb and strafe the huts. Unlike the scattergun defence with rifles and pistols that had met the previous raid, the guards now hit back with machine-gun fire from various positions inside the camp, while other guns blazed away from posts hidden in the surrounding jungle. None of it appeared to bother the Liberator pilots, who were able to aim their bombing runs with precision. 'Sticks of bombs fell across the area between the Japanese ammunition dump and our canteen and cookhouse,' Rivett wrote. 'Other bombs sliced across the area between the new hospital huts and the old, showering both with bomb splinters. One bomb crater was only fifteen yards from the slit-trenches in which over a hundred of us from the first new hospital hut were sheltering.'

Given the duration and precision of the attack, the toll of around 60 prisoners killed or wounded was surprisingly light. Direct hits on two huts caused both to collapse inwards, leaving most of the men packed into the slit trenches unhurt. Brigadier Varley himself was fortunate not to be killed by a delayed-action bomb that killed the camp adjutant, Captain Ray Griffin.

That night the survivors, dressed in rags and reduced to skin and bone by disease and malnutrition, stood four deep around the cemetery as their mates were put into the ground. A medical officer told Rivett, 'The raids are doing more damage to some of the patients than months without drugs.'

On the morning of 17 June 1943 the order came for prisoners to evacuate the base camp at Thanbyuzayat. Bar 50 or so who were too sick to leave their beds and would later be removed by train, every one of the camp's 3000 patients was ordered to pack his gear and move into the jungle. There would be no transport. Everything, including heavy mess equipment, would have to be carried.

Many men would not survive the next few days. Those not sick were still recuperating. Most had walked no more than a few hundred metres for weeks or even months. Some were barely capable of standing when they were kicked out of their beds and forced to drag themselves, their personal gear and their bedding up the sodden jungle road to 4 Kilo camp. The procession, Rivett wrote, was 'a gigantic Via Dolorosa of the halt, the lame and the blind . . . mere derelicts of the men they had been only a year before'.

Four Kilo camp had long been abandoned by prisoners, but enough shelter remained for the Thanbyuzayat camp administration to set up a new headquarters. For the rest, it was another exhausting six-kilometre march through the mud to 8 Kilo camp. The journey was too much for some, who stumbled and fell by the side of the road. Nagatomo was as personally culpable for their deaths as he was for those of the prisoners he ordered to be shot for trying to escape.

A rude shock awaited the prisoners when they reached 8 Kilo camp. The deserted camp had been ransacked and reclaimed by the jungle; only one hut still had a roof. Local villagers had pillaged whatever had not been torn to pieces by the monsoonal storms. Nearly a thousand prisoners—survivors from the *Perth* and remnants of Williams's Pioneers, Texan artillerymen and odds and sods from the Royal Navy, all suffering either from disease or ulcers—lay down for the night, sheltering from the incessant rain beneath branches, scavenged pieces of attap and whatever else they could find.

Over the next two days, the camp was put back together. Wigwams and humpies went up; cooks began to dish up meals; medical officers arrived to treat the sick. Meanwhile Allied planes continued to bomb the strategically important railway yards at Thanbyuzayat. There were five raids between 21 and 29 June; in a calculated act of reprisal the Japanese forced work parties of between 100 and 200 prisoners, all recently hospitalised, to clear rubble and fill bomb craters.

Jittery Japanese guards evacuated the camp each day between the morning and late afternoon, ordering prisoners into the jungle, from where they watched the Liberators flying over. Neil MacPherson recalls being mistakenly targeted by a Liberator returning from a bombing mission. 'It was a densely forested area. The Liberator was flying back with fully loaded machine guns. The crew must have thought I was Japanese and decided to strafe me. I stood behind a tree as the Liberator came straight at me, firing its machine guns. I knew that rear gunners always had a blast as they flew past, so as the plane went over I scurried back around the other side of the tree, just in case.'

Eventually the sickest patients were moved either to 18 Kilo camp or to the new main hospital camp at 30 Kilo. Many had to make the journey on foot, while others had the dubious privilege of travelling on the railway many of their mates had died building. It was not a comfortable ride, as the POWs on the train were well aware of the shoddy workmanship and casual acts of sabotage—such as crooked sleepers and loose embankments—that had been perpetrated during construction.

Further up the line another hospital was being set up at 55 Kilo with Lieutenant Colonel Albert 'Bertie' Coates in charge. Described by another doctor, Captain Rowley Richards, as 'the most outstanding medical officer and man on the Railway', Coates had been ordered to leave by ship for Java before the fall of Singapore but wound up in Sumatra, where he spurned several chances to escape before being taken prisoner by the Japanese.

Since May 1942 Coates had been the chief medical officer for Williams Force. Weary Dunlop remembered him as a 'short, upright figure with a ghost of a swagger, a Burma cheroot clamped in his mouth', who became 'the object of hero worship' for his surgical skill and his 'staccato flow of kindly, earthy wisdom'. Many Pioneers would owe their lives to Coates's makeshift amputations of ulcerated limbs using a butcher's saw that, according to Rohan Rivett, 'was duly returned after each operation, to cut up the camp meat ration'.

Hospitalised with malaria and suffering badly from ulcers on his legs, Rivett never forgot the agony of having his ulcers 'gouged' by the camp doctors. 'Having the raw flesh and exposed nerve scraped with a curetting spoon is about the most acute torture I have ever experienced,' he wrote in *Behind Bamboo*. 'It was no wonder that sometimes the air was rent with awful screams and groans which escaped, despite all efforts at control, from the patients' lips.'

For all his skills as a surgeon, Colonel Coates could do nothing about the loss of hospital accommodation that followed the abandonment of Thanbyuzayat. A desperate shortage of beds forced many sick men to be discharged and sent back to work on the railway.

Williams Force was now a shadow of its former self, although the Pioneers' commanding officer had lost none of his belligerence. Colonel Williams would clash with the Japanese 'at the drop of a hat', Rowley Richards told the author Peter Thompson. This defiance put Williams at odds not only with the Japanese but with his counterpart, Lieutenant Colonel Charles Anderson, whose approach was described by Richards as 'softly, softly, catchee monkey, let's educate the Japs'. According to Rohan Rivett, Colonel Williams 'had the honour of being regarded by the Japanese as No. 1 bad man in the prison camps. He defied them with sterling courage time after time and, despite many brutal attacks, never faltered in his opposition to the persecution of his men. No one could have fought more determinedly or revealed a greater contempt for the physical consequences.'

Of nearly a thousand Pioneers who had fought in Java, several hundred—including the lost souls from A Company—were now scattered across different camps in Burma and Siam, beyond the reach of their commanding officer. In January 1943, 165 Pioneers had been transported from various camps in Java to Changi in Singapore. They had no more luck than their predecessors in prising much-needed boots, clothing or Red Cross goods from the grip of 'Black Jack' Galleghan's 8th Australian Division headquarters. The majority were taken by train to Bampong in Siam and soon found themselves rock-cutting and building embankments on the Hintok section of the railway. Like so many of their mates up and down the railway, most were barefoot and had virtually no clothing, yet they all had to walk an average of eighteen kilometres per day just getting to and from the work site.

Another group, comprising 143 Pioneers under Captain Bishop, left Singapore by train on 7 January 1943 before joining a convoy bound for Moulmein in Burma. One ship carrying Japanese troops and Dutch POWs was sunk by Allied aircraft, while three Pioneers on another ship were killed. Working at 18, 80 and 100 Kilo camps, Bishop's small party had a tougher time than many others. Lacking even the rudimentary facilities provided to larger groups, they got no help or consideration from the Japanese. Numerous Pioneers died of malaria and septic tropical ulcers in what passed for a hospital at 80 Kilo camp.

As the wet season dragged on, the remnants of Williams Force moved gradually up the line, successively occupying 70, 80, 95, 108, 116, 122 and 131 Kilo camps. At each camp, a cemetery had to be laid out and graves had to be dug: the morbid routine never changed, only the number of men who died.

Japanese guards continued to steal from the pitiful rations allocated to the prisoners. The Pioneers who had fought so bravely in Syria and Java continued to die abjectly of malnutrition, dysentery, septic ulcers, cholera and simple starvation. The Burmese monsoon continued to make the lives of tens of thousands of POWs and labourers a misery. To the Imperial Japanese Army, however, only one thing mattered: each evening brought the railway a day closer to completion.

Chapter 11

ONE VAST HOSPITAL

———————

By the middle of 1943 smuggled reports of conditions inside the POW camps in Siam had begun to reach British authorities in Chungking, China, which since 1937 had been the headquarters of Generalissimo Chiang Kai-shek's provisional Chinese government. Eyewitness reports collected by the Swiss Consul, together with anguished appeals for money to buy medical supplies, were sent to the British Embassy in Chungking with a request for them to be forwarded to the Geneva Red Cross, the British Red Cross and the Vatican. The names of the informants and of the camps where they were being held were suppressed 'for fear of reprisals should this memorandum go astray'.

<u>One camp, April 7th, 1943</u>. We have 1,500 men here and practically no dressings at all. Occasionally we get a minute issue, quite inadequate, and occasionally we buy a few odds and ends from barges.

A second camp, April 20th, 1943. Emetine [for the treatment of amoebic dysentery] and morphia are of paramount importance as men are dying for want of the former and dying in pain for lack of the latter.

May 27th, 1943. During the past six months we have had 161 deaths of which 92 have died in the last two months.

June 18th, 1943. Death rate now about 4 a day. The above, of course, refers to this particular camp only.

A third camp, April 7th, 1943. Supplies of medical equipment are totally inadequate. A tremendous lot of malaria has caused anaemia, debility and prolonged illness. The incidence of dysentery is very high. There are a lot of vitamin deficiencies . . . no resistance to infection. We are most of us near the border line. There has been a lot of diphtheria . . . A lot of skin diseases due to overcrowding and shortage of clothing. Accommodation is very bad.

A fourth camp, June 11th, 1943. There are 1730 sick men in this camp; 28 died during the last month. We have no money and the men do not receive pay. We are urgently in need of money for food and medicines.

The Red Cross and the Swiss Consulate, acting on behalf of the British government, had both money and medicine ready to be distributed to the camps, but Japanese military authorities refused them access. As long as the Japanese warrior code extolled death over surrender, this disdain for the lives of prisoners was unlikely to change. After the battle of Attu Island, in which nearly 2400 Japanese soldiers died and only 28 were taken prisoner, a Japanese officer was reported to have told a foreign diplomat in Chungking, 'Our men fought to the end; if the enemy did as much there would be no trouble about Prisoners of War.'

Before the smuggled camp reports could be forwarded, a more detailed account was obtained from an unnamed medical officer in one of the Siamese camps. His report confirmed that the treatment of Allied prisoners inside the camps had 'gone from bad to worse, and . . . one of the reasons is that the railway is behind schedule and the Japanese responsible are being pressed from higher up.' The anonymous report paints a stark picture of conditions during the wet season of 1943:

At a working camp in the jungle near Tomchang a serious outbreak of cholera has taken place following the arrival of numerous Tamils, Malays and Chinese. Up to the present there have been 190 cases among the British and Dutch prisoners of whom 105 have died. The medical facilities for the treatment of these cases is really pathetic. Those stricken with cholera are placed on rice bag stretchers and left to lie on the ground in tents which leak badly. The Japanese have provided practically no drugs with which to treat these unfortunate men. Through lack of containers the men are forced to vomit and pass stools on the ground and they are so overcrowded they frequently vomit over each other.

. . . Owing to the Japanese not allowing sufficient orderlies and grave diggers, men who have died have had to be buried in communal graves with Tamils etc. The mortality among the Asiatics has been very high, and the Japanese have forced our Attend C men [prisoners medically unfit for duty] to leave their sick beds and dig graves and bury the dead, not only our own but all nationalities.

In Konyu a serious outbreak of cholera has occurred and out of 500 men, 200 have contracted the disease, resulting to the present in 125 deaths. Facilities for intravenous treatment were non-existent in this camp, but a large number of lives were undoubtedly saved by the liberal use of M&B 693 [an early form of antibiotic] in the milder cases. All M&B 693 is now finished.

. . . The same conditions prevail in a nearby Australian camp. The men have been up-river for four months and out of approx. 500 their present strength is about 300. They have lost a number of men due to cholera, but mostly from dysentery, avitaminosis [vitamin deficiency] particularly beri-beri, malaria, and black-water fever.

In another camp in the Konyu area they have, for several months past, averaged 91 deaths a month, mostly from the above-mentioned diseases.

The morale of the prisoners on the river is, on the whole, pitiful to see. Quite a few have gone insane and other unfortunate men are so weak that they are mere skeletons and have hardly enough strength to go to the latrines.

. . . The men have come to accept corporal punishment for the most minor offence as a matter of fact. They are often beaten up, often with deleterious effects on their health. One man died recently in Tasao following being beaten with a bamboo pole and laid unconscious on the ground. The Japs then jumped on his back fracturing two ribs.

. . . Many have no desire to live and lose all interest in their surroundings. At the present moment I reckon that not 10% of the men on this river can be regarded as fit for the job. In spite of this we are bullied into these long and arduous hours, and our latest misfortune is that 1,500 of us will have to shortly go up to the Thai–Burma border for heavy and rushed work on the railway. We can not find more than 200 men who can be said to be fit for the job. These, together with sick who will have to make up the balance of 1,500, will have a ten day march to their destination carrying their own kits, cooking utensils, tents, and the Jap equipment, and I fear heavy mortality as a result.

As far as I can ascertain, the mortality on the river is already about 4,000 and the rate of sickness and death is rising rapidly.

The medical officer, who described having to carry out surgical operations with a cut-throat razor because there were no other instruments, finished with a plea that news of the prisoners' plight 'may reach the proper authority and that something will be done to alleviate our misery'.

But who could alleviate their misery? The Allies were tied up in campaigns all over Asia and the Pacific, and the Japanese had no interest in alleviating misery. At Konyu and Hintok conditions were actually deteriorating. During May and June scores of prisoners died at Konyu. Six men did nothing but dig graves. A plague of flies descended on Hintok, attracted not only by food in the kitchens but by the suppurating wounds of hospital patients. The ash heaps used to burn kitchen waste became seething masses of flies. The Japanese refused to supply mosquito nets, so an inner tent fly had to be borrowed from the hospital to enable meat to be cut up. 'The camp is a sea of mud,' Weary wrote, 'and God knows how the cooks go on keeping fires going.' By the middle of June, Konyu central camp had become 'one vast hospital with no men working'.

With the roads reduced to bogs, the Japanese decided to build a second camp at Hintok, on the cliffs above a bend in the Kwa Noi River. The railway line had swung around from high up in the range down towards the river bank, tracing a great arc around the mountain. The notorious Compressor Cutting was practically in sight of the river camp. Unlike the mountain camp, which was difficult to reach during the monsoon, the river camp could be kept supplied by Thai barges. The two camps were about four kilometres apart.

Private Jack Thomas was one of a party of prisoners sent down from the mountain camp to establish the river camp. A precipitous muddy track connected the two. A tumble down the hillside could cause lacerations or worse: the start of a tropical ulcer. The glutinous black mud could suck the soles off a man's boots, if he still had any.

'The Japs were pretty much absent,' Thomas recalls. 'On the first evening I remember sitting on the river bank watching a beautiful sunset and thinking, "this is all pretty lovely". It was a little time of grace and I felt cleansed, refreshed for a while.' Not everyone could have found grace in such a setting, but it helped Thomas survive years of captivity when others did not. 'All things are relative,' Thomas says of that evening by the river. 'If things are pretty crook and the next day they're not so crook, things are pretty good by comparison.'

For a couple of days the fifteen to twenty men of the advance group had the place almost to themselves. But Jack Thomas's 'time of grace' could not last. With the arrival of the work parties, 'Speedo' was on again.

On 1 June 1943 every 'fit' man was sent to the Hintok River camp to work on a cutting two kilometres long. Behind them, other prisoners were laying the track. There were Tamil camps on both sides of the river, and when cholera broke out among the Tamils the disease spread to the POWs. At the height of the epidemic, medical staff at the mountain camp were working around the clock to produce saline solution. One of the Australians used to run two demijohns of saline solution twice a day down the track from the mountain camp. Despite the doctors' efforts, 27 Pioneers died.

When the rail layers caught up with the cutting gang, the Japanese pushed the cutting gang even harder. Jack Thomas worked hammer and tap, one man holding a steel tap drill against the rock while his partner belted it with an eight-pound hammer. A misdirected blow could crush your mate's hand or shatter his arm. He also did his share of heavy work with the pick and shovel.

For a while, when he was sick but not sick enough to be classed unfit for duty, Thomas was put on camp work, 'scouting around for wood for the kitchens and fetching water from the river in buckets'. Camp duties, although less gruelling than working on the railway, were hardly a soft option, especially for a sick man. According to the official Australian war history, the Japanese permitted no more than 70 prisoners to do all administrative and maintenance work for a camp of 1000. This allowed for 29 cooks, fifteen medical staff, eleven clerks, six men for antimalarial and hygiene work, five water carriers, one bugler and three batmen for the Japanese. Cookhouse staff often had to cut bamboo for firewood and carry all rations from the railhead or river—strenuous work, especially during the monsoon. At Konyu, casualties among cookhouse staff were as high as 50 per cent.

After a few weeks on camp duties, Jack Thomas found himself back on the railway. During his three years in captivity Thomas never had a day in hospital, although he was sick often enough. 'If you had dysentery, well that was all right. You could sleep in your shit, you got used to that. But I was lucky. I did not have cholera.' When the speedo was on, it fell to Dunlop and his fellow doctors to decide which of the sick were still capable of working. Thomas recalls, 'Weary had to send out people who were dying. He had to say, "I'm sorry, mate, but you've got to go to work." There was a quota to fill and the Japs didn't care how they filled it.'

Cholera swept through Hintok in July, hollowing out the workforce just as the railway engineers were making ever greater demands for labour. Suspicion for the source of the epidemic fell on the Tamils. Suspicion always fell on the Tamils, who succumbed in their hundreds and thousands. The rows of headstones at Kanchanaburi War Cemetery for POWs who died in July 1943 are testament to the cholera epidemic that struck the camps that month.

The situation was dire at Hintok but even worse at Konyu—'a real camp of death', in Dunlop's words. Lieutenant Colonel Ronald Frank Oakes had left Singapore in May with 600 Australians, part of a larger group of mainly British prisoners known as 'H' Force. Less than two months later, Oakes's camp was described by Dunlop as 'a shambles with cholera and the same starvation conditions of our tommys here. They have 96 deaths from cholera, etc. including 60 Australians.' Oakes himself, after testing positive for cholera, was quarantined from the rest. Yet despite the presence of cholera, 150 British prisoners, exhausted and half-starved, were marched into Konyu without being inoculated. They died in droves.

The pressure on Dunlop was immense. Responsibility and disease wore away at him. Like his patients, he suffered from malaria, dysentery and tropical ulcers. Failure to cooperate with the Japanese in filling work gangs earned Weary many a beating. 'Often he was made to kneel,' machine gunner Max McGee recalled. 'At about 6'3" he made the Japs feel mediocre. There was one parade where all the men were on show and the bashing started. A certain amount was always accepted. But when Weary got more than his fair share there was a sudden concerned growl from all the men. That was the only time I remember the Japs backing down. We would have got all of them even though a lot of us would have got shot.'

Any kind of infringement of camp rules was enough to get a man killed. On the evening of 22 June 1943 Sergeant S.R. 'Micky' Hallam was in the camp hospital with dysentery when a work party returned from the railway. When he heard that the party had returned short, Hallam hauled himself out of his bamboo bed and joined the exhausted workers in order to buy time for one of the stragglers still making their way back to the camp. For the crime of having left the hospital against orders, Hallam was pulled out of the line by the guards and bashed unconscious. The machine gunners' history records that 'Micky Hallam was a young Hobart journalist, a sensitive man, liked by everyone.'

In his wartime diary Weary Dunlop recorded that the young machine gunner was one of several sick men dragged out of the line that night and 'mercilessly beaten up by the Nippon Engineer Sgt "Billie the Pig" and his assistant, "Mollie the Monk"'. The defenceless prisoners suffered 'blows with a fist, hammering over the face and head with wooden clogs, repeated throwing over the shoulder heavily onto the ground with a sort of fireman's lift action, then kicking in the stomach and scrotum and ribs etc., thrashing with bamboos frequently over the head, and other routine measures . . . This disgusting and brutal affair continued for some hours altogether.'

Afterwards Hallam was returned to the camp hospital 'deadly pale', his face swollen, cut and bruised from his neck to his knees and with a sprained right ankle. His temperature was 103.4°F (nearly 40°C). Three days after the bashing he was dead. The Australian War Memorial's roll of honour states, euphemistically, that Sergeant Hallam died of 'illness'.

The cause of death recorded by the camp doctors was 'contusion to the heart causing cardiac arrest—a result of beating by a Nippon engineer Sgt whilst suffering from malaria on the night of 22nd June, 1943'. Weary had no doubt who was responsible. Hallam was buried in the camp cemetery with what Dunlop described as the 'usual simple military honours', adding that he 'was slain by these Nipponese sadists more certainly than if they had shot him'. Jack Thomas did not witness the bashing but remembers placing a poppy on Micky Hallam's grave.

The Japanese engineer who ordered the bashing was Lieutenant Hirota, described by Dunlop as a 'pug-faced, fit-looking fellow with a charming, show the teeth expression which does not conceal the fact that he is a vicious, spoilt child at heart'. After a particularly savage argument about forcing sick men to work, Dunlop told Hirota, 'You can shoot me, but then my 2 I/C is as tough a man as me, and after him you will have to shoot them all. Then you will have no workmen. In any case, I have taken steps to one day have you hanged, for you are a black-hearted bastard!' Four years later, on 21 January 1947, Hirota was executed at Changi for his crimes against POWs.

On 20 July 1943 three of Des Jackson's comrades in the Hintok River camp contracted cholera in the space of just twelve hours. Jackson slept between two of them while the third man occupied the bunk opposite. All three died, but Jackson survived; he spent the resk of his life wondering why.

The question that haunted Jackson must have haunted every survivor of the railway. Jackson came close to death several times, once fading to a mere seven stone in weight (five stone lighter than when he was captured) after a severe bout of bacillary dysentery. After impaling his foot on a sharp bamboo stump, Jackson was sent to a so-called 'convalescent hospital'. The months he spent there, while his comrades were being worked to death on the railway, saved Des Jackson's life.

The same day that three of Jackson's comrades died of cholera, a consignment of letters from home finally reached the men at Hintok camp. The earliest had been written a year and a half earlier. Weary received a letter from his wife, Helen, who 'would have been shocked to see me having these stuffed in my pocket in the cholera area so as not to touch them, me with two days growth of beard, shabby, haggard, growing very old and grey and limping about with my tropical ulcer burning like a coal.'

Nearly every day saw the death of another prisoner from cholera: three on 20 July; six on the 22nd; two on the 23rd. In August Private Frederick Souter, a 23-year-old machine gunner, died at Hintok camp, but not of cholera. 'There was no sign of impending disaster with this patient,' Dunlop wrote in his diary. 'He was a tall pale freckled boy, very thin; rather large but healing tropical ulcer and recent malaria.' As well as malaria and a tropical ulcer, Souter had been ill with enteritis and beri-beri. Although Souter's body was racked with disease, Dunlop still considered the young machine gunner's death to be 'sudden'. He suspected that the antimalarial drug quinine might be a factor in the deaths of men like Souter who also had beri-beri.

With more and more sick men to care for, money was a constant worry. Not only were the Japanese always behind in paying the prisoners' wages but the sick were not paid at all. By the middle of August the 'huge preponderance of sick over workers' forced Weary to cut his hospital budget to a measly 10 cents per day for each patient—which was less than he had been spending on tinned milk alone. Within two days, even this amount had to be halved. A third of each man's pay was now going to the regimental fund to provide for the sick, while the rest was pooled and paid evenly by rank to all earners. Weary was grimly aware that 'with the proposed rate of hospital expenditure some sick men will die'.

As the number of sick at Hintok mountain soared, the Japanese decided to evacuate large numbers of patients by barge to hospitals downriver. Hintok was not the most brutal POW camp in Siam, yet after five months 57 Australians had died there. The toll at the neighbouring British camp was much higher; Dunlop was told that 220 men had died there in just thirteen weeks.

While Dunlop did what he could to help the British POWs, his first priority was always to minimise the suffering of his own men. 'Their state is pitiable,' he wrote after a British soldier died of cholera, 'but then, Oh Lord! hygiene is a menace to us who live alongside them.'

Private Wally Holding described an English camp near Nieke which

> had a terrible lot of sickness so they could hardly get any of their blokes to go out to work. A lot of us were sent up there to help out. The English camp was a shocking mess: the latrines were not kept up, nothing was working, the cookhouse was not working properly . . . so Major Hunt got the Japanese to give us two days off to try to sort out this camp. They had fouled the ground and it was a hell of a job to get it cleaned up . . . After we had finished the clean up the Lieutenant-Colonel in charge of the camp had us on parade. He thanked us for coming up and . . . said his chaps had got to the stage they had just thrown in the towel, they were dying of starvation and they just did not have the will to keep on going. It was a shocking bloody camp.

Something about the British prisoners rubbed the Australians the wrong way: their lassitude; their inability to look after themselves; their tendency to give up. 'The English camp here is most dismal,' Ray Parkin wrote while at Hintok. 'The morale is low. They have little sense of hygiene: they wash their mess gear in the creek *below* our showers, where men with dysentery wash.'

The cholera epidemic at Hintok subsided after July, but men went on dying from dysentery, malaria and malnutrition. The living and the barely alive were now succumbing in ever greater numbers to tropical ulcers. A visit in the first week of October 1943 to the ulcer wards at Tha Sao base hospital, 25 kilometres from Hintok, appalled even Dunlop, who described the wards as 'a butcher's shop'.

Except for Pte Abbott, I have never seen ulcers like these and they are not limited to the lower legs but include the thighs, buttocks and upper limbs. Evidence of cross-infection is quite irrefutable. Huge numbers of men with naked, necrosed bone exposed and sloughing great masses of tendon. I was most particularly shocked at changes in the conditions of men who were all doing well when I saw them last and are now in great danger of loss of limb or life. This infection writes its grisly tale on the face and frame very quickly, the pale, lined, harassed face and haunted eyes telling of toxaemia, pain and loss of sleep—I well remember the pain and sleeplessness myself.

While a prisoner at Tarsao in Siam, Sergeant Alf Sheppard boiled water in his billy can to clean the ulcers on his legs, but 'it never seemed to do much good'. One day, as he filled his billy in the river, 'I left off my bandages while I was standing in the water. I felt tickling sensations around all the ulcers . . . I just stood there in the water till it stopped.' When Sheppard came out of the river he found the ulcers quite clean; all the pus had gone. For the next few weeks 'I stood in the river to let the fish clean out the pus and then I washed the ulcers with hot water—as hot as I could stand. They started to heal up slowly after that.'

The railway was days from being completed, but the demand for workers did not slacken. When Corporal Okada, who was responsible for medical arrangements, demanded to know 'why more sick every day?' Dunlop told him to look for the answer in the camp cemetery.

Okada and Dunlop butted heads repeatedly. Their relationship was volatile but not always antagonistic. In his diary Dunlop recorded Okada giving him lunch, 'both of us sitting cross-legged in the N hut with a small table between. Disadvantage: seen by the majors of English battalion, who looked at me with dropped jaws.' On 18 October Dunlop commented that Okada was 'ubiquitous and appears to work very hard in the interests of the sick' but that he was 'mortally afraid of Lt-Col Ishi whom he detests'.

Weary was crafty as well as brave and would have understood that his dealings with Okada were inseparable from Okada's dealings with Colonel Ishi. Relations between the pair—and among all Japanese soldiers of different ranks—were outlined by Major Ted Fisher in a penetrating footnote to the official history. Any Japanese soldier of whatever rank, Fisher wrote, if alone

had no hesitation . . . in giving orders to a battalion [of prisoners]; but in response to orders from a rank one step higher than his own he was an automaton. The Emperor was God, but to [other ranks] any officer was a demigod. Similar prestige attached to seniority among officers; the Japanese commander of P.O.W.s in Burma was known to bash his second-in-command till he lost his feet and then kick him down the stairs, injuring his back severely: he was then sent out in disgrace to a working camp where he stayed in hospital for six weeks under the care of a P.O.W. medical officer. Nevertheless there were some curious features. A guard commander during his tour of duty, though holding no rank, was supreme in his own domain and even the camp commander could not or would not interfere with one of his guard during a period when he was regarded as the direct representative of the Emperor. Consequently redress for offences by a guard commander or his guard could not be obtained.

Fisher, who for a while was in charge of the base hospital at Thanbyuzayat, could be an awkward character himself. Rohan Rivett sketched him as 'a brilliant but temperamentally difficult Macquarie St specialist with a biting tongue and a dictatorial manner which earned him the title of "the Fuehrer"'. Colonel Albert Coates, the senior Australian surgeon in Burma, was more generous, remarking after Fisher's death that '[b]eneath a stern exterior, a heart of gold and a brilliant mind resided'.

In his 1946 sworn statement to the Australian War Crimes Board of Inquiry, Weary Dunlop accused Corporal Okada of having 'daily over-ruled experienced medical officers, forcing them to send sick men to work under the most exhausting conditions and brutality and thereby directly causing many deaths.' Recounting a visit to Hintok camp by a Japanese general on 10 May 1943, Dunlop stated:

Okada promised me that if 43 sick men were removed from the hospital into the jungle, they would not have to work, and the sick figures would thus be improved. The men were to return to hospital after the general's inspection. Instead of this, Cpl Okada handed these men over to the engineers, and though these 43 were suffering from huge tropical ulcers and were bloated with beri-beri, they were compelled to roll heavy drums of oil some miles over rough mountain tracks ... Cpl Okada was well known for trading in the belongings of PW [prisoners of war] and was responsible for delaying the evacuation of the sick unless they sold watches etc at a fraction of their value.

Of Corporal Okada's tormentor, Colonel Ishi [or Ishii], known as the 'Laughing Colonel', Dunlop said that he was 'responsible for the deaths of hundreds of men by his neglect to ensure provision of sufficient food, clothing, shelter and medicines to the working camps during 1943'. Having visited the death camps at Konyu and Hintok, Ishi was 'completely aware' of the 'brutality and violence' suffered by POWs—'in point of fact, his visits were accompanied by an especially increased severity in the ill-treatment of the sick men'. During one of Ishi's visits, Dunlop pointed to tents full of emaciated men with dysentery and protested about the Japanese refusal to supply drugs. 'I told Ishi that the only possible alternative treatment was by starvation and fluids. He asked, "How long no food," and I told him 2–3 days. He then replies, "In future remember—no food one week."'

Colonel Ishi was tried and hanged at Changi as a war criminal for his treatment of prisoners on the railway. Lieutenant Osuki, the 'young, sleek, Japanese officer' remembered by Ray Parkin as having 'looked us over like a schoolmaster receiving a new crowd', was also hanged. In a letter written in 1992 to the historian Hank Nelson, Dunlop described Osuki as 'a whisky sodden no-hoper'. Corporal Okada—'Doctor Death'—was sentenced to ten years in prison.

Chapter 12
WHERE ARE THE REST?

———❦———

The monsoon had passed. The prisoners working from the Burma end of the railway had crossed the border into Siam. The men of the No. 1 Mobile Force, including Colonel Williams and his Pioneers, were working eighteen-hour shifts. During the previous month, living conditions in the Burmese camps, especially those near the border, had been the worst the Australians had ever known. Private Doug Hampson recalled living 'in a sea of mud . . . like knee deep bogs. Sections of some of the camps were under water, stepping off the sleeping platform into a running stream . . . Life at that stage was pure hell.'

Food was always scarce, consisting mostly of infinite varieties of what Les Cody called the 'soup de jour—melon, radish, jungle weed, tumeric, chilli, bamboo shoots, pepper, yams'.

Meat and fish were rarities, the former sent up the line on unsteady legs or in boxes. 'Much of the boxed meat received during this period was green and flyblown,' the official historian reported, and the small cattle ... that found their way into the camp were often diseased and would normally have been condemned. The green portion of the boxed meat would be cut away, the maggots washed off, and the remainder of the meat would be eaten. The wisdom of Solomon and the patience of Job were sometimes required to decide whether or not diseased cattle should be used in the cookhouse. One battalion commander who lacked the qualifications needed to decide whether or not an animal should be eaten, developed the practice of asking each of his butchers in turn what he would do if it were thrown out. If the majority said they would eat it themselves, the animal was added to the camp rations.

Lieutenant Hoshi was so nauseated by a reeking consignment of boxed meat delivered to 105 Kilo camp that he demanded it be eaten without delay. When the Australian commander refused, Hoshi ordered it to be buried because, even from 300 yards away, he could not bear the smell. But even bad meat was better than no meat, and in the end much of it was eaten.

At 115 Kilo camp there was only room in the hut for half the work force, but since the men were working alternate 24-hour shifts, it was enough. Collapsed cuttings held up the track layers, and in order to catch up, the Japanese forced the prisoners to work 33 hours without a break.

On 12 October the first train passed the 100 Kilo mark at Regue, where prisoners had been dying at the rate of nearly four a day. Relatively few of the dead were Australians. The official history attributes some of the deaths to 'depression caused by the damp, dank surroundings and the unsuitable food'.

The declassified records of the US Office of the Provost Marshal General are more specific about the reasons why so many prisoners died. At 100 Kilo camp, staff sergeant J.L. Summers recalled living in a hut built in a swamp at the base of a hill. As the rains continued, springs from the side of the hill started flowing and the floor of the hut was covered by water from 6 inches to one and a half foot in depth. It was impossible to divert this water around our hut, due to the rocky formation near the surface of the ground. The food conditions in 100 Kilo camp were the worst that we had experienced, and this together with the long hours of work, resulted in the deaths of more than 50 of our men during the time that we were in this camp. We were without meat and vegetables for as long as ten (10) days and two (2) weeks. At other times we were furnished dried fish that was infested with maggots; these were held over the fire until the smoke forced the worms to leave. The prisoners were forced to eat dogs and snakes and there were many instances of prisoners eating rats. These conditions existed until the railway was completed and we were moved into Thailand in December 1943.

Loss of appetite could kill a starving prisoner as surely as disease. Rations by now consisted of little more than boiled rice and white radish. 'To men racked with malaria, and groggy with quinine, the tackling of plain boiled rice demanded the utmost will-power and perseverance,' Rohan Rivett wrote. 'When breakfast consists of boiled rice, with hot water to drink, lunch of boiled rice, with a rich stew of hot water and pepper, and dinner of boiled rice and an exquisite dish of more peppered hot water with odd pieces of wood-like radish or bamboo root floating in it, few fever cases are capable of taking sufficient nourishment to feed a babe in arms . . . for most of us there were days when rice was the anathema of all anathemas.'

Colonel Coates had drummed into the Australian troops that 'Your ticket home is in the bottom of your dixie', and a survey of prisoners' eating habits showed that his advice was being followed. If food was edible, the Australians forced themselves to eat it. The American and

Dutch prisoners were more fastidious, and died disproportionately as a result.

F Force was a group of 7000 POWs brought from Changi in April 1943 to work on the railway. Just over half the prisoners were Australian, the rest British. By May 1944, after the railway had been finished and the survivors sent back to Changi, 1060 out of 3662 Australians had died. British losses were even higher: in just twelve months, 2036 British soldiers died. Between May and December 1943 the average monthly death rate had been more than 360.

Lieutenant Colonel Charles Kappe, who led the AIF contingent of F Force, suggested various reasons for the lower Australian death rate, including 'a more determined will to live, a higher sense of discipline, a particularly high appreciation of the importance of good sanitation, and a more natural adaptability to harsh conditions.' Kappe's own 'will to live' came at the expense of the men he commanded. In his book *Descent Into Hell*, Peter Brune describes Kappe's record as one of 'incompetence, sheer neglect and the total abuse of the privileges of command'. Watching his men starve did not harm Kappe's appetite. 'One of his first acts,' a fellow officer, Captain Fred Stahl, wrote, 'was to issue an instruction that he was to receive double rations. The reason was, he said, "Somebody must go back to tell the story of this bastardry and I am the best qualified to do it."' Private John Boehm told Brune that Kappe 'didn't have any patched clothes . . . he looked physically well . . . the doctors and kitchen staffs hated his guts because he . . . demanded what he wanted . . . his nickname was Kappe-yama.'

The British commander of F Force, Lieutenant Colonel Stanley Harris, who saw British prisoners dying at twice the rate of Australians, believed that the Australians benefited from being 'all members of one volunteer force with a common emblem and outlook' and that their average physical condition was 'incomparably higher than that of the mixed force of regular soldiers, territorials, militiamen, conscripts and local volunteers' who formed the British half of F Force. Harris also believed the Australians had more experience of looking after themselves under 'jungle' or 'bush' conditions.

Ray Parkin was more scathing. 'These English are careless,' he wrote. 'They drink from wayside pools . . . their own officers make no provisions for getting the men boiled water . . . [the English officers] are waited on by batmen, and spend their time in self-seeking and self-protection.'

The end of the monsoon brought some respite for Colonel Williams and his Pioneers, but it was only relative. The 'speedo' was over and the mud was drying, but the sick were still sick and food was scarcer than ever. 'There were in fact no fit men,' the official history comments in a footnote, 'only men who were fit compared with others who were sick.'

On 17 October 1943 track layers working from both ends of the Siam–Burma railway met at Konkuita in Siam. The men working from the Burma end, who included many of the 2/2nd Pioneers, had laid 152 kilometres of track. Those working from the Siamese end, including the bulk of Brigadier Blackburn's 2/3rd machine gunners, had laid 263 kilometres. A month later, the POWs were given a rest day to mark the official opening. A party of *Kempeitais* (military police) descended on Kinsayok camp, allegedly to protect a Japanese general from possible assassination by the prisoners. Parkin hid his diaries.

On 20 November 1943 the Japanese held memorial services for the men who had died building the railway. Crosses were erected at the cemeteries, and Colonel Nagatomo read a letter of condolence to the POWs at 55 Kilo camp, while his representatives read the same letter to prisoners at other camps. In camps throughout Siam and Burma, men were given two days' rest. After everything they had witnessed and endured during the preceding year, few were interested in hearing Japanese soldiers express their 'condolences'. To Les Cody, the ceremony 'remained a bitter memory'. Rohan Rivett quotes Nagatomo's letter in full, noting that the comments from Australian prisoners were 'colourful and blasphemous'. Des Jackson did not bother to mention it.

The truth, as every prisoner knew, was that their mates had died from malaria, dysentery, beri-beri and a dozen other treatable diseases because the Japanese had no interest in saving them. 'The hospitals on the Burma railroad were death traps,' the SEAC POW report concluded. Noting that there was 'no provision for trained medical personnel in the hospital camps, saving where by accident a prisoner himself was a doctor', the report told the story of Commander Epstein, of the US Navy, who

> was reported as having performed major surgical operations with equipment consisting of one small scalpel, a syringe with a broken needle, and a few drugs. An Australian medical officer was reported as having performed amputations successfully with similarly limited equipment, to the amazement of Colonel Nagatomo ... The use of clothing, rags, and other materials for bandages was common ... medical supplies were frequently looted by the Japanese under the pretext that 'medicine was for the troops'.

According to the SEAC report, the only known inspection of conditions inside a POW hospital by 'Japanese medical personnel' was a visit to 80 Kilo camp by a 'dental student of three weeks' experience'.

> No reports from other areas (except on the Sumatra railroad) even approximate to the extremes of the 'death camps' on the Burma railroad ... [it] seems to have been a universal policy to prevent any but those too ill to stand from remaining in bed or otherwise recover[ing] their strength. The conclusion has already been made inescapable. The Japanese policy toward the sick was to let them die.

Die they did, in increasing numbers.

Lieutenant Colonel Nagatomo's crocodile tears for the prisoners who died building the railway did not save him when he faced justice at the war crimes trials. Nagatomo was the most senior of six Japanese officers charged after the war with having caused the deaths of 'many' POWs and the 'bodily injury, damage to health and physical suffering of many others' during the construction of the Siam–Burma railway. Nagatomo and two officers were also charged with ordering the shooting of recaptured POWs. Nagatomo, two officers, one NCO and four Korean guards were found guilty and hanged.

The ceremony honouring the dead POWs was followed by a macabre day of what Rivett described as 'enforced merrymaking', including a four-hour concert by the Japanese which was 'so awful that many of the troops arose and departed' and an athletics meeting at which '[t]he bookies made a killing'. According to Cody, 'It was the prisoners' first opportunity in a long time to relax their guard and dare allow themselves a little bit of fun. Even then the enjoyment . . . was tainted by a "demand" performance by Lt. Hoshi the hated Camp Commander. The theme of his presentation . . . "The Triumph of Good over Evil".'

Colonel Dunlop, battling a new and deadly epidemic of cholera at Hintok, mentioned neither the Japanese condolences nor the 'celebrations' that followed. On the same day that Cody and Rivett were watching Lieutenant Hoshi perform his 'spirited dance in costume' at 105 Kilo camp, Weary was struggling to save the lives of two Australian prisoners with 'extremely serious extensive ulcers'. The two prisoners, both 'losing gound rapidly', had their legs amputated.

In just ten months a railway had been hacked out of rock and jungle using little more than hand tools, but at what human cost? According to the official Australian history, 330,000 workers, including 61,000 prisoners of war, were employed on the railway. The Allied war graves registration units concluded in 1946 that 12,399 POWs had lost their lives; this total included 6318 British prisoners, 2646 Australians,

2490 Dutch and 589 prisoners of unknown nationality. The toll on 'volunteer' labourers from Burma, Malaya and Siam was much higher: perhaps as many as 90,000 out of a coolie workforce of around 270,000.

With the railway completed, the demand for work slackened. While 'fit' prisoners were to stay in the jungle to maintain the line, 'light sick' would be sent to Bampong in Siam and 'heavy sick' to a new base hospital at Nakon Pathom near Bangkok. On 2 December, 500 'fit' Australians were sent to Bangkok to be returned to Singapore by ship. A fortnight later they were delivered by truck to Changi, where they were met by a welcoming party including 'Black Jack' Galleghan, the man whom Dunlop had accused of doing 'nothing' to help the Java Rabble and whom Ray Parkin had mocked for 'preserving an élite corps which is being trained with broomsticks'. The Australian soldiers who emerged from the trucks a year later were 'almost unrecognisable shadows of the men who had gone away; many were hatless, bootless and obviously ill on their feet'. Told that the new arrivals were 'all present and correct', Galleghan asked in disbelief, 'Where are the rest?'

Major Noel Johnston of the 2/30th Battalion replied, 'They're all here, Sir.'

According to his biographer, Black Jack walked in silence along the line of ragged and emaciated survivors from his own 2/30th Battalion, 'tears streaming down his face'.

Chapter 13
STOPPO!

In the last weeks of 1943 food was scarcer than ever for the POWs left behind in the railway camps. 'Five bags of potatoes and five bags of rice arrived today,' Williams wrote in his diary on 10 November. 'The guards took the bags of potatoes to be cooked by us for their consumption. Meals very poor today: dirty water and rice.' Eight days later, 'Private Irvine died at 0230 hrs this morning suffering from beri-beri. He was blown up like a balloon last night and unconscious.'

Prisoners at 131 Kilo camp did not see a scrap of meat or fish during the whole of November. With conditions worsening by the day, Colonel Anderson wrote a long letter to the new Japanese commander protesting bitterly about conditions in the Siamese camps. 'Pellagra and malnutrition are rife,' Anderson wrote, 'and it is no exaggeration to state that a large number of patients will die within the next eight weeks unless something is done to save them.' Men were eating 'rats, snakes, and . . . jungle leaves' in order to survive.

'The hunger didn't go away,' wrote Les Cody, 'nor did the malaria, diarrhoea and dysentery or the ulcers and skin infections or the beri beri and happy feet [lower leg neuropathy caused by vitamin B deficiency] or the tremendous weariness that had penetrated their very souls ... Every man in the camp was subject to recurring attacks of malaria and chronic dysentery or diarrhoea.' Of 884 men in what had once been No. 1 Mobile Force, a mere 24—including Colonel Williams—were classified as fit in December 1943.

As much as 50 per cent of the prisoners' food was routinely stolen by the guards. Williams described the process in his diary. 'When the rations reach the dump from the rail the Japanese in charge of the dump proceed to take out half of the contents of the baskets for private use. 30 bags of pomelos arrived. The Japs made 60 bags out of them, issued 30 and put the other 30 in their own storeroom.'

Urging the Japanese commander to see the truth for himself by making 'an inspection of ALL prisoners in all camps', Colonel Anderson warned that the failure to improve conditions for POWs would be 'an everlasting blot on the name of Japan as a nation, which hitherto has always been respected for its honourable actions'.

In December 1943 it would have been difficult to find another Australian prisoner willing to commend Japan for its 'honourable actions', but Anderson's preference was always for guile and diplomacy ('softly, softly, catchee monkey', as Captain Rowley Richards put it) over confrontation.

Christmas brought an unexpected gift for some men: mail. Sackfuls of letters had been sent from Australia by the families of POWs, but few were ever distributed to the prisoners. Captain Ernest Lawson's wife, Margaret, wrote a letter to him every week for the three and a half years he was imprisoned in Java, but none of them reached him. The machine gunners' history records that before leaving the camp, prisoners 'discovered a room in the Japanese officers' area filled with bags of mail from Australia'. Jack Thomas did not receive a single letter during his entire time in captivity. Des Jackson was luckier, receiving mail on five different occasions—amounting to a haul of 70 letters in all. 'Usually they were at least fifteen months old and, of necessity, brief and uninformative,' Jackson recalled. 'Nevertheless, it was always an emotional moment to be handed letters, particularly if they contained sad news.'

Les Cody believed the arrival of letters from home gave men back 'not only dignity and hope, but a direct line to all the familiar memories that had slowly been buried in the struggle for life in the jungles of Burma. They had an identity again.'

Although the railway was finished, Allied bombing of the line meant that prisoners were still needed for track maintenance. While some repair gangs remained in Burma, the Japanese began a mass transfer of Allied POWs across the border to Siam.

The Japanese had given little thought to evacuating large numbers of sick men safely from the river camps to base hospitals in Siam. The usual method of removing the sick was for them to hitch a ride on returning barges or trucks or railway wagons. Often this meant lying in transit for days, exposed to the sun and rain, untended and with little or nothing to eat. When they did manage to get a lift, the transports were often so overcrowded that the sick were forced to lie on top of each other. Sick men were offloaded and made to walk or else left lying for hours beside the tracks without water. After journeys lasting four or five days, they were delivered without warning to the understaffed and overwhelmed base hospitals.

The new base hospital at Nakon Pathon, near Bangkok, staffed by Australian doctors, gave hundreds of sick prisoners a second chance at life, but for many of their mates it came too late. 'Unloading the barges or the rail trucks was a shocking experience, the stench arising from dysentery and ulcer patients, confined for days in cramped conditions, was unbearable,' Les Cody wrote. 'In many cases it was the dead they had to unload.'

Those who made it to the hospital benefited from the much improved rations and from the arrival of Red Cross medical supplies. Priceless drugs and surgical dressings saved many lives.

After a 'fairly easy time' at 131 Kilo camp, the remnant of Williams Force were moved progressively back to 114 Kilo and then 105 Kilo, where they joined the main body of Australians left in Burma. Poorly fed, they were made to go out every day to chop wood to feed the locomotives. 'The axes weren't too bad,' Harry Walker recalled, 'the food was a little better, and the guards weren't so severe.' The trees they were chopping down were teak, up to 40 feet high. 'We cut the straightest and the best . . . cut it into 2 or 3ft lengths, and packed it into heaps.' The work lasted for a couple of months. Then Walker was given another medical inspection and vaccinated against smallpox.

It was at 105 Kilo camp that Neil MacPherson came closest to dying. Racked with malaria and dysentery, he knew that his body could not take much more. He was lucky, however, to have just received some letters from home. Horrified by the thought of his mother having to read a telegram saying that her son had passed away, MacPherson read those letters every day to remind himself that 'there was another life waiting for me outside'. Eventually he recovered.

As if the lives of POWs were not precarious enough already, two Liberator bombers machine-gunned 105 Kilo camp in March, killing a Dutch prisoner. Three days later, the last of the Australians under Colonel Williams were moved to Kanchanaburi in Siam.

By the end of the month, the bulk of Allied prisoners, bar some who had been sent to Singapore, had been moved to camps in Siam. One consequence of this redistribution was that, nearly two years after the surrender in Java, soldiers from the 2/3rd Machine Gun Battalion and the 2/2nd Pioneers were reunited in Siam, although some machine gunners were still behind wire at Bicycle Camp in Batavia.

Jack Thomas was among a party of machine gunners moved from Hintok to a camp near Kanchanaburi. Conditions in the new camp were better than at Hintok—'not good,' Thomas recalls, 'but better.' There was little for the prisoners to do: one of Thomas's jobs consisted of 'digging up palm trees and replanting them at the gates of the camp'.

Bill Haskell fluked a transfer to Bampong and spent a while working on barges, loading and unloading attap. 'We had quite a nice job going for us there . . . we had access to markets and the Thais used to toss us a bit of stuff every now and again. The food was very good and we were only a small working party . . . I must have been Johnny on the Spot at the time they wanted someone. I was with a crowd of Queensland artillery men so I must have been just filling the gap at the time . . . It was probably the best job I ever had in Thailand.'

The transfer of POWs away from the jungle camps did not signify a change of heart in the Japanese but rather a belated realisation of the disastrous consequences of their previous mistreatment. According to the official Australian history, the Japanese 'had begun to feel apprehensive about the heavy casualties of 1943'. High-ranking Japanese officers from Tokyo visited some Siamese camps and propaganda photographs were taken that purported to show healthy prisoners singing as they worked in the gardens. Other photographs showed well-equipped hospitals in camps at Chungkai, Tamuan, Tarsau and Kanchanaburi.

By mid-1944 the war had turned decisively against Japan in the Pacific and in central and east Asia. Japanese forces had suffered a string of defeats in the Solomons and New Guinea and were on the run in Burma. There was good reason for Japan's political and military leaders to fear the consequences of their country's barbaric treatment of Allied POWs. But retribution was not their only worry; there was also the logistical problem of what do with the exhausted remnants of the railway labour force. The majority of the survivors were now too sick to be useful.

The destruction of the POW labour force through starvation, neglect and physical abuse was not just morally inexcusable but self-defeating. In a report dated 5 October 1945, Weary Dunlop, by then a medical liaison officer in Bangkok, wrote:

The IJA [Imperial Japanese Army] showed complete indifference to the fate of the sick and labourers. This policy was economically so stupid that one can only suppose that it was due to sheer sadism. On one occasion, one of them killed a patient by putting a pick through his skull, apparently . . . to see how effective a weapon it was. The Nipponese orderlies used to enjoy going about the hospital with a bottle of chloroform and a 10 cc syringe, administering the chloroform intravenously to patients chosen at random and watching the subsequent convulsions and death.

The Japanese homeland was now desperately short of workers. Some way had to be found to restore the prisoners to health—or at least some ruined approximation of it—and recycle them to where they were needed.

After the deprivations of the jungle camps, some men suspected that they were being 'fattened up', although it didn't feel like that to Jack Thomas. Articles of clothing—often bizarre and unsuitable—were distributed to prisoners who had spent most of the previous year wearing nothing but a loincloth. Thomas remembers being given 'a pair of pink cotton pants—the sort a lady would wear'.

Harry Walker was one of a group of Pioneers declared fit and sent to Tamarkan to join a large number of Pioneers already awaiting transfer to Japan. At Tamarkan, 'we met some of our fellow prisoners who had been treated at the hospital for two or three months. The stories they had to tell us were mouth watering. They had meat, they had onions, they had vegetables. They had put on weight . . . I could hardly recognise them. Some had put on three or four stone.'

But the generosity would not last; rations were already starting to dwindle. Neil MacPherson found a way of supplementing his allowance by volunteering to carry water up the mountain to the Japanese guards at the lookout post—a task that earned volunteers the right to eat any leftovers from the guards' evening meal. It was back-breaking work for the two-man teams, clambering up a steep mountain track with a cut-down 44-gallon drum slung on a bamboo pole. Each time MacPherson vowed it would be the last, only to volunteer again when hunger pangs gripped his stomach.

Initially the plan had been to select 'technical' workers for heavy industry. Later it was decided to send 10,000 of the fittest prisoners to work in general war production industries and in coal and copper mines in Japan and its occupied territories. At first the Allied POW administration was simply given quotas to fill. As the operation grew, the Japanese took control of the process themselves.

At Tamarkan a Japanese medical officer (a dentist, according to Les Cody) and his assistants stalked up and down the line of haggard survivors from the jungle camps, identifying those fit enough to be sent to Japan. If a prisoner could stand unsupported, he was deemed fit enough to go. Cody records that '[o]nly men in hospital or with amputations, serious ulcers, skin complaints or currently suffering a malarial relapse, or were considered too old or who had dark skin (even freckles) were automatically excluded'.

According to Neil MacPherson, there was another criterion for exclusion: red hair. 'For some reason they didn't want to send chaps with red hair,' he recalls. 'I've got no idea why. Maybe they wanted to breed us and didn't want any red-headed Japanese. I was selected but my mate Bluey Rowe, he had red hair and wasn't taken. Until then we had been together throughout the war. We didn't meet up again until we were back in Australia.'

Corporal Walker was one of those eager to be sent to Japan, believing that conditions could not be any worse and might even be better. 'If we were to stay in the jungle there didn't appear to be any hope for us,' he recalled. 'Malaria . . . would beat us in the end.'

MacPherson, who had nearly lost his sight to conjunctivitis, was another who thought of Japan as a place where he could escape from the tropical diseases that had killed so many of his mates.

Singapore and Saigon became staging posts for the mass transfer of prisoners from Southeast Asia to Japan. Since 1942, when the first Allied prisoners were sent to Japan , the journey time had grown steadily longer. Ten-day direct voyages were not unusual in 1942. By 1944, when prisoner ships were forced to hug coastlines and follow convoluted routes to avoid submarines, the voyage could take seven times as long.

Machine gunners Jack Thomas and Bill Haskell stayed only a short time in Singapore before embarking for Japan on a ship they christened *Byoki Maru*, literally 'sick ship'. The ship was an English-built rustbucket. A crack ran right across the ship where the original bridge superstructure had been, and both halves of the ship were held together with steel girders spot-welded to the deck. 'It had been sunk at Singapore and refloated,' Haskell recalled. 'All the midships had been bombed out and the steering was from a little attap enclosure . . . at the stern of the ship. There were loose planks all over the deck . . . The toilet facilities, we used to call them sidecars, were little boxes on either side of the ship. They had about four of them . . . All that was holding the ship together were steel box girders running the length of the ship.'

The *Byoki Maru* sailed on 1 July 1944 with around 1000 Australian prisoners stuffed into its holds. Before leaving Singapore, Jack Thomas was given a pair of black leather boots. 'The boots were size 10,' Thomas recalls. 'They were too big for me. I gave them away to a friend who was not on the Japanese draft. He would have flogged those boots for a pound of tobacco.'

Sailing very slowly via Borneo, the Philippines and Formosa, the convoy containing the *Byoki Maru* clung to the shoreline, rarely straying out of sight of land. At one point the ship lay at anchor for three weeks in Manila Bay. Thomas remembers a barge coming out with food: 'It was a bargeload of chokoes. They were very appetising!'

The convoy set off again but was only two or three hours out of port when American submarines attacked. 'We were the lead ship on the port side going up,' Haskell recalled. 'The subs came in and they cleaned up the two tankers behind us . . . the Korean guards went berserk. They were firing rifles everywhere . . . I was actually in one of those side cars and I saw the result of this torpedo . . . debris flying in the air and bodies and decking . . . so I scurried back down below.'

With ships exploding and depth charges going off, an Australian bugler started piping out a popular tune. The prisoners joined in: 'I'll tell you the tale of the Nancy Lee/The ship that got shipwrecked at sea/ And the bravest man was Captain Brown/And he played his ukulele as the ship went down.' At the sound of the men singing, the Korean guards 'went mad', Haskell recalled, waving their guns and shrieking 'Stoppo! Stoppo!'

After surviving the submarine attack, the *Byoki Maru* was hit by a tropical cyclone off the Philippines, with waves 50 or 60 feet high. Sergeant Gordon Maxwell of the 2/19th infantry battalion described the scene to Hank Nelson for the ABC radio series *Prisoners of War: Australians under Nippon*:

[T]he old Byoki Maru started to sway and creak and groan, and various bangs—not quite as loud as a rifle shot—started to occur and we wondered what the devil was happening. And we suddenly found out because all the spot welds were breaking along the girder. Some mates and myself got ourselves at a spot near the old bridge and we were sort of astride the crack than ran across from side to side, and the crack started to open up and close as the ship went over waves. The welds were parting. We wondered how long this was going to go on.

It took the *Byoki Maru* 70 days to reach the Japanese port of Moji, the steel girders somehow holding the heaving ship together. 'We didn't leave the ship,' Thomas recalls. 'We were between decks the whole time.' Several ships fell away from the convoy and some were sunk, but no prisoners died.

The ship arrived on 8 September 1944. Before landing, the POWs were 'glass rodded' to check for cholera, but it was more than 10 weeks since they had been exposed to the disease and the results were negative. Despite being passed fit, they were a 'pretty dejected-looking crowd' after 70 days afloat. Thomas recalls being 'lined up on the wharf and sold off in batches to various organisations that wanted labour. I was sent to Honshu. A group of us were designated to go to a coal mine. We had our own barge and were supervised by a Japanese man with an American education. He spoke very good English. He welcomed us and gave each of us a freshly baked bread roll. That bread roll was heaven.'

Lance Corporal Rockliff remembered the buns, but in his version each prisoner received half a bun, with the Japanese keeping the rest. 'The Japanese camp staff had sold a hundred buns,' wrote Rockliff. 'Typical!'

The prisoners were taken across the inland sea to the coal mine at Ohama, which was unlike any they had ever seen. 'It only had one exit,' Thomas recalls. 'The mine was under the sea so there was no ventilation shaft that I could see—the only ventilation was at the entrance to the mine which was 200 metres from the sea. As you went down the ramp into the tunnel, there was a compressor station at one side ... for the pneumatic drills. At the coal face there was so little air that it was hard to keep a cigarette alight.'

Experienced Welsh and English coal miners were already working at the Japanese mine when the Australians arrived. With the help of these old hands, the Australians soon got the hang of working underground, although Haskell and Thomas—both around six feet tall—had to stoop to fit inside shafts dug by much shorter Japanese miners. Even the cords on the miners' lamps were too short for the Australians: Haskell had to strap the bracket to the back of his hand.

The northern hemisphere winter was approaching, and all the POWs had to wear was black cotton shorts and a little black cotton vest, both of which would get wringing wet inside the mine. The cold and damp were a fatal combination. Two years of near-starvation had reduced the Australians to skeletons; most suffered from recurring malaria. They had survived the horrors of dysentery and cholera in the tropics but would die by the hundreds of pneumonia.

Mining beneath the sea unnerved the Australians. 'We didn't know how far above us the water was,' Haskell recalled. 'Towards the end when they used to sow the inland sea with mines you would have all these detonations going on. They were loud bangs and the walls would be shaking and you'd think, "When is the top going to come in?"'

The Japanese winter of 1944–45 would be the coldest in half a century. Jack Thomas improvised shoes for himself by winding belts around his feet. Being underground offered some relief from the freezing temperatures outside. There was a boiler for cooking the rice. Before a shift Haskell and his mates would huddle around the furnace 'like chickens around an incubator'. Afterwards there was a warm bath, then a dash to get into bed before the cramps started. 'You used to get an awful lot of cramps. It was bitterly cold and we had practically nothing in the way of warmth.'

The accommodation at Ohama consisted of a barracks purpose-built for mine workers, with circulated water and furnaces for heating. Each POW carried a wooden 'ticket' inscribed with a number written in Japanese. The tickets hung in rows outside the rooms where the prisoners slept. Any man going outside to use the latrine had to turn his ticket around for the guards to see. One day Jack Thomas forgot to turn his ticket. He recalls being 'caught out by a young soldier, maybe 17 years old. The young fellow knocked me to the ground. He flattened me. As I lay on the ground I just felt that I had had enough. That man hated and despised me. I was exhausted.' It was the only time during his three and a half years as a prisoner of war that Thomas doubted his ability to survive.

While many Australian prisoners remember Japan as the place where random bashings stopped, others had a different experience. In some camps the guards lashed out with impunity. Private George Kennedy, a prisoner at Fukuoka No. 15 camp between May 1943 and August 1945, described how the camp, although nominally under the command of a lieutenant, was 'virtually controlled and administered by a Japanese sergeant known as "The Bull" and later by a Japanese corporal known as "Degus" and a Japanese sergeant-major named Iwanuma commonly known as "Lemmy Caution".'

Many times Kennedy 'watched whilst "The Bull" and others brutally and viciously attacked prisoners of war with sticks, fists or boots'. When this happened, Kennedy 'noticed that [Lieutenant Suematsu, commonly referred to as "The Old Man"] wore a disgusted expression and would quickly pull on his cap and hurry away from the scene.'

While George Kennedy, an infantryman from Brisbane, spent the bulk of his captivity in Japan, others would never set foot on Japanese soil.

At the beginning of September around 1000 POWs left the River Valley Road camp in Singapore to board two transports, the *Rakuyo Maru* and the *Kachidoki Maru*, bound for Japan. Harry Walker and Neil MacPherson were among a group of Pioneers separated from the rest of the battalion to make room for extra British prisoners. They remained in Singapore when the convoy containing the *Rakuyo Maru* and the *Kachidoki Maru* left Keppel Harbour on 6 September 1944. Six days later, the convoy was attacked by American submarines in the South China Sea. Both transports were sunk.

Private Lawrence Hock was one of the 2/2nd Pioneers aboard the *Rakuyo Maru*. 'I was asleep in the hold when we was hit and I jumped out and then went over the side onto a raft,' Hock wrote in his diary.

'There were about ½ dozen men besides myself on the raft. We drifted about a mile from the boat and 3 of us decided to swim back to the ship. It was the longest mile I ever swam in my life. I was exhausted by the time I climbed the roap on to the ship. We got on to a life boat which they left behind.'

Japanese ships picked up all the Japanese survivors, and the *Rakuyo Maru* sank at around 5 p.m. By then the *Kachidoki Maru* had also been torpedoed and sunk. On the morning of the third day, '3 Nip escorts appeared on the horizon and they approached us and picked us up . . . We were 54 hrs adrift in an open life boat.'

Private Hock was transferred to another ship and taken to Japan. Of that second convoy of three transport ships and two escorts, Hock's diary records that '[e]very boat was sunk but ours'. Hock reached Japan with nothing but 'a sailor's coat, a pair of pants and a hat . . . I ate my rice and stew out of my hat and all what I used was my fingers to eat with. Quite an experience.'

After days clinging to life rafts or floating wreckage, around 150 Australian and British survivors from the *Rakuyo Maru* and *Kachidoki Maru* were rescued by American submarines. A total of 543 Australians and more than 1000 British POWs died. Among the dead was Brigadier Arthur Varley, who had commanded several thousand Allied POWs at Thanbyuzayat in Burma.

MacPherson, Walker and the others left behind in Singapore were put to work building a dry dock. It would be Boxing Day 1944 before they finally embarked for Japan aboard one of the few surviving large Japanese merchant ships, the *Awa Maru*. Like earlier convoys, this one followed the coast of China, anchoring overnight in sheltered bays, while air patrols scoured the seas for submarines.

Crammed into the ship's hold, the prisoners were accommodated on three tiers of timber decking. There was no room for them to stand up, only to kneel. Rations consisted of rice and vegetable water. Periodically they were allowed on deck. 'We used to get the fire hoses and sluice ourselves down a bit,' MacPherson recalls. The temperature dived as the convoy sailed north. MacPherson often saw snow on the decks. 'As we got closer to Japan it was so cold that only a few of us went up on deck except to use the latrines.' That, too, was a hazardous operation, with prisoners perched over the side of the ship and only a freezing rail to hold onto.

On 15 January the *Awa Maru* anchored at Moji. After the now obligatory 'glass rod' test for cholera, conducted on this occasion by Japanese women (MacPherson remembers them giggling), the prisoners spent hours shivering on the snow-covered wharf while being 'sold off' in groups to their new owners. MacPherson remembers being issued with a one-piece overall made of 'not very warm' material, as well as a more impressive suit of clothes manufactured out of wood pulp. He was also given a pair of canvas boots with the distinctive Japanese split toe. 'They were anxious to dress us up,' he says, 'and make it look as though we were being well treated.'

At Moji the Pioneers were separated. As a general rule, the bigger the camp, the harsher the conditions. Neil MacPherson was sent to No. 24 POW camp, in Fukuoka Prefecture near the village of Emukae. Harry Walker's destination was the much larger No. 17 POW camp, in the provincial manufacturing town of Omuta. For the next eight months both men would work as slave labourers in the coal mines.

The camp at Emukae had been built to house Japanese miners; the huts were relatively warm and comfortable, with twelve prisoners to a room and plenty of hot water for washing. It soon became clear to MacPherson that the camp commandant was under instructions from the Sumitomo mine manager to ensure the prisoners were healthy and well looked after; apart from petty harassment, they were not mistreated by the guards. The Japanese miners under whom the prisoners worked were helpful rather than hostile. Rations, however, were poor. Towards the end, the Japanese miners at Emukae were getting little more in their lunchboxes than the prisoners.

Fleas were MacPherson's biggest enemy. In *The Burma Railway, Hell-ships and Coalmines*, MacPherson describes the 'stampede of the fleas' when a prisoner lay down on his bed and the clicking noises made by hordes of fleas as they 'hopped across the matting' towards the nearest human. Quite often 'we would see the camp commandant, a major, sitting on the step of his quarters going through his garments looking for fleas'.

Three years as prisoners of war had changed the way the Australians behaved towards each other. Some barely spoke. 'Everyone knew every-thing about everyone,' MacPherson recalls. 'We got out of the habit of conversation.' Like everyone else, MacPherson was identified by the number on his wooden ticket: 13061. Japanese guards and miners would address a prisoner by the last two digits, spoken in Japanese. MacPherson remembers the Australians falling into the same habit, addressing each other not by name but by their prisoner number in Japanese.

At Omuta Harry Walker found himself assigned to the extraction team, whose job was to shovel coal onto the conveyor belt after blasting. It was heavy work, and the men on extraction were supposed to be the best fed. 'We did get an additional bun,' Walker recalled. 'But we had to shift a fair amount of coal to earn it. After three months that small privilege was stopped.'

There was a desperate need for coal to keep Japan's war industries going. Many coal mines that had become too dangerous to work were reopened to meet the demand. The mine at Omuta was more than a century old; some of the shafts were flooded and there were frequent power blackouts, during which the miners would be trapped in the darkness, listening to the creaking timbers and hoping nothing would collapse. Exposed and damaged cables were a lethal hazard. In his tape-recorded memoirs, Walker describes one fatal accident:

At one time I went to get some timber . . . I found three Koreans lying face down in the water. They must have been standing in the water and touched something. I had to make a very quick decision as to whether I would try to roll them out or whether I'd duck back into the burrow. I looked both ways and as there was nobody there I went back without the timber. A bit later on there were people running around everywhere and the power was cut off, and I think the short was fixed up. It was quite dangerous.

Discipline was much harsher at Omuta than at Emukae. Any suspicion of malingering could result in a beating. A POW from Deniliquin was forced to stand outside for hours in the snow after being overheard by a guard telling another prisoner not to work too hard. He got frostbite and had to have both legs amputated.

Japanese cities were now being bombed heavily by the Americans, and many of the huts at Omuta were flattened in night-time raids. Although the camp had air-raid shelters, the safest place to be was underground. The same sadistic bashings that the POWs had endured in Siam and Burma began happening again in Japan. A couple of men were paraded naked in front of their mates with a card saying 'We are thieves' hanging around their necks—punishment for having been caught scavenging for oats that had blown out of the horses' feed trough. The hunger, the cold, the beatings, the ever-present threat of being bombed by their own side—to have survived the death railway for this was more than some prisoners could bear.

Many times during his three and a half years as a POW, Harry Walker had been told by his captors, 'Either we will win the war or you will never be released.' Even 'Christian George', one of the more even-tempered guards on the railway, would make the same promise. Japan had not been defeated, but by 1945 its armed forces had nothing left to fight with. As American bombs rained down, Allied POWs began to feel that something extraordinary would have to happen for them to survive the war. Harry Walker was convinced that he would not live to see his family again.

Chapter 14

DO NOT OVEREAT

Strange things happened at Fukuoka No. 17 POW camp in the last days of the war. On the morning of 9 August 1945 acting bombardier Tom Uren, a veteran of Timor and the Siam–Burma railway, was standing in the camp compound when he saw the south-west sky change colour. At 11.02 a.m. an atomic bomb nicknamed 'Fat Man' exploded over the factory district of Nagasaki at a height of around 1800 feet (550 metres). While the distance by road from Omuta to Nagasaki was 170 kilometres around the northern rim of the Ariake Sea, the distance across the water was less than 70 kilometres. '[W]e didn't see the mushroom cloud,' Uren recalled, 'but we saw the discolouration of the sky and it was that crimson colour, that beautiful sunset magnified about a hundred times over.' Harry Walker, too, saw a lurid red sky that reminded him of a 'mallee dust storm'.

No one knew what had caused the sky to turn red. Uren and his mates thought it must be a 'big ammunition dump' going up. And then 'several days later' the Japanese came in and said a 'big bomb' had been dropped and the war was over. 'They started bringing out the Red Cross parcels ... and soon after that General MacArthur ... made an announcement over the air that the prisoners of war in Japan were to be the "garrison" of Japan.'

A week after the bomb was dropped on Nagasaki, Neil MacPherson was underground at Emukae when he was told to stop working and return to the camp. Nothing else was said until they reached the camp, where the commandant announced, 'The order has been given to stop the fight.' MacPherson remembers one of the Australian prisoners calling out, 'Who won?'

Bill Haskell was on the day shift. 'We were working down the mine and we came back and the afternoon shift were going down. They said, "She's all over." We said, "Yeah! She's all over, my foot." This had been going on for weeks and weeks and weeks. "No," they said, "It's all over this time."'

Back at the camp, the guards had spent the day huddled around a wireless set. There had been no bashings. Instead of being sent down the mine, the men on the afternoon shift were told to go back to the camp, as there would be no work. The guards on the gate let everyone straight through. Nobody was belted for failing to salute. A little later the Japanese announced a Red Cross distribution of one parcel for every four men; Haskell had no idea there were any Red Cross supplies in the camp. '[Y]ou can't imagine just what a little bit of cheese or cake would do,' Haskell recalled. 'It was just heaven to eat white man's tucker again ... It just tasted so glorious.'

Many prisoners refused to believe the war was over. There were rumours that the Americans had landed and that all POWs were to be taken underground. Walker remembered being given his share of a Red Cross parcel but being warned to save the food, not eat it. When the camp lights were left on and there was no air raid, it was clear to everyone that something momentous had happened. The Red Cross food parcels were full of American cigarettes—Lucky Strikes, Chesterfields and Camels. Being allowed to smoke in the huts—previously an offence that could result in a man being beaten to death—was another sign that the world had changed . When the Japanese second-in-command of the camp came into Walker's hut he made no attempt to reprimand the smokers, brushing aside the prisoners' hasty salutes and telling everyone to sit as they were.

In POW centres all over Japan, optimism about the war's end was mixed with trepidation. According to the machine gunners' history, 'there seemed little doubt preparations were being made to exterminate' Allied prisoners. Parapets had been built around the parade ground at Omuta, and prisoners had been told that in the event of an American invasion they would all be shot. Instead the commandant announced three days of mourning for the dead, assuring prisoners that they would soon be returning to their own countries. Retribution would come later. For now, MacPherson recalls, 'everyone had only one thing in mind and that was getting home'.

But after three years living on the edge of starvation, there was a more urgent priority: food. Japan had been bombed to a standstill. The transport system was in ruins. According to Haskell, a high-ranking Japanese staff officer who visited the camp was told by an Allied officer, 'You've got to do something about food because this mob are just about starving on their feet.' He replied, 'All the population is starving.' The Allied officer said, 'I'm not concerned about your people. I'm concerned about my people and I want you to get some food.' The Japanese delivered a bargeload of melons.

Private Lawrence Hock, a Pioneer who had survived the sinking of the *Rakuyo Maru*, was a prisoner at Niigata No. 15 POW camp when planes from an American aircraft carrier flew over on 25 August 1945.

'US Navy planes came over our camp and dropped ciggerettes and papers,' Hock wrote in his diary. 'It was a very exciting day for us. We learned the news and we went mad with happiness.'

Among the 'papers' mentioned by Hock was a typed pamphlet bringing news of the Japanese surrender:

WAR ENDED: JAPAN AGREES TO
UNCONDITIONAL SURRENDER.
TERMS OF ALLIED ULTIMATUM

The Second World War, history's greatest flood of destruction and death, ended Tuesday night with Japan's unconditional surrender . . .

The pamphlet picked up by Private Hock had a message on the back, handwritten in pencil by an American sailor. Faded, folded and torn from many readings, it is preserved in Private Hock's file at the Australian War Memorial. The message read:

From the hearts of sailors to you whom we've been reaching out to for many months. The guys on this aircraft carrier wish it were more, and it will be more if you'll spell out the more necessary articles on the ground. We haven't much of an idea of what you've been through, all we know is that you are ours and we're proud of you and the sooner we can bring you back among us the better we'll feel. This is one job our pilots were tickled to take on and vowed that their best pin-point technique would be employed in hitting the [target?]. We're here to stay until you are free. God bless you all and bring you to us.

Two days later, American planes swooped low over Niigata dropping bundles of K rations [US combat rations] and sundries. 'Oh boy!' Hock wrote in his diary. 'What a time we had eating good food instead of rice and barley.'

Prisoners were told to paint on the roof the number of men held in each camp, and to mark with a white circle the best place for supplies to be dropped. At Ohama, Jack Thomas went up on the roof with a tin of white paint and daubed the number '400' after the letters 'P.W.' It was rumoured that every man would get 80 cigarettes and some sugar. Two days of bad weather made deliveries impossible. When the sky cleared and the American bombers appeared overhead, 44-gallon drums tumbled out of the open bomb bays, floating to earth beneath brightly coloured parachutes. Inside the drums were tinned meat, fruit juice, vitamin tablets, cigarettes, candy. Ray Parkin remembered the bounty coming with a health warning: 'DO NOT OVEREAT, DO NOT OVERMEDICATE'. One bale landed just outside the camp gates. When the starving prisoners tore it open, they discovered it contained 'Boots . . . bloody boots!'

Many of the steel drums ruptured when they hit the ground, scattering Hershey's tropical chocolate [a chocolate bar specially formulated to withstand tropical heat] and tins of Campbell's pea soup. Bill Haskell remembered picking up a tin of pea soup that had burst open and 'just sitting there spooning up cold pea soup on my finger and eating Hershey's tropical chocolate'. Relief rations also included dehydrated food. 'You'd eat it and your tummy would swell up. Our stomachs had shrunk . . . because we'd been starved so long. It took a bit of getting used to but gee, it was nice getting crook on good tucker.'

Some drums broke free of their parachutes and became deadly projectiles. Hugh Clarke told Hank Nelson about an American medical orderly named Joe Truey who 'got hit on the head with a case of Spam and was killed instantly'.

After fourteen days of air-drop rations, American doctors conducted what they called a 'cursory examination' of prisoners at the Ohama camp. The results were included, along with each prisoner's age and next of kin, on a typewritten list of 386 names. The health of Jack Thomas and Ray Parkin was described as 'good'; Bill Haskell's condition was described as 'poor' due to 'malnutrition'. While the majority were listed as either 'good' or 'fair', scores were diagnosed with ailments such as 'chronic abdomen'; 'chronic chest'; 'chronic malaria'; 'optical neuritis' and 'unexplained fever'.

Harry Walker remained at Omuta for a month after the war ended and 'never stopped eating. I could never find enough to eat. It didn't matter how much we were given, we just ate and ate.' Lawrence Hock reported on 2 September 1945 that 'we are averaging 6 bars of chocolate a day'. The next day Hock went to Mass, 'which was celebrated by a German missionary priest'.

Demobilised Japanese troops were handing their weapons in to the police stations. 'They had been told to lay down their arms by the Emperor and they just accepted it,' Haskell recalled. While awaiting orders from General MacArthur, liberated Allied prisoners were free to roam around the countryside. Some trains were still running. 'You didn't need any money . . . you could go anywhere on a packet of cigarettes.' Neil MacPherson still has 'pleasant memories' of 'hikes into the surrounding countryside, invitations from farmers to visit their homes, sharing scarce food, prisoners in turn sharing the bounties from the US planes.'

A week after the Japanese surrender, Harry Walker travelled overnight by train to Nagasaki. This time there were four, not 24 men to a carriage. In daylight he witnessed the destruction caused by the atomic bomb, from total devastation within the inner blast zone to damaged roofs on houses perched on mountains that surrounded the city on three sides. Where the bomb had exploded, Walker saw no broken masonry or concrete, only dust.

Some Australian POWs had been in Nagasaki when the bomb was dropped. Gunner Ted Howard of Hobart would later describe how a 'tremendous blue flash' ran through the prison building, which began to collapse around them. 'I threw myself on the floor and was lucky to get out without a scratch,' Howard told newspaper reporters on his return to Australia, 'then everything began to burn and we got out as soon as we could. We made our way in tremendous heat through a city that was burned and blasted flat.' Other witnesses said the explosion was accompanied by red, blue and white flashes. Ships in the harbour burst into flames, while trees on nearby hills were incinerated.

By the time they returned to Sydney, returning Australian soldiers were dismissing reports of radiation sickness as 'a lot of nonsense' and claiming that the only after-effects they suffered from spending time in the radioactive ruins of Nagasaki was a temporary loss of appetite.

As well as supplying seemingly limitless quantities of food, the Americans brought clothes. At the wharves Walker and his mates were fumigated, deloused and given new outfits before boarding an American aircraft carrier, where they were plied with real coffee and donuts.

Rigorous medicals on American hospital ships awaited each liberated prisoner. 'Dozens' of doctors were stationed in what Haskell described 'a kind of lucky circle . . . you'd move from one to the other and one would be looking at your eyes and others [at] your nose and ears and chest. Of course we were still carrying malaria and all sorts of stuff . . . they'd say, "Go to bed. You're a sick person. You're hospitalised." But we'd never felt better.'

On his discharge from the hospital ship, Haskell was taken by tender to a Liberty ship that was to take him home. '[A]ll of the crew and the medical staff . . . lined the side of the ship and they were cheering and a flight of Liberators went over and waggled their wings. It was kind of reassuring. We thought, "We've been accepted back in the human race."'

The returning prisoners did not come under Australian command until they reached the Philippines, where their identities were checked against photographs. At the same time, men were asked to identify any of their mates they knew for certain to be dead. Many soldiers who had previously been reported dead turned out to be alive. The arrival of a telegram about a missing son had often been a source of dread, but thousands of Australian families now received telegrams reporting that their sons had been 'recovered' safe and well.

Bill Haskell's father was at home when the telegram boy knocked on the door.

The young fellow gave Dad the telegram and he opened it and saw that I was recovered and he was just jumping out of his skin . . . he ran out [into] the street, and it was a little short street, with this telegram and he was running up and down yelling out, 'It's Bill, it's Bill.' Of course all the neighbours knew that they'd been waiting for news on me and the longer they waited the worse it looked as though it was going to be. When they got the news that I'd been recovered there was a fair amount of rejoicing.

In the Philippines, Harry Walker joined around 800 released POWs aboard HMS *Speaker*, which berthed at Pyrmont in Sydney on 15 October. After a night in a military camp he travelled by train to Melbourne. His family was waiting for him at Spencer Street station. That night they put a big dinner in front of him, but Walker could not manage more than a couple of mouthfuls. His family had not realised that prisoners like Harry had been eating almost nonstop since the day of their release. During those two months Walker had put on 64 pounds (29 kilograms). By the time he reached Australia, food was the last thing on his mind.

Neil MacPherson was taken by train from Emukae to Nagasaki, where he boarded an escort carrier, the USS *Chenango*. Except for news received sporadically and at great risk via clandestine wireless sets, Allied POWs had heard little besides enemy propaganda during their years of captivity. The last three years of the war had happened without them. On board ships like the *Chenango*, every effort was made to bring prisoners up to date with the events of the missing years through newsreels, movies and lectures.

MacPherson was among a group of Australian POWs sent to Okinawa, where some Japanese soldiers were still refusing the order to surrender. In his written memoirs Jack Thomas remembered spending an idyllic evening on Okinawa sitting on his American army blanket 'on a gentle hillside, full of turkey and apple pie and Coca Cola, with a few of my companions, watching . . . black and white movies'. In one of the movies 'a herd of dairy cows [was] walking in file alongside a post-and-rail fence. The music was soft and lilting, and a lady was singing . . . "Don't Fence Me In", which I had never heard before . . . My cup was full.'

From Okinawa the homecoming POWs were flown in American bombers to Manila, in the Philippines. It was in Manila that MacPherson learnt that both his brothers had joined the Australian armed forces: Jim had fought in Borneo, and eighteen-year-old Jack was in training at Flinders Naval Depot, near Melbourne.

On 6 October about 900 released Australian POWs, including Private MacPherson, boarded the British aircraft carrier HMS *Formidable*. A week later the ship sailed into Sydney Harbour.

During the three and a half years that he spent as a prisoner, MacPherson had never been allowed to forget the shame of the surrender on Java. But the soldiers of the 2/2nd Pioneer Battalion and the 2/3rd Machine Gun Battalion had been humiliated and disarmed not on the field of battle, but by order of a Dutch general. Politics, not fighting spirit, had decided their fate. During those three and a half years, the Australians might have been lost but they had not been forgotten. Many were overcome by the multitudes lining the streets of Sydney on 13 October 1945 to welcome them home. Others were too sick or badly injured to appreciate the crowd, hundreds being taken direct from the hospital ship *Wanganella* by ambulance and special train to Concord hospital.

Few of those families waiting on the docks or at railway stations could begin to guess the horrors endured by their homecoming sons and brothers and fathers. Brigadier Blackburn, who had recently returned by plane, spoke for every returning soldier when he addressed a civic reception on 24 September. 'There never has been a finer body of men than those men,' he told the audience at Adelaide town hall. 'It is going to mean a tremendous amount to those who are coming back if the public knows that it was not their fault that they were taken prisoner. They wanted to fight on, even though we had practically no equipment or medical supplies and it was probable that half of them would lose their lives.'

Described by the *Adelaide News* reporter as 'gaunt and thin', Blackburn recounted how his force of 2500 men—including 'clerks, transport drivers, members of a mobile laundry and the postal and pay corps'—had been given the job of 'holding up a crack, well-equipped Japanese division'. The fighting had lasted for three days. 'By sheer, stark bravery our men held them off, and at the end of that 72 hours the Japs had not advanced a yard.'

Describing their captivity, Blackburn struck the same jingoistic note. 'The Japs,' he said,

> more than anything else wanted the British to 'kow-tow' to them—but that was the one thing they could not make them do. Our men took knock after knock just for that reason. I saw one Australian knocked down because of the way he looked at the Japs. They kicked and punched him while he was on the ground. And when he picked himself up he put his chin out and looked at them in just the same way as he had before.

The jingoism was understandable—it was barely three weeks since the Japanese surrender—but Blackburn had a more serious message to deliver about the damaged men returning home:

There are a large number of these chaps coming. They have had a tough time, tougher than the officers. We were humiliated and ill-treated—but we did not suffer any atrocities. They are all nervy and worn out ... While we were prisoners we thought we might be treated as invalids and neurotics when we came back. We wondered how 'gaa-ga' we were. We had been together for three and a half years, just us, and we didn't know whether we were all silly or not.

Although separated from them, Blackburn had suffered many of the same physical privations as his men; in captivity his weight had dropped from 77 kilograms to less than 46 kilograms. Since his release from a camp in Manchuria, Blackburn had been constantly on the move, landing in China, India and Ceylon en route to Australia. Masking his own fragile mental state, he asked for sympathy and understanding and 'unobtrusive treatment' for his soldiers. Practically every man returning from Japanese prison camps, he said, would be suffering from 'neurosis', but 'relatives and friends or anyone with whom he came in contact should give no sign that he was being regarded or treated as suffering from neurosis'. Everyone's approach should be, "Glad to see you back and now for a happy future."'

Under the headline 'Brig. Blackburn's Plea', the Adelaide *Advertiser* reported his appeal for returning soldiers to be

sifted and watched without their knowledge and ... released from hospital only when they are perfectly fit again. The minimum of regimentation will help greatly in rehabilitating them. A relaxation of some of the usual restrictions and discipline associated with military establishment will assist them to rehabilitate themselves. For years they have been bashed from pillar to post ... regimented to the nth degree, and have undergone terrible hardships. Australia has had little, if any, experience of such neurosis before, and we must begin now to understand it before it is too late.

Chapter 15

WE HAVE DEVELOPED QUEER HABITS AND OUTLOOK

In a letter to Blackburn after the war, Weary Dunlop described 1943—the year of the Siam–Burma railway—as a 'nightmare of starvation, disease, and death'. Dunlop had witnessed the horror up close; Blackburn had not, although he saw its aftermath. Weary's letter went on:

We had a dreadful problem with cholera, dysentery, malnutrition, malaria and tropical ulcers, finishing the Railway with almost every man broken in health. I can genuinely say that the AIF outworked and out-suffered any nationality ... and the lads from Java showed fortitude beyond anything I could have believed possible. I saw them flogged to work reeling with sickness and I've carried them to the engineers' lines when they could no longer stand up, to do more work sitting down. But through that long ordeal with sick parades going on in pouring rain into the late hours of the night I never saw an

Australian refuse to go out in another man's place when the necessity arose nor a man's spirit break until the time came to turn his face to the wall and die. They showed an unselfishness that has never been exceeded.

The honour roll of the 2/3rd Machine Gun Battalion lists the names of 139 soldiers who died as prisoners of the Japanese. The 2/2nd Pioneer Battalion's losses were higher: the battalion history records that 178 Pioneers died in captivity in Burma and Siam. Fifty-five more died on 12 September 1944, when the hell-ship *Rakuyo Maru* was torpedoed by an American submarine. With so many junior officers left behind on Java, the dead of both battalions consisted overwhelmingly of private soldiers, corporals and sergeants; each battalion lost only a single lieutenant during the years in captivity in Burma, Siam and Japan.

It was said that every sleeper on the Siam–Burma railway had cost a prisoner's life, but most of the Australians who worked on the death railway did not die. Neil MacPherson and his red-haired mate from the Pioneers, Bluey Rowe, survived the Middle East, Java, the hell-ships and three and a half years as prisoners of the Japanese. Jack Thomas and his friend Ray Parkin, the sailor who escaped the sinking of the *Perth*, both made it back to Australia, as did the majority of the men in Thomas's machine-gun platoon. Pioneers and machine gunners who had fought side by side against the Vichy French in Syria in 1941 disembarked together in Sydney in 1945.

By his own estimation, Jack Thomas's survival was anything but remarkable. 'I had a couple of ulcers for which I had no treatment. I very seldom reported to the doctor. Yes, I had malaria but not as bad as many, many people. I had dysentery, as everyone did—I know what it was like to wipe your bum on the grass or on a stick. What else? Beri beri—we all had vitamin deficiency.'

Lieutenant Gordon Hamilton, whose brother Murray also fought with the Pioneers, recovered from debilitating bouts of dengue fever, bacillary dysentery, amoebic dysentery and malaria. The psychological effects of his years in captivity were harder to diagnose and more insidious. 'Mentally we have become very slow and stagnant, and have developed queer habits and outlook,' Hamilton told his family in a letter quoted by Linda Holmes in *Four Thousand Bowls of Rice: A prisoner of war comes home*. '[H]ope that diet and environment will soon correct that, but the past three and a half years must have left its mark. It is only when we come in contact with outside people that we realize our peculiarities.'

Neil MacPherson, who suffered malaria and dysentery but never had a tropical ulcer, was initially judged too healthy for any kind of invalid pension. After reaching the age of 65, he was granted a so-called extreme disability adjustment—belated official recognition of the toll of having been a prisoner on the railway. Yet MacPherson maintains that his years of captivity 'didn't worry me mentally. I came out of it very well, all things considered. I never had nightmares.'

But many did. Bill Haskell suffered for 'years and years and years' from nightmares about his experience on the railway. 'Everyone did, I think, and that was one of the legacies of the situation—the horrible nightmares. Always in the nightmares I was back in that Hintok camp where there was mud and slush and god knows what in the height of the monsoon season. You were never far away from the horrible stench.'

It was returning to Siam—now Thailand—with Weary Dunlop in 1985 that put an end to Haskell's nightmares. Everything about the visit was the antithesis of his experience as a prisoner: the Kwa Noi River (now more familiar as the River Kwai) was tranquil rather than bursting its banks; the sun shone; and when Haskell walked through the railway cuttings he had helped to dig, he was wearing boots. 'I don't think I had a terrible dream after that to speak of,' Haskell recalled later.

For Jack Thomas, going back to Thailand would have the opposite effect.

Like thousands of other soldiers, Thomas returned from the war determined to pick up the life he had left behind. His time in the army had been, in his words, 'very sober ... I didn't drink, I didn't smoke and I didn't gamble. Nearly 100 per cent of my pay was allotted back home. I lost my mother when I was a young boy so my father put it aside for me.'

From Sydney, Thomas travelled by train to Melbourne and Adelaide, where he was met by an old schoolmate, Jack Bullwinkel, who had flown Spitfires over the Western Desert. Jack's sister Vivian was the sole survivor of the infamous 1942 massacre of Australian nurses on Bangka Island by Japanese troops.

After a week in Adelaide—including a couple of days in hospital being examined and 'de-wormed'—Thomas headed back to Broken Hill, where a job in his father's grocery store awaited him, along with a few hundred dollars in army pay. With no battalion friends in Broken Hill, he 'forgot' about the war. 'I didn't have time to cry in my beer,' he recalls. 'I was too busy working with my dad. It was hard, hard work.'

It was not until 1973, when he took the Indian Pacific train to Perth for a battalion reunion, that Thomas's experience as a POW began to catch up with him. In Perth he met Weary Dunlop for the first time (although Thomas had been one of 'Weary's thousand' in Siam, the two men had never actually spoken). Eight years later Thomas made his first return visit to Konyu, where in January 1943 he had stood at the bottom of that 'bloody steep hill' feeling 'worried' about his chances of surviving the war. Thomas stayed in a hotel just a few miles from the site of the disease-ridden camp at Konyu, where in June 1943 Dunlop was told just 60 of 600 POWs were fit for work. He visited the Kwa Noi River, the jungle lifeline that had brought a steady supply of duck eggs and other precious things to Thomas and his starving mates.

For some former POWs, returning to the railway was a way of exorcising demons, of laying the past to rest, but the visit left Thomas 'troubled . . . deeply troubled'. As a result of the trip he felt reconnected to a place that had been a source of deep suffering.

The civilian future Thomas had pictured for himself—a future that could be bought with 'hard work'—had not materialised. The world had changed, especially for small shopkeepers. The business his father had passed on to him—a business in which orders were scribbled down in pencil and handed to boys on bicycles—no longer existed. By the start of the 1980s the grocer's shop in Broken Hill was 'falling around my shoulders'.

Memories of Konyu occupied Thomas's thoughts 'night and day'; he could not stop thinking about the men who never returned. Back in Broken Hill, troubled by his memories of the war, Thomas began to feel 'drawn back into the battalion'. At the age of 61 it dawned on him that he had no connection at all with the Department of Veterans' Affairs; that— except for a small pension of 'a few bob a week' given to him when he was repatriated—he had been going it alone since leaving the army. On the advice of a pensions officer from Legacy—the veterans' support group that had taken him back to Konyu—Thomas applied for a pension and was rejected out of hand. In his appeal against the decision, he submitted a twelve-page paper 'about the way I saw the world' before putting his case in person to a three-man tribunal in Adelaide. A fortnight later he was awarded a TPI (totally and permanently incapacitated) pension—an acknowledgment not just of the mental and physical hardships Thomas had experienced as a prisoner but of the emotional stress he continued to suffer.

In 1983 Jack lost his wife, Joyce. His old comrades from the 2/3rd Machine Gun Battalion attended Joyce's funeral 'en masse'. Their presence brought Thomas back into the fold. Since then he has made two more visits to the site of the Siam–Burma railway, attending the Anzac Day dawn service at Konyu in 2013.

After closing his grocery shop, Thomas developed a successful business selling timber and building supplies. In 1986 he married Shirley Temby, who had written to him often during the early years of the war and who had since become widowed. A condolence card sent after she learnt of Joyce's death turned out to be the spark that rekindled their friendship.

In late 2017 Jack Thomas had to readjust to living alone again, in an aged-care home in the suburbs of Adelaide, close to one of his sons. At 97 he felt 'a bit old' to be starting another life, but Thomas still had his special gift for finding moments of grace when he needed them most. His new life had given him 'a realisation of how contented I can be here'.

In April 2018, at the age of 95, Neil MacPherson made his sixteenth visit to the site of the death railway. MacPherson is almost the last of the 2/2nd Pioneers who sailed to war in April 1941 aboard the *Queen Mary* and *Queen Elizabeth*. Many of Blackburn's machine gunners and Pioneers were teenagers when they joined up; they were prisoners of war before they turned twenty. Speaking at the 2004 Anzac Day service at Kanchanaburi War Cemetery, MacPherson told his audience: 'We matured quickly . . . we adapted, we learned self-discipline, most importantly we discovered mateship. No prisoner on the railway survived who did not have a mate.'

When MacPherson was at his lowest ebb, hollowed out by dysentery and malaria at 105 Kilo camp in Burma, it was rereading letters from his mother that helped keep him alive. Two and a half years older than MacPherson, Jack Thomas found something else to sustain him. 'I worked as hard as anyone else and I got as many hidings as anyone else and I had the same food as anyone else, but something kept me going. I think it was the thought of a beautiful young woman at home that kept me alive. If I'm quite honest about it, it was a woman who kept me alive. When I got home she was married . . . but that was OK.'

ACKNOWLEDGEMENTS

This book could not have been written without the generous help of Neil MacPherson OAM and Jack Thomas, who shared their memories during multiple interviews. Both experienced the war as private soldiers—young men who (in the words of the Pioneers' historian) 'bore the brunt, who endured the worst conditions and the greatest dangers. The great mass of them did not win decorations; they went about their duties quietly and confidently, expecting no reward and receiving none except the respect and admiration of those who associated with them.' Neil's name is not mentioned in E.F. Aitken's history of the 2/2nd Pioneer Battalion, and Jack's appears only in an appendix to John Bellair's history of the 2/3rd Machine Gun Battalion. Valuable as those histories are, it needs to be remembered that Aitken and Bellair were not with their battalions in Java or on the Siam–Burma railway. Both were officers. Aitken, especially, obtained his information largely from officers (he names them in his 'Acknowledgements'). Neither Neil MacPherson nor Jack Thomas claims to be anything other than an 'old soldier with nothing much to skite about', but both men lived through every minute of the doomed campaign in Java and its brutal aftermath. While we need the accounts of commanders such as Brigadier Arthur Blackburn to understand the narrative sweep of the war, it is the memories of private soldiers like Jack Thomas and Neil MacPherson that enable us to grasp its human texture.

I am indebted to Andrew Faulkner for his guidance during the early stages of this project; to Michael Kramer for sharing information from his visits to Leuwiliang; and to Dr Karl James at the Australian War Memorial, who pointed me towards useful material in the AWM's collection and elsewhere. Thanks also to the staff at the AWM's research centre for their help and advice.

Finally, I am grateful to the Australian Army for an Army History Research Grant to enable me to research an underappreciated campaign in what sometimes seems an overanalysed war.

BIBLIOGRAPHY

Aitken, E.F., *The story of the 2/2nd Australian Pioneer Battalion*, 2/2nd Pioneer Battalion Association, 1953

Beattie, R., *The Death Railway, a brief history of the Thailand–Burma railway*, T.B.R.C. Co, 2009

Bellair, J., *From Snow to Jungle: A history of the 2/3rd Australian Machine Gun Battalion*, Allen & Unwin, 1987

Brune, P., *Descent into Hell: The fall of Singapore—Pudu and Changi—the Thai–Burma Railway*, Allen & Unwin, 2014

Carter, T., & MacPherson, N., *The Burma Railway, Hellships and Coalmines*, Parker Pattinson Publishing, 2008

Coast, J., *Railroad of Death*, Commodore Press, 1946

Cody, L., *Ghosts in Khaki: The history of the 2/4th Machine Gun Battalion*, Hesperian Press, 1997

Day, D., *The Great Betrayal: Britain, Australia and the onset of the Pacific War 1939–42*, Angus & Robertson, 1988

Dunlop, E.E., *The War Diaries of Weary Dunlop*, Penguin, 2009

Ebury, S., *Weary: The Life of Sir Edward Dunlop*, Viking, 1994

Faulkner, A., *Arthur Blackburn VC: An Australian hero, his men, and their two world wars*, Wakefield Press, 2008

Ford, J., *Allies in a Bind: Australia and Netherlands East Indies relations during the Second World War*, Australian Netherlands Ex-servicemen and Women's Association, Queensland Branch, 1996

Holmes, L.G., *Four Thousand Bowls of Rice: A prisoner of war comes home*, Allen & Unwin, 1993

Jackson, D., *What Price Surrender? A story of the will to survive*, Allen & Unwin, 1989

Long, G., *Australia in the War of 1939–1945, series 1, Army, vol. II: Greece, Crete and Syria*, Australian War Memorial, 1953

McCormack, G. and Nelson, H., *The Burma–Thailand Railway*, Allen & Unwin, 1993

Nelson, H., *Prisoners of War: Australians under Nippon*, ABC Books, 1985

Parkin, R., *Into the Smother: A Journal of the Burma–Siam Railway*, Hogarth Press, 1963

Parkin, R., *The Sword and the Blossom*, Hogarth Press, 1968

Richards, R., *A Doctor's War*, HarperCollins, 2005

Rivett, R., *Behind Bamboo: An inside story of the Japanese prison camps*, Angus & Robertson,1946

Russell, E., *The Knights of Bushido: A short history of Japanese war crimes*, Cassell & Co, 1958

Saggers, I., *To Hell-Fire, Purgatory and Back*, self-published, 2000

Shepard, S., 'American, British, Dutch and Australian coalition: Unsuccessful band of brothers' (Masters thesis), University of Virginia, 2003

Starck, N., 'Machine Gun Memoirs: Four veterans tell their stories of war', booklet published by 2/3rd Machine Gun Association, 2015

Summons, W., *Twice their Prisoner*, Oxford University Press, 1946

Van der Post, L., *The Night of the New Moon*, Hogarth, 1970

Walker, A.S., *Australia in the war of 1939–1945, series 5, Medical, vol. II: Middle East and Far East*, Australian War Memorial, 1953

War History Office of the National Defense College of Japan, *The Invasion of the Dutch East Indies*, translated by Willem Remmelink, 2015

Wigmore, L., *Australia in the War of 1939–1945, series 1, Army, vol. IV: The Japanese Thrust*, Australian War Memorial, 1957

Australian War Memorial

2/2nd Pioneer Battalion, unit diary

2/3rd Machine Gun Battalion, unit diary

Affidavits and sworn statements to war crimes trials by Brigadier Blackburn; Colonel Lyneham; Captain Kennedy; Lieutenants Handasyde and Hands

Australian War Crimes Board of Inquiry: Report on War Crimes committed by Enemy Subjects against Australians and others

Blackburn, A.S., diaries and letters

Blackburn, A.S., evidence to the Australian War Crimes Board of Inquiry

Blackburn, A.S., 'Report on Operations of the AIF in Java Feb/Mar 1942'

Hock, L., diaries and letters

McGee, M., 'The War of Maxwell Lawrence McGee', memoir

Rockliff, A., 'The War Time Memories of Adye Rockliff', manuscript

Schilling, W., 'Report on operations Western Java 1942'

Sheppard, A., 'Wanderings of a Warrior', memoir

Sitwell, H.D.W., 'Operations in Java—24 February to 20 March 1942'

Starrett, E.B., 'The Force Code named "Stepsister"', manuscript

Walker, H., tape-recorded memoirs

Williams, J.M., POW diary

Interviews

Neil MacPherson

Jack Thomas

Websites

http://www.2nd2ndpioneerbattalion.com/associationFRAMESET.html
(accessed 31/01/2018)

http://2nd4thmgb.com.au/story/cocking-released-australian-prisoner-
    of-war/
(accessed 31/01/2018)

https://anzac.dpc.wa.gov.au/Resources/Stories/holding_w_pte_20050225.pdf
(accessed 9/02/2018)

http://www.australianbiography.gov.au/subjects/uren/interview1.html
(accessed 31/01/2018)

Video interview with Private Bill Haskell available at
http://australiansatwarfilmarchive.unsw.edu.au/
(accessed 31/01/2018)

https://www.cia.gov/library/readingroom/docs/DOC_0000710366.pdf
(accessed 31/01/2018)

SEAL POW report; records of the Office of Provost Marshal General;
records of the Office of the Judge Advocate General (Army) held at
http://www.mansell.com/pow_resources/camplists/death_rr/
    deathrailwaycamplist.html
(accessed 31/01/2018)

https://search.archives.un.org/uploads/r/united-nations-archives/3/b/3/
    3b3ee5f2686e4f921d98937192ef14222949f54a75f1ed8542df19187b87
    7e9a/17373-00008.pdf
(accessed 1/12/2017)

http://lemare.org.uk/43%20special%20mission.pdf
(accessed 31/01/2018)

INDEX